The Historic Gardens of England
Hampshire

For Valerie Joynt

First published in 2016 by Stephen Morris
www.stephen-morris.co.uk
T: 0208 946 8705
E: smc@freeuk.com

©Timothy Mowl and Jane Whitaker

ISBN 978-0-9930554-4-7

British Library Cataloguing-in-Publication Data
A catalogue record for this book is available from the British Library

Designed by Stephen Morris, smc@freeuk.com www.stephen-morris.co.uk
Hoefler Text 10.5/13.5
Printed in the Czech Republic via Akcent Media Ltd

Opposite: Cartouche from Isaac Taylor's 1759 Map of Hampshire. *Hampshire Record Office: 110M89/P67*

The Historic Gardens of England
Hampshire

Timothy Mowl

Jane Whitaker

STEPHEN MORRIS

Preliminary scheme for the garden at Little Boarhunt, drawn by Harry Inigo Triggs.
By kind permission of Norman & Daphne Davidson-Kelly

Contents

Acknowledgements

Our first thanks go to The Hampshire Gardens Trust, whose members have been so helpful in advising us on gardens to visit and owners to contact. We are especially grateful to Gilly Drummond, founder and first Chair of the Trust, Valerie Joynt, to whom this book is dedicated, Sally Miller, Janice Bennetts, Janet Hurrell, Peter Atkinson and Caroline Hubble. The County Archivist, David Rymill, has guided us expertly through the archives at Highclere and his colleagues at the Hampshire Record Office in Winchester have answered all our research queries with keen interest and professionalism. We are indebted to a number of close friends who have given us support and advice throughout the research and visting, particularly Min Wood, Carole Fry, Robin Whalley, Helena Gerrish, Helen Lawrence-Beaton, John & Carol Lawrence, Susan Wilson, Laura Mayer, Marion Mako, Wendy Bishop, Kate Felus, Laura Dance and Christopher Francis.

We would like to acknowledge those owners and their employees who have welcomed us to their houses and gardens and shared with us their personal knowledge. They include the Earl and Countess of Carnarvon, the late Lord Montagu of Beaulieu, Sir James & Lady Scott, Penelope Chamberlayne-Macdonald, Susan Grey, Kim Wilkie, Rosamund & John Wallinger, John Jervoise, Clive & Anna Standish, Miel de Botton, Phil Wells, Robert Adam, David & Belinda Stride, Katherine & Edward Wake, Rosaleen & Peter Wilkinson, David Hill, Terence Lyons, Duncan MacDougall, Karen & Graham Potts, David Blake, Maureen & Christopher Burton, Jane George, Christine Tulk, Hilary Parsons, Trisha Rickards, Mark Smith, Anthony Hughes-Onslow, Sarah Parry, Laura Westbury, Nicola Robinson, Cathy Hutton, Philip Daubeney, Karen Gaster, Debbie Goodfellow, John Ford, David Key, Martin Edwards, Norman & Daphne Davidson-Kelly, Robert Radley, Abigail Williams, Neil Simpson, John & Samantha Hunt, Megan Pritchard, Major Ian Mattinson, Mick Wray, Hamish McKeown, Lamin Koroma, Peter & Bettina Mallinson, Peter Douglas, Nathalie Heinst, Paul Pettifor, Gordon Hawke, Sloan Hickman and Louise Wilkie.

Other archivists who have been helpful include Susan Tomkins, Sue Woolgar, Joanne Smith, Tricia Buckingham, Lorraine Coney, Jen Burford, Justin Hobson, Julia Sandison, Elizabeth Hughes, Jenny Geering, Graham Deacon, Mia Jackson, Katy Ball and Lucy Waitt, while Michael Richardson of the University of Bristol's Special Collections has brought many important texts to our notice. Stephen Morris has achieved an elegantly designed volume, Alexandra Denman has proofed the typescript most conscientiously, and Douglas Matthews has produced another definitive index.

My daughter Olivia and my son Adam have supported me through a very busy spring and summer, the one from home and the other from Los Angeles through regular texts and emails. Jane Whitaker has been the perfect companion on our travels and, as well as researching and organising visits, has written four of the chapters in this study; she has been supported unfailingly by her husband Alistair Strang, to whom we both record our gratitude here. She would also like to thank her children – Katy, Jonathan, Laura and Annabel – for their encouragement. Finally, I should like to thank John Coke, who has most generously offered his grounds at Bury Court for the launch of this book.

The future of traditional publishing is uncertain and Hampshire has had to be financed by personal funds rather than underwritten by advances from a publisher or grants from charitable bodies. As well as the mainland, it was also to have covered the Isle of Wight, but on a reconnaissance visit there Jane soon realised that there were too many gardens that would have to be included. It is our intention to go back next year and, with the help of John and Christine Harrison and the Isle of Wight Gardens Trust, scope out a further book in the series. In our frantic age it will be a welcome relief to be transported back to the 1950s and to spend a summer slowly criss-crossing that idyllic island.

Timothy Mowl, Bristol, May 2016

Green Meads, Sculptured Landforms Eclectic Landscapes and an Eighteenth-century Apollo

The list of acknowledgements in the last book of the Historic Gardens of England series, *Cambridgeshire and the Isle of Ely*, ended with my postscript that, 'after twelve years of garden visiting and writing' it was time 'to take a break and to look for new publishing ventures'.[1] It was intended to be the last book in a series that had begun with *Gloucestershire* in 2002. There were to be no further volumes, nor revisions of earlier books; the volumes that had been published up to 2013 would have to stand alone. Consequently, I embarked upon research for a proposed book on Regency gardens and another, returning to my first love, of twelve architectural walks in my home city of Bristol. But I missed the excitement of the chase, and the lure of new garden discoveries was too great to resist. Accompanied by Dr Jane Whitaker, a former PhD student of mine, and an expert on the mediaeval, Tudor and Elizabethan periods, I hit the road again.

I had always steered clear of Hampshire in the past, put off by the professionalism and intimate local knowledge of the research team of the Hampshire Gardens Trust, the first county body to be set up under the authoritative and commanding figure of Gilly Drummond. What could we possibly discover in a county so well served by its garden aficionados? Not surprisingly, Gilly and her fellow Trust members, especially Valerie Joynt, to whom this book is dedicated, have been wonderfully supportive and they have directed us towards gardens we would otherwise have missed. But we have made our own discoveries too and the resultant book should provide a fascinating overview for county dwellers and outsiders alike. *Hampshire* is in no way meant to be comprehensive; it is a snapshot only of, in our view, the most important historic garden and landscape interventions over the last thousand years. Due to the constraints of word and picture limits there are some 120 sites covered in detail here. Lost gardens particularly intrigue us, as do certain periods for which we have an affinity: my favourite is the eighteenth century, Jane's the sixteenth.

However, what this series has proved, through the research and site visiting for the last thirteen books, is that it is never advisable to make generalisations about the garden history of any county. Hampshire is no exception. It is received wisdom, for example, that most major houses were once sited at the centre of expansive deer parks, their environs paled around to secure the deer, their vast green acreage studded with veteran oaks. Certainly an estate like that at Brockenhurst in the New Forest still retains the appearance of a mediaeval deer park, but a 1635 'Plott of the Mannor of East Tisted' carried out for Sir Richard Norton (1) reveals that the Tudor house at Rotherfield was at that time surrounded by hedged fields – 'meades' – and had no deer park whatsoever.[2]

Maps such as John Hudson and Thomas Kington's East Tisted survey have been the research lifeblood of the series and Hampshire is fortunate to have a magnificent county map of 1759, surveyed by Isaac Taylor, that marks all the important estates in meticulous detail. Furthermore, it has a key listing all of the owners in possession in the mid eighteenth century. It was from this rich visual source that many of the lost Eclectic landscapes of the 1740s like Dogmersfield Park could be retrieved through vignettes of their garden buildings. Then there are the usual landscape architects' plans and specifications, especially Lancelot Brown's vast, but sketchily detailed, six-foot wide plan of Highclere, for which he charged £40 in 1770, and Humphry Repton's Red Books – some surviving, as at Stratton Park, some lost, though mentioned in letters, like that for his commission at Herriard Park – with their 'before' and 'after' views of his proposals. It is not often, however, that plans of garden layouts are used as endpapers to contemporary books. Henry Avray Tipping directed his publisher to do just that in his 1933 survey *The Garden of To-Day*, which features George Herbert Kitchin's drawing of his busy garden at Compton End (2). The two were close friends and Tipping often stayed at Compton, which he described as 'a deliciously enjoyable multum in parvo'.[3]

Compton End, the house and garden that Kitchin remodelled for himself between 1895 and 1925, and in which he lived until his death in 1951, signals one of the themes of the county. It was home to several influential architects and landscape gardeners who made houses and gardens for themselves in the shire. As well as Kitchin in the Edwardian period, Harry Inigo Triggs and Mervyn Macartney both lived and gardened in the county, while earlier, the architect and garden writer John James had settled in 1724 at Warbrook House, Eversley, where he laid out a vast axial garden around the skirts of his austere classical house. The great Baroque architect and garden designer Thomas Archer did the same after 1715 at Hale Park, near Fordingbridge, creating possibly the earliest *ferme ornée* in the country.

The soft contours and mellow brick and flint of the county attract architects and landscape gardeners alike and the Winchester-based classical architect Robert Adam continues the tradition today, having devised for his

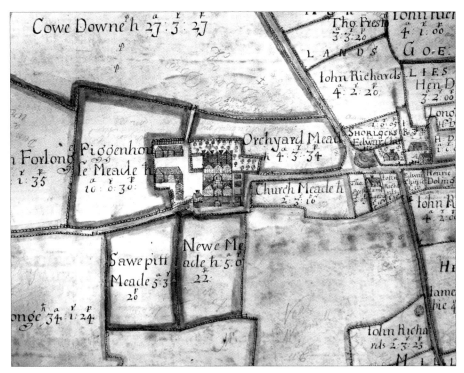

1 John Hudson & Thomas Kingston's 1635 'Plott of the Mannor of East Tisted' shows that the field pattern around the Tudor house at Rotherfield was retained well into the seventeenth century. *By kind permission of Sir James & Lady Scott*

own English vernacular house, Crooked Pightle at Crawley, a delightful Doric pavilion (*colour 1*). Finally, the county has sculptured landforms, including a spectacular terraced amphitheatre at The Holt, near Upham, designed by Kim Wilkie, one of the most sensitive of our contemporary landscape practitioners, who lives at Franklin Farm, Bishop's Waltham, where he has designed another striking garden.

The county had a particular presence in our national psyche while this book was being researched and written. As we approached the completion of our eight months of travelling down the A34, the M3 and the M27, the sixth and last television series of ITV's *Downton Abbey* was about to be aired. The programme has been filmed in the Earl and Countess of Carnarvon's Highclere Castle, which is set in a breathtakingly beautiful landscape park devised, if not actually constructed, by Lancelot Brown. It was through our researches into the shadowy Robert Herbert, who created the early eighteenth-century landscape which preceded Brown's at Highclere, that we made what is probably the most fascinating, if bizarre, discovery in the entire county, one that features England's Homer. One tantalising clue was there in Isaac Taylor's 1759

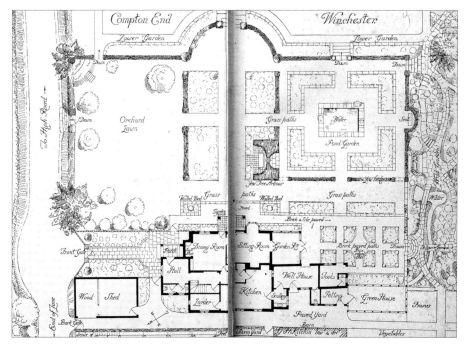

2 This plan of George Herbert Kitchin's compartmented grounds at Compton End
was used for the endpapers of Henry Avray Tipping's 1933 *The Garden of To-Day*.
By kind permission of Laura Westbury

map; the other was a pair of extraordinary portraits hanging in the Drawing
Room at Highclere.

Taylor's detailed map marks the old house and church at Highclere, while
to the south there is the 'Arch' on Sidown Hill, known as Heaven's Gate.
Further south at the corner of a wood a 'Grotto' is marked as a pointed-arched
structure (3), which might possibly have been another building added to the
Highclere landscape by Robert Herbert, or it could have related to Cruxeaston
nearby. Set this research conundrum, we found that the Grotto did, indeed,
connect with the 1740s Eclectic landscape at Highclere, but that it had been
built and decorated in the 1730s by the nine Lisle sisters, who lived at the
manor house in Cruxeaston. One of these, Harriet, was a competent artist and
had made pastel studies for the Grotto, copied from 'ancient portraits', two of
which, of Sir Richard and Lady Kingsmill, were in the possession of the 2nd
Earl of Carnarvon in 1795.[4] These are the two portraits in the Drawing Room,
across the way from a Jonathan Richardson painting of Robert Herbert as a
young boy. The Lisle pastels (*colour 2 & 3*) are delicately painted head-and-
shoulders studies set in extraordinary Rococo frames, which are constructed of
gilded shells and, as such, are extremely rare and important survivals of the
1730s. Edward Wedlake Brayley and John Britton, who saw the Grotto in 1804

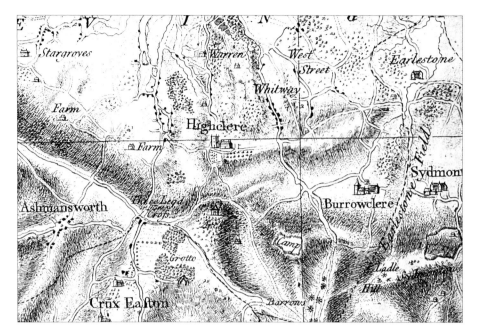

3 A detail from Isaac Taylor's 1759 Map of Hampshire showing the Cruxeaston
Grotto at the edge of woodland to the south of the Highclere estate.
Hampshire Record Office: 110M89/P67

on their topographical tour of the county, reported that 'On the trees of the
grove surrounding the Grotto', Harriet 'painted the portraits of several of her
acquaintance, in a manner which produced a singular effect, as they appeared
to form parts of the trees themselves'.[5] These were long gone by 1804.

One of the more celebrated visitors to Cruxeaston was Alexander Pope,
who stayed with the Lisles in August 1733 and wrote the following 'Inscription
on a GROTTO of Shells at CRUX-EASTON the Work of Nine young Ladies':

> Here shunning idleness at once and praise,
> This radiant pile nine rural sisters raise;
> The glitt'ring emblem of each spotless dame,
> Clear as her soul, and shining as her frame;
> Beauty which Nature only can impart,
> And such a polish as disgraces Art;
> But Fate dispos'd them in this humble sort,
> And hid in desarts what wou'd charm a court.[6]

The Revd Jeremiah Milles, who kept a topographical diary of his travels
through the county, saw a 'beautifull little square Grotto adornd with shells' at
Cruxeaston on his 1743 tour of Hampshire with, close by, 'an arched seat made

of flint stone & a rural Theatre in ye wood'.[7] When Brayley and Britton saw it only the shell of the Grotto remained, but their brief description suggests that it must once have been a wonderfully numinous and atmospheric building: 'The front was of flint; the interior studded with shells, scoriae of iron ore, and other substances: it contained a seat for each sister, with a niche for the presiding magician'.[8]

The 4th Earl of Carnarvon, who wrote a biographical history of the Herbert family, in describing the Grotto gives a hint as to the identity of the 'presiding magician': the 'nine Muses...built a grotto in the wood with nine niches for themselves and a tenth for Mr. Pope as Apollo'.[9] Another account suggests that the sisters 'stood in the niches, Pope being placed in the midst, as Apollo'.[10] The poet also wrote an extempore epigram, 'On seeing the LADIES at CRUX-EASTON Walk in the WOODS by the GROTTO', describing the sylvan place as a paradise 'where these bright angels walk'.[11] Pope was called many things in his lifetime, mostly related to his prodigious scholarship, but the image of the diminutive poet posing as a strapping God is hard to take. One can more readily see Robert Herbert acting as that magician, with nine women in thrall, in much the same way as Gilbert White's brother Henry would double later as the hermit to entertain the Battie sisters at the Hermitage on top of the Hanger at The Wakes in Selborne. Herbert's lovelorn character suggests the strong possibility that he would have enjoyed the role. He will feature in Chapter Four on the Eclectic Garden; for the moment we must begin this survey chronologically with the county's rich heritage of former ecclesiastical foundations and the gardens that once served them.

1

'A gardyn saw I ful of blosmy bowes'
Mediaeval Gardens

St Swithun's Priory, Winchester Castle, Wolvesey Castle

The Hospital of St Cross, Bishop's Waltham Palace, Beaulieu Abbey

Odiham Castle, Winchester College

The centre of Winchester, close to the Cathedral and beside the River Itchen, was the site of several mediaeval gardens associated with monastic buildings. Medicine was an important Christian mission and the monks and nuns maintained herb gardens to produce a ready supply of medicinal plants. Among the documents translated from Latin into Anglo-Saxon for King Alfred in the ninth century was the *Herbarium*, attributed to Apuleius Platonicus (now called Pseudo-Apuleius). Derived primarily from Dioscorides, this was the principal illustrated Latin herbal of the Middle Ages, originally made between the second and fourth centuries.[1] It lists about 183 known herbs with descriptions of their appearance so that they could be used as Simples in medicine. It also gives directions for the best time to pick plants, or verses to be said while picking them. It remained popular and was copied for a thousand years, throughout the Middle Ages. The copy now in the Bodleian Library may reproduce an exemplar written towards the end of the tenth century at Winchester.[2]

Another medical text associated with Anglo-Saxon Winchester is the *Leechbook of Bald*. This was written in the vernacular, which was unique before 1100 for medical literature in Western Europe. The copy now in the British Library belonged to Bald, an Anglo-Saxon physician or 'leech', and was made in the middle of the tenth century at Winchester, although the material was probably assembled at the time of King Alfred.[3] The book is a collection of medicinal recipes, some of which are straightforward. For a man who 'hath mickle ache in his eyes' it recommends groundsel, bishop's wort (*Betonica officinalis*) and fennel, boiled in water or, better, milk.[4] Other recipes were long and complicated, involving a wide range of herbs. A remedy for 'thigh ache', or sciatica, requires a drink made with pepper, wine, walwort and honey, 'also in addition, apple tree, thorn, ash, quickbeam, everthroat, ashthroat, helenium, bishopwort, ivy, betony, ribwort, radish, spraken (*Rhamnus frangula*), pepper, mastic, costmary, ginger, sal ammoniac, nettle, bind nettle, work this to a drink'.5 For 'a lithe drink against a devil and dementedness' the *Leechbook* prescribes the following remedy:

> Put into ale cassuck, roots of lupin, fennel, ontre (radish), betony, hindheal, marche, rue, wormwood, nepeta, helenium, elfthone (nightshade), wolfs comb (wild teasel); sing twelve masses over the drink, and let the man drink, it will soon be well with him.6

The copying in Winchester of these rich sources of medical knowledge implies that the monks and nuns carried out their mission of healing there, requiring both a knowledge of the many herbs involved, and the means of obtaining them. This gives clues about the variety of herbs that would have been grown at the religious houses.

Very little survives of the mediaeval **St Swithun's Priory**, the oldest of these religious houses, which once dominated the centre of the city. Part of the Prior's lodging in the Cathedral Close remains, with a thirteenth-century porch, and a fifteenth-century Great Chamber.7 The fourteenth-century monastic Pilgrims' Hall, where visitors stayed, is incorporated into the Pilgrims' School,8 and the site of the monks' dormitory is now a tranquil garden, dedicated to Dean Garnier,9 but it was once a large and wealthy abbey. According to the *Anglo-Saxon Chronicle*, the Priory was founded in 634 in honour of Saints Peter and Paul, by Cenwalh, King of Wessex.10 It was the first Christian church in Winchester, the heart of Anglo-Saxon Wessex, and later became known as the Old Minster, as well as becoming the Cathedral. Today its outline is traced in red brick, just north of the present Cathedral.11 Winchester was King Alfred's capital city, and when he died in 899 he was buried in the Old Minster. His son Edward the Elder, following his father's wishes, founded a New Minster in 901. A vernacular charter records King Edward's acquisition of land 'so that I might found a monastery there, for the salvation of my soul and that of my venerable father King Alfred', and Alfred's remains were removed to the New Minster soon after the foundation.12

The Old Minster was rebuilt on a vast scale and re-consecrated in 980 by Bishop Ethelwold. The name of St Swithun was added to its former patrons; it retained the name of St Swithun's Church and Priory until the Dissolution. The Old and New Minsters, together with St Mary's Abbey, which was the nuns' minster, known as Nunnaminster, formed the greatest ecclesiastical group in Anglo-Saxon England, and Winchester became an unparalleled literary, artistic and monastic centre.13 But after 1066, William the Conqueror replaced Winchester's last Saxon bishop with his own royal chaplain, Walkelin, who set about building a huge new church in the Norman Romanesque style. The Old Minster was demolished and its stones were used for the new Cathedral, which was consecrated in 1093 with a great ceremony attended by almost all England's bishops and abbots.[14]

Some old accounts survive which provide more information about the later gardens of the Priory, and what grew there. It is known that they produced medicinal herbs for the monastic community, continuing the Anglo-Saxon tradition, but that some herbs were also sold. In 1312 the produce of the *herbagio Gardini Elemosinarii*, the Almoner's herb gardens, contributed 9 shillings.[15] Robert of Basing was *Custos Gardini Conventus*, keeper of the Convent Gardens, in 1334-5.[16] Many payments were necessary for work associated with garden upkeep; the accounts for 1337 include payments to the *Talpanarius*, or mole-catcher, and the *Gardinarii*, the gardeners, of 12d each.[17] We know that apples were grown in the gardens because a fourteenth-century roll containing a Consuetudinary for the Refectory states that the gardener was to provide apples on Mondays, Wednesdays and Fridays in Advent and Lent; the sub-prior, third prior and fourth prior, the fraterer and other officers were to have ten apples each; if the prior was present he was to have fifteen. The same was to be done on St James's Day, when there was the blessing of apples.[18] Apples were clearly an important part of the produce of the gardens, and there was a press in the garden for making cider.[19]

As well as herb gardens cultivated for medicine, and gardens for food, monasteries had pleasure gardens for the monks to walk in prayer and contemplation. At St Swithun's before 1335, there were large pleasure grounds of around three acres, described as *viridaria et deambulatoria*, plantations of trees and covered walks.[20] They were approached through a *garite*, a watchtower or gazebo.[21] In 1336 the monks obtained a licence from the King to build a gallery over the city wall and what is now College Street, in order to have private access to their gardens.[22] We also know that these monastic gardens were usually enclosed. The Almoner's accounts in 1399 include the cost of a new dike ten perches long, *'cum vivis plantis plantando'*, planted with live plants, presumably to make a quickset hedge.[23] Six cartloads of underwood were bought for the enclosure at a cost of 10s 8d,[24] and the garden gate was repaired with one great plank and other boards, together with a lock and two keys, costing 10d.[25] Finally, a new entrance was made between this garden and 'the newly made Gardener's garden called Southgarden', which was sited within the precincts of the monastery.[26]

Other enclosure materials were used too. In 1536-7 there were payments for chalk and soil for the Sacrist's garden wall, and a 'Tiler' was paid £2 for roofing it.[27] The accounts of 1410 include costs for a new wall made in the north of the Hordarian's Garden of 60s 8d, with 20s more for timber.[28] The Hordarian had charge of the material resources of the convent and was responsible for providing bread and beer, meat and fish for the Refectory. This may be the same garden as that described as *Le Praiel*, the little green close of the

Hordarian, where the walls between that and the '*Coquinee*' garden were repaired in 1382.[29] Carpenters were also hired to make forks of wood to cover the walls of both the *Coquinee* and *Le Praiel,* and these were probably to attach plants and fruit trees.[30]

The accounts for 1409 include costs of 4s for two carts of underwood used for enclosing a garden called *le Joye*, in the Convent precincts, which was possibly the garden known as 'Paradise'.[31] This was an enclosed garden to the north-east of the Cathedral, planted with apple trees, which was also called 'The Dean's Paradise', the fifteenth-century doorway of which still stands.[32] 'Paradise' must have included grass, because the 'Herbage of Lower Paradise' was sold for 6d in 1536-7.[33] 'Paradise' was enclosed by Paradise Wall, which ran across the present Cathedral Green, up to the north face of the Norman transept.[34]

The Great Hall, completed in 1235, is the only substantial surviving part of **Winchester Castle**. It is the largest and finest surviving mediaeval hall after Westminster, and was built by a master mason called Stephen in the shape of a double cube, using stone from the Isle of Wight, Bath and Caen, with arcades of pale Purbeck marble.[35] The surviving door at the lower end of the Hall led to the King's apartments.[36] Inside, the Hall was originally brightly decorated and the huge Round Table hanging on the west wall was probably commissioned for Edward I in 1290.[37] The Castle, built by William the Conqueror in 1067, was situated in a commanding position at the top of the hill, within the Roman walls.[38] It was designed to control the West Gate of the city, which is still in use today, and was both a residence and a fortress.[39] At first, the principal royal palace remained in its ancient position in the centre of the city, by the Cathedral, but by around 1100, the royal seat had moved up the hill to the Castle. In that year, William Rufus died in a hunting accident in the New Forest, and his brother, Henry I, who had been with him, rode immediately to Winchester to secure the royal treasure, which was in the Castle.[40] After the city was burnt in 1141, when Henry de Blois, Bishop of Winchester and brother of King Stephen, laid siege to the Empress Matilda, Henry II rebuilt the Castle between 1155 and 1189, as a royal residence.[41] The enclosed area was only about four acres,[42] and so the gardens within the Castle walls were restricted to relatively small spaces between buildings. Work is recorded on the King's chambers and those of his Queen, Eleanor of Aquitaine, as well as the Hall.[43] Within the walls a herber was made for Henry in 1178, and planted with grafts five years later.[44] Outside the West Gate, below the Castle, Henry purchased a property in 1181-2 and converted it into a mews for his falcons. The King's Mews contained quarters for the falconers, a chapel, a dove-cote, and an upper chamber. The buildings were known as 'La Parroc'.[45]

Henry III, known as Henry of Winchester, who was born in the city in 1206 and a frequent visitor, repaired and strengthened the Castle after it was taken by the Dauphin, the future Louis IX of France, in 1216, and recaptured the following year.[46] Henry spent considerable sums extending and improving the royal apartments. In 1222, he pulled down the earlier hall and began the construction of the present Great Hall, completed by 1235 at a cost of over £500.[47] In the same year, Henry ordered the making of 'three herbers in this castle', thereby providing it with pleasure gardens.[48] As Albertus Magnus wrote in *De Vegetabilis et Plantis*, in around 1260: 'It is then delight rather than fruit that is looked for in the pleasure garden'.[49] Such a herber, or pleasure garden, was 'mainly designed for the delight of two senses, viz. sight and smell'.[50] It required the site to be levelled, the weeds cleared, and the plot to be covered with 'rich turf of flourishing grass', since 'the sight is in no way so pleasantly refreshed as by fine and close grass kept short'.[51] Around this lawn sweet-smelling herbs such as rue, sage and basil would be planted in a square, together with flowers such as violet, columbine, lily, rose and iris.[52] There would be a higher bench of turf at the edge, 'flowering and lovely', and 'sweet trees with perfumed flowers', such as apples, pears, and sweet bay.[53]

Much more work was carried out on royal gardens soon after Henry's marriage to Eleanor of Provence in 1236. At Winchester, there was work from 1247 to 1269, with several gardens recorded in mediaeval accounts. A lawn is mentioned in 1252 between the new Chapel, built for the Queen, and the King's Chapel of St Thomas.[54] This was the King's herber, and another herber between the Queen's chamber and the Chapel is also mentioned.[55] Some queens brought with them gardeners from abroad and there was a Provençal gardener directing the royal gardens at Windsor when Eleanor was Queen.[56] Henry was succeeded in 1272 by his son Edward I, who married Eleanor of Castile in 1254. Eleanor was fond of gardens and there was considerable spending on them for her. At Leeds Castle in Kent, a large lake was formed with a Gloriette, or summerhouse, on an island accessed by a two-storeyed bridge, between 1278 and her death in 1290.[57] At King's Langley in Hertfordshire, she had a new garden made planted with vines and fruit trees from 1279, for which she brought gardeners from Aragon.[58] She may also have used her Spanish gardeners at Winchester, where she stayed.[59] In 1302, Edward I and his second Queen, Margaret, were in their chambers at the Castle when fire broke out and severely damaged the royal apartments. The damage was never repaired, and subsequent royal visitors stayed elsewhere.[60] It is unlikely that the gardens were maintained, and there is no further record of spending on them.

The palace of the Bishops of Winchester in the Cathedral City was, and still is, at **Wolvesey Castle**, situated beside the River Itchen just inside the city walls (4). The entrance to this mediaeval palace is from College Street, through wrought iron gates between stone piers. The ruins include the East Hall, a Chapel, kitchens and a tower. The large stone building known as the West Hall was built by the Norman bishop, William Giffard, in about 1110,

4 An aerial view of the ruins of Wolvesey Castle, now known as the Old Bishop's
   Palace. The Palace was largely built for Henry de Blois between 1129 and 1138.
   RCAHMS Enterprises

and this now largely lies beneath the garden of the present Bishop's House.[61]
The diocese of Winchester was the wealthiest in mediaeval England, and
Wolvesey Castle, now known as the Old Bishop's Palace, has been an important residence of the Bishops of Winchester, and a centre for administration
of the diocese, since Anglo-Saxon times. In the mediaeval period, over thirty
Hampshire manors were included in the estates, as well as almost as many
more in six other counties. Most of this vast territory came to the bishops
before the Norman Conquest through the gifts of Anglo-Saxon kings.

Wolvesey Castle was largely built for Henry de Blois, Bishop from 1129 to
1171, brother of King Stephen.[62] The Winchester Annals of 1138 describe how
Henry had built a 'house like a palace' at Winchester, with a 'strong tower'.[63] The

palace was approached through a gate in the city wall, and was surrounded on three sides by a broad moat. The buildings were arranged around an inner courtyard, the site enclosed by a wall. In the sixteenth century, John Leland described the 'castelle or palace of Wolvesey' as 'well tourrid [and for the] most part watered [about]', suggesting an appearance more like a castle than a palace.[64]

After the fire at Winchester Castle in 1302, the royal chambers were not rebuilt and royal visitors usually stayed at Wolvesey. When Queen Margaret accompanied Edward I to Winchester in the spring of 1306 she was awaiting the birth of a child, and arrangements were made for her to stay there. A new garden was laid out for the Queen at the then considerable cost of £2 3s 9d, and it is described in the records of the King's Remembrancer as a turfed enclosure with water running through the middle.[65] William of Wykeham carried out a major programme of repair in the late fourteenth century, and Cardinal Beaufort carried out further work in the early fifteenth century, including the courtyard cloister walk.[66] In 1403 Henry IV and Joan of Navarre stayed there for their wedding, while in 1554 Mary Tudor and Philip II of Spain were also accommodated there after their marriage in the Cathedral on 25 July 1554, and their wedding breakfast was held in the East Hall.[67]

Sited by the water meadows of the River Itchen, below St Catherine's Hill, about a mile from Winchester Cathedral and outside the mediaeval walls, the **Hospital of St Cross** is one of England's oldest surviving almshouses. To walk through the mediaeval entrance gate today is to pass into another time; the tranquillity of the enclosed site with its church, hall and tower leads the visitor into a lost era. St Cross is a rare survivor of the mediaeval period which has continued in occupation for almost 900 years. It was founded between 1133 and 1136 by Henry de Blois, brother of King Stephen and grandson of William the Conqueror. De Blois was appointed Bishop of Winchester in 1129 at the age of twenty-eight, and the almshouses at St Cross were funded by tithes from fifteen Hampshire parishes.[68] The Hospital housed and supported thirteen old, poor men, 'feeble and so reduced in strength that they can scarcely, or not at all, support themselves without other aid', providing them with clothing, 'daily a good loaf of wheaten bread…three dishes at dinner, and one for supper, and drink in sufficient quantity' as well as 'beds fit for their infirmities'.[69] In addition, under its charter, the Hospital provided food for 'one hundred other poor persons', who ate in the Hundred Men's Hall, in the outer court, taking away what they did not eat for their families.[70]

De Blois put St Cross into the hands of the Knights Hospitallers of St John in 1151, but instead of supporting it, they bled it of funds, and it was returned to the Bishops of Winchester in 1204. Mention is made of a garden at St Cross in 1282-83, when the bishop was paid three shillings for water flowing through it.[71] In 1392-93 the accounts of the Master, John de Campeden, record that a wooden wall was constructed for the 'enclosed garden' and a 'house for the garden' was made.[72] This was possibly either a summerhouse, or a house for the gardener. Campeden also planted 245 trees called *Notebenius* in various places in the garden.[73] The name simply means 'well known' trees, but exactly what they were is not in fact known, although this was probably an orchard, as two orchards are recorded less than ten years later.

In 1401, when William of Wykeham was Bishop of Winchester, the precincts of the Hospital were surveyed and described as having orchards and gardens, as well as a lake in the water meadows, and three water mills. The records are from *Wykeham's Register,* one of a series of bishops' registers kept in Winchester Cathedral. There were two orchards, the 'Northgardyn' and 'Connyger', which were quite large, together amounting to 7 3/4 acres. The fruit from these was likely to have been for cider making, as at St Swithun's and Beaulieu Abbey, though the name North Garden may imply that other plants were also grown. There were four more gardens: the 'Homegardyn', the 'Portersgardyn', the 'Wortgarden', suggesting coleworts, cabbages and other potherbs were grown there, and the 'Letulpicl' garden, the name meaning the 'little piece of ground'. The water meadows had descriptive names including 'Seintecrosmede', some of which was rushy and marshy, and some good for hay, 'Gretmullemede' and 'Southmullemede', named for the mills.[74]

There are earthworks (5) to the south of the church in St Cross Park, which have been the subject of a study by archaeologist Christopher Currie.[75] Ditches form three sides of a large square; the size of them suggests that they may have been a moat. The area enclosed by this moat was probably the orchard called Connyger, described in the 1401 survey.[76] Between the moated orchard and the lodgings is a square area which was once walled, which could be the 'enclosed garden' mentioned in Campeden's accounts.[77] The Lockburn stream would have run through here at one time, making this a peaceful enclosed mediaeval garden, enlivened by running water.[78] St Cross has a rare surviving example of a mediaeval *servatorium*, a pond for fish breeding. It is turf-edged and clay-lined, and would have provided the community with a supply of fresh fish.[79]

A Tudor cloister walk connects the Porter's Lodge with the Norman church. Its arches command the inner quadrangle, which is enclosed by the fifteenth-century brothers' quarters and the fourteenth-century Brethren's Hall. Today there is a grass lawn in the quadrangle, but it would probably have been a formal square in the mediaeval period. The Hospital survived the Dissolution in the 1530s, despite a visitation from one of Thomas Cromwell's team, because, as a lay foundation not a monastery, it did not come under the terms of the Act of Suppression. Visitors arriving on foot are offered the ancient tradition of Wayfarer's Dole of bread and beer if they request it, as refreshment for the weary on their journey.

A 1783 engraving of the complex records a dovecote set into the wall of the

5 The River Itchen runs through the valley, passing Winchester Cathedral and Winchester College in the background. The Hospital of St Cross is in the foreground sited beside water meadows, which may have contained gardens. *RCAHMS Enterprises*

6 This 1783 engraving of St Cross from Francis Grose's *Antiquities of England and Wales* shows a round dovecote built into the wall of the precinct, which would have provided meat and eggs for the mediaeval community, as well as manure and feathers for mattresses. *University of Bristol Library, Special Collections*

inner precinct (6), and there is still a semi-circular recess in the wall where it was sited. The Domesday Book shows no records of dovecotes, suggesting that they were introduced after the Norman Conquest, and this one was probably built in the twelfth century to provide for the community.[80] The law allowed pigeon-houses or dovecotes to be built by a lord of the manor and by monasteries, but tenants could not build them without their lord's licence.[81] Dovecotes were, therefore, a symbol of status, and would have contained on average between 500 and 1500 nesting boxes.[82] The site of the dovecote is in the Compton Garden, which was opened by HM Queen Elizabeth the Queen Mother in 1986. The garden commemorates Henry Compton, Master of St Cross from 1669-1676. He later became Bishop of London and created the gardens at Fulham Palace, introducing plants from the New World.

As well as Wolvesey Castle in Winchester itself, the bishops, among the wealthiest prelates in England, possessed houses and parks outside the city. The ruins of the palace of the Bishops of Winchester at Waltham – **Bishop's Waltham Palace** – southeast of Winchester, are beside the modern town. The original entrance was through an outer gatehouse from the town into an outer courtyard with barns and stables.[83] But the gatehouse is now gone, and the modern bypass cuts through the site of the outer court.[84] The visitors' entrance is directly into the square inner court, which is enclosed by the ruins of the Great Hall, Chapel, Cloister and inner Gatehouse, as well as ranges of lodgings and service buildings. In the mediaeval period the palace had a large garden that lies to the south of the inner court, accessed through a doorway in the south range. Beyond the garden was the Great Park to the south, which was mentioned in Domesday; this is an exceptionally early date when there were only thirty-five such hunting parks in England.[85] There were also fishponds to the west, which survive in reduced form.[86] The palace is surrounded by a wide moat on all sides which is still partly filled with water, known as the 'River of the Lord'.[87]

The Waltham estate was acquired by the bishopric in 904, but the present palace was begun in the twelfth century, when Henry de Blois established it on his return from exile in 1158. He built Waltham as a fortified house with timber and earth ramparts, a moat, and twin corner towers. The west tower, which still stands, linked the Hall to the bishop's apartments, and there was a chapel on the east side of the inner court.[88] This early palace was transformed by William of Wykeham between 1378 and 1402. He rebuilt the two principal ranges in a grand style, replacing the timber buildings with flint and stone, and added a new bakehouse, brewhouse and kitchen in the inner court. The work was under the direction of his master mason, William Wynford, and cost over £1,500.[89] Further additions were made by Cardinal Beaufort between 1406 and 1442, including glazing the windows of the Hall, building a cloister in the courtyard, creating a new chapel, and adding an extra floor onto the tower.[90] Bishop Langton added further buildings between 1495 and 1501, including facing the lodgings with red brick, and building the base court, which has now gone, of brick and timber.[91] Langton's garden (7) was made by enclosing part of the park with a brick wall which had elaborate corner turrets.[92] There were originally three turrets, but today only two remain.[93] This walled garden was accessed from a door in the inner courtyard that opened onto a bridge across the moat. Leland, in his *Itinerary*, described the palace as 'a right ample and goodly manor-place, moted aboute, and a praty brooke renning hard by it'.[94]

Some fragmentary information of the mediaeval gardens at Bishop's

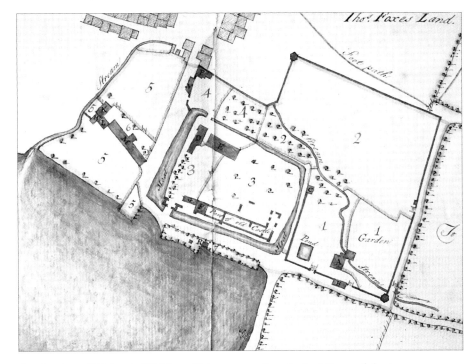

7 A 1785 plan of Bishop's Waltham Palace recording the buildings of the inner court-yard surrounded by a moat on all sides, while a stream runs through the gardens. *Hampshire Record Office: 78M1/P1*

Waltham can be gained from the surviving Pipe Rolls. We know that in 1208-09 there was a gardener employed at the manor who was paid 3s a year, the same rate as oxherds and carters.[95] Each of these men also received an allowance of about two quarters of grain, usually barley, and they were styled *famuli*, or servants, because most work at the manor was done by tenants as part of their feudal service.[96] The same payments to the same number of men, including the gardener, recur in 1210-11.[97] The gardener also received a new spade and hoe in 1208-09 at a cost of 4d, to be used *ad opus gardinarii*, to work the gardens.[98] Not every manor is recorded as having a garden, but one was needed at Waltham because it was a residence of the bishop, so produce to serve his household needs was grown there, as at Downton, another episcopal house.[99]

There must have been apple orchards at Waltham because six tuns of cider are recorded as being produced in 1208-09,[100] and twelve tuns were recorded in 1210-11 as *facte de gardino de Waltham,* made from the garden at Waltham, clearly a better year.[101] These orchards were maintained for at least three centuries, because a lease granted in 1490 mentions the Bishop's Apple Orchard and his malt mill.[102] It is known, too, that both honey and nuts were produced and sold,[103] and today there are niches for bee skeps in the garden walls. The manor also sold four tuns of wine in 1208-09, suggesting that there was a vineyard, though it is possible that this came from vineyards at other manors, since nine sent supplies of different produce in the year to Waltham.[104] There is also a cost of 'cord to tie up the Bishop's palfrey in the garden',[105] which suggests that the garden was partly, at least, grassed and could be used as pasture. This reinforces the fact that mediaeval gardens were expected to be productive, even if they had elements of the ornamental and were used for pleasure as well. In similar vein, in 1210-11 there were expenses recorded for 'Walter the fisherman' for three days, either for fishing the ponds, or possibly harvesting the moat.[106]

On the wider estate, two warreners called Adae and Walter were paid 60s 10d in 1208-09, a considerable sum which probably covered the expenses of breeding rabbits rather than just their wages.[107] There was also clearly extensive hunting in the deer park, as the *leporarios domini Episcopi,* the Lord Bishop's greyhounds, and the dogs of the King when he visited for the feast of St James, were fed bread made from 26 quarters of grain in 1208-09.[108] Seventy-one fox skins were sold to a Winchester tradesman, though this may have been a by-product of the warreners trapping foxes to protect rabbits rather than evidence of fox hunting.[109] In 1210-11, we find payments to Gervase the huntsman,[110] the expense of 'two of the Bishop's men with greyhounds for 10 days,[111] and 38s 4d in the expenses of the King's fewterer, or dog handler, with four men and twenty-four bratchets (a type of hound), a terrier and six greyhounds staying for twenty-seven days.[112] The palace was burned by Parliamentarian troops during the Civil War, and subsequently uninhabitable.

As well as important episcopal houses, there were several large abbeys in mediaeval Hampshire. The site of the great Church of **Beaulieu Abbey** is marked in outline in the grass, enclosed by the ruined mediaeval walls. Beaulieu was the largest Cistercian house in England.[113] It was founded in 1204 on land gifted to the monks by King John, in atonement for past oppressions, together with 300 marks for building work, 100 cows and ten bulls for their pastures, and a gold chalice for the altar.[114] Some of the mediaeval buildings still remain, although most were demolished at the Dissolution and the stone used to build a series of coastal defensive forts for Henry VIII in the 1540s.[115] The Abbey buildings were grouped around a central Cloister (*colour 4*), which is planted with herbs grown in the mediaeval period.[116] The refectory is now Beaulieu Parish Church, and the *Domus*, the monks' dormitory, now displays a series of embroideries depicting the history of the Abbey.

The grounds have been developed into a mixture of formal and informal gardens. Cistercian abbeys were built in remote and isolated places, 'far from the concourse of men'.[117] But since agriculture was their principal activity, the monks chose places where there was fresh water and the land was fertile.[118] Beaulieu Abbey is situated on the south coast, on the edge of the New Forest, six miles from Southampton, overlooking the River Beaulieu. The master mason was a Frenchman, Durand, who had been responsible for building Rouen Cathedral.[119] Building was complete by 1227, and the Cloister dedicated by the Bishop of Winchester in 1246, in the presence of King Henry III and Queen Eleanor of Provence.[120] Beaulieu was often visited by kings, with Henry III recorded as visiting again in December 1268, while Edward I and Eleanor of Castile were also frequent visitors.[121] After the Dissolution, a Tudor house was built on the core of the Great Gatehouse of the Abbey.[122] In common with other abbeys, the Beaulieu estate aspired to be entirely self-supporting. As the Rule of St Benedict requires:

> The monastery should, if possible, be so arranged that all necessary things, such as water, mill, garden, and various crafts may be situated within the enclosure, so that the monks may not be compelled to wander outside, for that is not at all expedient for their souls.[123]

The grounds of the Abbey were enclosed by a wall about 12 feet high and a mile long, of which substantial sections survive. This enclosure, known as the Precinct, was around 58 acres, while the wider estate was called the Great Close, surrounded by a dyke, parts of which also survive, known today as 'manor bank'.[124] At Sowley, on the western edge of the estate, the monks dug a large pond for fish breeding.[125] Lay brothers tended the sheep for wool, their main source of income. They also managed woodland, and kept bees to supply wax for candles for the church, as well as honey. They grew grapes for wine and grain for bread, and caught fish for the table. The gardens were filled with a wide variety of vegetables. By the end of the thirteenth century, there were around 200 men living and working at the Abbey, and all had to be provided for.[126]

There are surviving monastic accounts, covering a single year from autumn 1269 to autumn 1270, which throw some light on the Abbey's gardens and their produce in the mediaeval period. These show expenditure for the various activities which combined to support the monastery as a self-contained institution, including a forester, shepherd, piggery, stables and forge. There were two infirmaries, a guesthouse, a cellar and brewhouse, a granary, a mill and a bakehouse.[127] In its fields, the Abbey grew wheat, peas, vetches and oats.[128]

There are entries for digging and preparing the ground for vines, as well as tending, staking and pruning them. The accounts show Beaulieu using 375 vine stakes.[129] This implies that the monks were planting vines in 1269-70, although they did not yet have any wine in production.[130] Beer was the usual drink, but wine was served when the abbot entertained special guests.[131]

The Abbey had a 'Curtilage' or Kitchen Garden, which employed five men, who also cultivated the land between the monastic buildings and workshops, and looked after the graveyard.[132] The keeper of the curtilage provided fresh beans for pottage, each bushel being worth 3d, and pottage plants for the convent, infirmatory and guest house in return for the manure of the stables.[133] The receipts from the garden included sales of leeks and vegetable seeds, as well as 2s 6d for five gallons of honey.[134] The *Gardinarius* produced enough apples from the orchard to make eighteen barrels of cider. He also produced beans and leeks. His expenses included collecting and spreading dung, digging the gardens, and buying and making spades and shovels.[135]

Along with Winchester Castle, **Odiham Castle** was the main seat of royal power in Hampshire. It was the only stronghold built as a completely new foundation by King John, to add to the ninety-four he already owned.[136] The site was chosen because it lay halfway between the important mediaeval centres of Windsor and Winchester, on a loop of the River Whitewater, which provided a natural defence. There had been an earlier royal residence at Odiham, but John chose a new 20-acre site on meadowland and the Castle was built between 1207 and 1212 as a royal retreat, at a cost of £1,154.[137] A contemporary chronicle describes how it was built '*pour lui deporter*', in order to enjoy the hunting.[138] By the sixteenth century it had fallen into decay and only the earthworks and ruins of the great tower remain. The ruins are accessible on foot along the towpath of the Basingstoke Canal, which was cut through the site of the moated garden.[139]

The accounts of the Castle's construction, recorded in the Pipe Rolls, give an idea of its scale. They describe the digging of great 'square moats', the raising of banks and palisades, the building of the '*domus Regis*', or 'King's house', and the stocking of the moats with fish.[140] They were about 10 metres wide and enclosed two large rectangular areas around the Castle, in total about an acre.[141] The keep is in the northern half of this moated enclosure, while the southern part may have been a walled garden, surrounded by a terrace and the moat.[142] The terrace suggests that this was probably a pleasure garden, bounded by water. Entry to the Castle was across a bridge, and through an imposing Gatehouse.[143] Other buildings on the site included a Hall and a kitchen, which stood over the water.[144] The keep had a lead roof, and iron windows; inside there were carved stone corbel-tables, and there was also a whitewashed Chapel with an altar.[145] The King visited frequently and rode out from there to place his seal on Magna Carta in June 1215.[146]

The Castle remained in royal hands and in 1236 it was granted to Eleanor, Countess of Pembroke, sister of King Henry III. The deer park was adjacent to the Castle, and there was a lodge in the centre of the park, about a mile along the river. A garden associated with the lodge was made for Eleanor, in 1236-37.[147] In 1238-9 she married her second husband, Simon de Montfort, Earl of Leicester, the Castle being held by them until 1258. In 1275 Odiham was assigned to Queen Eleanor of Castile, wife of Edward I, and the pleasure garden in the park seems to have been improved for Edward I's arrival in 1291-92.[148] The location of the garden beside the river meant that water ran past, if not actually through it. A similar arrangement existed at Woodstock, where Ever-swell, later called 'Rosamund's Bower', was a self-contained living unit, separate from the Woodstock Manor a few hundred yards away. Henry III made a herbarium there around one of the pools in 1239, and it provided a pleasure garden where the King and Queen could retire from the formalities of court life.[149] Piero de'Crescenzi of Bologna, in his *Liber Ruralium Commodorum* of 1305, describes 'the gardens of kings', who can 'by reason of their riches and power...make gardens having many delights':

> They should, therefore, choose a flat place...in which there is a spring flowing through the place...Suitably high walls should surround it, and in the northern part it should be planted with a grove of various trees. In the southern part there should be built a handsome palace [summerhouse or arbour], in which the king or queen may linger when they wish to escape from heavy thoughts and to renew the spirit by means of joys and solaces.[150]

In 1330, Odiham was granted to Queen Philippa for life.[151] Daughter of the Count of Hainault in the Low Countries, Philippa had married King Edward III in 1328 at the age of thirteen, a year after his accession to the throne. Edward himself was only fifteen, and Philippa was crowned Queen in 1330. Shortly afterwards, in 1332, the pleasure garden in the park was re-made for her, and enclosed with 124 perches (around 620 metres) of new hedge, which cost 3/4d per perch.[152] This implies that the hedged garden extended to around 5 acres, and as the cost of this work was £3 17s 7d it was an expensive royal garden. Four men worked for twenty-four days, felling six oak trees to make 742 boards for fencing,[153] which would have enclosed a smaller area, perhaps an acre, making a more private inner garden, within the hedged enclosure. This garden had five doors, and seats, or benches, protected by turfed roofs, and a garderobe screened by a hedge.[154] This private inner sanctum, known as a *herbarium,* was possibly used for entertainment for hunting parties, since it was closely associated with the lodge. At a later date such a detached garden would have been called a 'pleasance', like that made on the far side of the Great Pool at Kenilworth by Henry V.[155] Royal gardens in the mediaeval period were the particular preserve of royal ladies,[156] and they may have influenced the planting. The Worshipful Company of Gardeners was founded in 1345, when Philippa was Queen, and enjoyed the privilege of presenting a bouquet of flowers to the Queen at coronations and royal marriages, as it still does.[157] Although there is no record of the plants in the garden at Odiham, accounts of 1275, at which time Eleanor of Castile was Queen, record the purchase of roses, lilies and peonies for royal gardens.[158] With this evident degree of royal interest and involvement it is plausible that the gardens at Odiham, in both the Castle and the deer park, were well provided with these flowers, as well as with herbs and fruit trees. According to the contemporary physician, Henry Daniel, Queen Philippa had an important herber containing unusual flowering plants.[159] It was from her herber that a scented pink was brought to Daniel's botanic garden in Stepney. He wrote that: 'It is a wonder sweet and it spiceth every liquor that it be laid in'.[160] Philippa was also responsible for the introduction of rosemary to England about 1338. In that year the Countess of Hainault sent a copy of a treatise on rosemary, and probably a cutting or small bush to her daughter.[161]

Another notable connection with thirteenth-century royal gardens was the poet Geoffrey Chaucer, whose wife was Queen Philippa's lady-in-waiting. In 1366 an annuity was granted by the exchequer to Philippa Chaucer, damoiselle of the Queen, which was often collected for her 'by the hands of' Geoffrey Chaucer.[162] Between 1371 and 1373, Chaucer was an esquire of the King's chamber, a member of the inner household which travelled with the King wherever he went, and he later rose to the position of Clerk of the King's Works, which he held until 1391.[163] It is likely, therefore, that the poet would have seen royal gardens such as Odiham when travelling with the court, and has left a description of one:

A gardyn saw I ful of blosmy bowes,
Upon a ryver, in a grene mede,
There as swetnesse everemore inow is,
With floures whyte, blewe, yelwe and rede,
And colde welle-stremes, nothyng dede,
That swymmen ful of smale fishes lighte,
With fynnes rede, and skales sylver bryghte.
On every bow the bryddes herde I synge,
With voys of aungel in here armonye.[164]

Returning to the centre of Winchester, another important mediaeval complex is **Winchester College**, founded by William of Wykeham, Bishop of Winchester and Lord Chancellor. Wykeham was a great believer in education, and founded both Winchester College and New College, Oxford, for training clergy, in order to provide educated men dedicated to God and public service, able to run Church and State. He obtained his charter for Winchester College in 1382; building began in 1387, and the College was first occupied in 1394. To this day Wykeham's seventy scholars live in College. The original community was self-contained in the mediaeval manner, comprising 115 men, governed by the Warden and ten Fellows, with two schoolmasters, three chaplains, sixteen quiristers (choristers) and three lay clerks. In addition, Wykeham allowed the education he provided to be shared at their own expense by ten commoners, the sons of gentry and particular friends of the College.[165]

As Clerk of the King's Works, Wykeham was responsible for overseeing the re-building of Windsor Castle by Edward III. In Winchester, his building work provided for the first of a new tradition of English public schools, and the master mason for both Winchester College and New College was William Wynford, who established a design precedent for the Oxford and Cambridge colleges.[166] The site was acquired from St Swithun's Priory, which was nearby, on the other side of the city wall.[167] It was slightly less than 5 acres, and was within the pleasure gardens of the monastery, in the Bishop's soke, next to the 'Priors' Garret', a summerhouse.[168] It is likely, therefore, that the College inherited some elements of the earlier monastic gardens. Built close to the Cathedral, around two courtyards, its planned layout was innovative for a school. The College was accessed from College Street through an outer Gate-house, begun in 1394, which survives today with its original door.[169] It leads into the Outer Court, the service court where the brewhouse, granary and stables were located.[170] From there, a second gatehouse led to the Chamber Court with its Chapel and Hall, and the chambers of the scholars and fellows. The Hall is on the upper floor, and below it is the original schoolroom. Beyond the courts is the secluded Cloister.

The gardens at the College were for growing food for the community, but also for quiet rest and scholarship, and so, as well as kitchen gardens, there was also a pleasure garden. Items relating to these gardens appear in a series of accounts made between 1394 and 1437.[171] Food requisites in 1396 included 1lb of onion seed, costing 9d, and garlic for 4d. In the following year, an assistant was hired to help the gardener 'make the garden ordained anew', and in 1398 Henry Knyght spent six months surveying the new pleasure garden and super-vising the work. In 1399, 'little plants' costing 7s/6d were planted by the gardener, Thomas Daisy. The College pleasure garden was called 'Rosemoundes Bowre', named after the famous bower at Woodstock mentioned earlier.[172] The College garden had arbours and alleys, and the accounts mention a payment in 1404 to two labourers for clearing and cleaning 'les alures' in 'le Bour' (the alleys in the bower).[173] A gardener is recorded buying rods and canes for the making or re-making of arbours in 1406. This pleasance was enclosed by a hedge, and entered through a gate, and in 1408 an expensive knife was bought at 1s 8d to

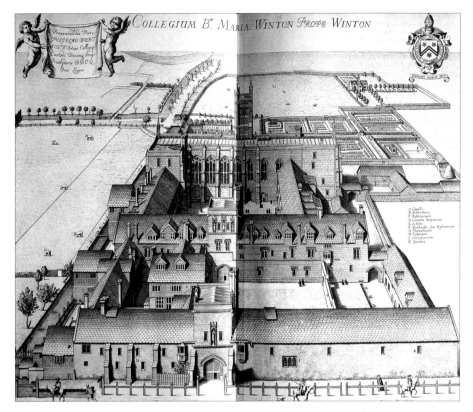

8 Winchester College was built around two courtyards, with the Lockburn stream
running beside it. David Loggan's view from his *Oxonia Illustrata* of 1675 shows the
gardens that were laid out on the meadows behind the College. *Reference Library,
Bristol Central Library*

cut and trim the hedges, and two labourers were hired to weed the bower for
six days.[174] The accounts frequently mention the purchase of branches, rods
and osiers, to make and repair trellis and fencing.[175] Hemp cord and measuring
lines were bought to lay out the walks, while rods were bought for the bower
and to form railings, called 'lez traylynges', most likely trellis.[176] David
Loggan's engraving (*8*) for his *Oxonia Illustrata* of 1675 shows gardens laid out
behind the College on the meadows between the buildings and the river, and
this was probably also the site of the earlier gardens. A running stream was very
desirable, and the same stream that served the Priory, the Lockburn stream,
was divided and made to flow on either side of the College.[177] The garden
probably offered the students a pleasant place to study in hot weather, as well
as for recreation. This combination of productivity and pleasure continued to
characterise gardens well into the Tudor period.

2

'Various entertainments of scent and sight'
Tudor and Early Stuart Gardens

Warblington Castle, The Vyne, Basing House, Netley Abbey
Titchfield Abbey, Hursley Park, Elvetham Hall, Bramshill House

There are no complete surviving Tudor gardens in England, and Hampshire is no exception, although elements of some of the gardens remain, including the walled garden at Basing House with its corner turrets, the walled enclosures at Bramshill House and the chain of ponds at Titchfield Abbey. The Dissolution of the Monasteries in the 1530s led to one of the greatest changes of land ownership in England's history, and Netley Abbey and Titchfield illustrate how monastic buildings were converted into domestic houses by wealthy courtiers. Hunting remained a popular sport for the Tudor aristocracy, and Hursley Park was one of many deer parks of the period. The role of gardens as symbols of status and as venues for courtly entertainment continued through the age, and often landscapes were constructed specifically for royal visits, including the digging of a new lake at Elvetham Hall. Queen Elizabeth I travelled through the county six times on her summer progresses, and there were royal visits by Henry VIII, Edward VI, Queen Mary and James I.

All that remains of **Warblington Castle**, east of Langstone, once a substantial residence, is one of the tall octagonal towers of the Tudor Gatehouse, now stranded in the garden of a farmhouse. After the Castle was slighted during the Civil War, this single tower was left as a landmark for passing shipping.[1] The Castle was built on the site of earlier buildings for Margaret, Countess of Salisbury, between 1514 and 1526.[2] Accounts for the years April 1517 to April 1519 survive;[3] they describe works to the new buildings, including the brewhouse, gatehouse, stable, tower, hall and park gate, as well as the hanging of bells.[4] A large quantity of materials, including 11 tons of Caen stone and 210,000 bricks, was used that year.[5] After the Countess's attainder in 1539, Warblington was granted temporarily to Sir Thomas Wriothesley, and entailed on Sir Richard Cotton in 1551.[6] It remained in the hands of the Cotton family until the Parliamentarians seized it in 1643.[7]

The house was the first brick building on such a large scale in Hampshire.[8]

It was surrounded by a square moat, at least 10 feet deep, enclosing an area of about an acre, part of which still exists, overgrown with wood.[9] There are foundations of some of the buildings beneath the lawn of the modern house and in the paddock to the south.[10] To the north of the Castle is a field of about 5 acres surrounded by a mound and ditch.[11] This probably represents the area of the formal gardens of the house, described in a survey of 1632 carried out for Sir Richard Cotton:

> The scite of the principall mannore house of Warblington is a very fare place Well moated about...Wth a fare grene court Wth in and buildings round the said court Wth a fare gallery and Diverse Chambres...And there is a fare grene court before the gatt of the said house...and there is a very spacious garden Wth plasent Walkes adioyning to the house...and neare to the said place a grove of trees...2 orchards and 2 little meadows...And a fare fishe ponde neare the said place.[12]

Although so little remains (*colour 5*), this description presents a clear image of an important house with extensive gardens amounting to some 6 acres, as well as orchards, meadows and a fishpond, the latter which survives to the east of the Castle. One of the gardens is described as a spacious garden with pleasant walks, which was probably a large formal enclosure, adjoining and so over-looked by the house. In the Tudor period, such a garden would have been known as the Great Garden, and this one would have been similar in size to those at Montacute in Somerset and Hardwick Hall in Derbyshire. The green court in front of the Gatehouse was also a standard feature of Tudor design, and was probably used for games, as well as forming an impressively large entrance court.

One of the most visited houses by Henry VIII, as well as by Elizabeth, was **The Vyne**, near Basingstoke, which the visitor approaches today across a broad lawn sloping down to a long lake. This lawn is the site of the Tudor base court and the approach from the north is the same as it would have been in the sixteenth century. The building, however, was much reduced in size in the middle of the seventeenth century, with only the central section and the southwest wing, along with the Chapel and a three-storey tower at the east end of the north front, surviving from the Tudor house.[13] Sir William Sandys inherited the manor in 1496, and subsequently converted the mediaeval build-ings, and added to them, to create this very large Tudor house. Leland writes: 'at the tyme ther was no very great or sumptuous Maner Place, and was only conteinid within the mote. But he so after translatid and augmented yt, and besides buildid a fair Base Court that at this time is one of the Principale Houses in all Hamptonshire'.[14]

An inventory drawn up in February 1541, after Lord Sandys's death, describes a substantial and well-furnished house, which was in part, if not entirely, surrounded by a moat. Because earlier buildings were 'translatid' into the new house, it may not have had a regular layout of courtyards compared with similar houses of the period, but it was certainly on a large scale.[15] According to dating of the roof timbers, the bulk of the building work was done between 1524 and 1526.[16]

Sandys was well placed to carry out these extensive works. He was already prominent in Court circles in the reign of Henry VII, and became a Knight of the Body to Henry VIII when he succeeded to the throne in 1509. Sandys was appointed Knight of the Garter in 1518, created Baron Sandys in 1523, and became Lord Chamberlain in 1526. It was between these latter dates that most of the building was completed. The King visited him at The Vyne in 1510, in 1531 and again in 1535.[17] Such a leading courtier required an appropriate house and gardens to reflect his status and to entertain royal visitors in a suitably impressive style.

There was an extensive mediaeval deer park around The Vyne, which would have played a part in the entertainment of Henry VIII. However, much of this parkland was leased out in 1608-09 and has remained as farmland ever since.[18] A survey in 1776 recorded a rabbit warren, orchard and hop yard to the east of the house; [19] these may have survived from the Tudor period, when all would have been common garden or park features. There were formal gardens to the northwest in the sixteenth century, on the far side of what is now the lake.[20] These were probably just outside the moat, which originally extended close to the lake.[21] The lake itself was formed in the eighteenth century from a series of Tudor fishponds,[22] again common in grand houses of the period, both to supply fish for the table and as an ornamental feature. An eighteenth-century painting shows a parterre and bowling green beyond the lake, which may have had their origins in the Tudor gardens.[23] Across the moat was an outer gatehouse, as well as an inner gatehouse, both mentioned in the 1541 inventory, suggesting conventional inner and outer approach courtyards.

There were also gardens to the east of the house, and in these is a brick Summerhouse (9) built, according to tree ring dating, in about 1632.[24] It was part of a formal garden layout, and there is an identical Summerhouse to the west, now much altered, but shown in an eighteenth-century painting by JH Müntz.[25] The ground plan is a Greek cross, which contains a circular dome and four two-storey projections, each topped by Tuscan pediments.[26] The Summerhouses may have been added to pre-existing Tudor gardens, or extended gardens may have been concurrently laid out in the 1630s. The buildings may have been commissioned by Alethea Sandys, widow of the 4th Baron Sandys, who died in 1629, and whose connection with the circle of Inigo Jones may indicate an attribution to Isaac de Caus.[27] There may well also have been formal Tudor gardens to the west of the house, since it would have been normal for the long gallery, especially one as magnificent as that at The Vyne,

9 This 1630s Summerhouse at The Vyne, built in the form of a Greek cross, probably
overlooked a formal garden surviving from the Tudor period

to overlook such flowery enclosures; but again, no trace of these remains. Lord
Sandys acquired Mottisfont Priory in 1536 at its Dissolution, and after his
death in 1540 Mottisfont became the principal Sandys family seat. Nonethe-
less, The Vyne remained an important residence and must have been well
maintained, since Queen Elizabeth visited in 1569, 1591 and 1601.[28]

The Marquess of Winchester's **Basing House** was one of the most important Tudor houses in England and again frequently visited by royalty (*10*). It
was sited in a prominent position on a hill overlooking the valley of the River
Loddon, just to the east of Basingstoke. Approaching the ruins of this once-
magnificent house, the path runs between the river and a chain of three Tudor
fishponds. The visitor can peer through Hampshire County Council's trans-
parent re-creation and see the palatial residence projected onto the skyline.
Although the house itself was destroyed during the Civil War, some of the
outlying buildings have survived. Taking his inspiration from Hampton Court,
Sir William Paulet built his new house in two stages, reflecting his rise to
power and wealth under Henry VIII, by whom he was ultimately promoted to
Treasurer of the Royal Household. After the Dissolution, many of the confiscated church estates were given to the new nobility, and in Hampshire Paulet
acquired Netley Abbey and Bishop's Waltham from the rich see of

10 This aerial view of Basing House shows the ruins of the circular Citadel or 'Old House' at the centre and the surviving Walled Garden to the right.
RCAHMS Enterprises

Winchester, making him one of the wealthiest men in the country.[29] He inherited Basing and received a knighthood in 1525, and in 1531 he obtained a licence to crenellate, and to empark 300 acres.[30] The first house, known as the Citadel or 'Old House', was built on the site of a twelfth-century castle. It was constructed of a red brick wall on the outside of the circular castle rampart with buildings around the inner face.[31] The entrance was over a bridge across the moat, and through a large gatehouse, of which only the footings survive. It was described in the diary of the 5th Marquess of Winchester as 'the loftie gatehouse with foure turrets looking northwards'.[32] The house was decorated with Renaissance features created by Italian craftsmen, including terracotta roundels of busts of Roman emperors similar to those by Giovanni da Maiano at Hampton Court.[33]

The Old House was evidently suitable to Paulet's status at Court and fit for entertaining royalty, as Henry VIII visited in 1535, and Edward VI in 1553, two years after Paulet was created Marquess of Winchester.[34] In 1554 Queen Mary and Philip of Spain stayed at Basing after their wedding in Winchester.[35] The second stage of building, the 'New House', was built around a square adjacent to the Old House. The entrance was through a gatehouse from the bailey of the earlier Castle.[36] An inscription among the surviving ruins, which reads 'all these new works up to a d 1561', suggests that the New House was complete by then.[37] Queen Elizabeth I visited Basing on four occasions. On her first visit in 1560 the young Queen stayed for five days with the elderly widowed Marquess, who was her Lord High Treasurer.[38] She was clearly entertained well, probably in the park and gardens of her host, as a letter from Francis Allen to the Earl of Shrewsbury records:

> She liked so well my Lord Treasourer's house, and his greate cheare at Basinge, that she openly and meryly bemoned him to be so olde; 'for ells, by my trouthe,' says she, 'if my Lord Treasurer was a young man, I could fynde in my harte to have him to my husbande before any man in Englande'.[39]

In September 1601 Elizabeth stayed at Basing with the 4th Marquess, 'whereto she took such great content...that she stayed there thirteen days to the great charge of the said Lord Marquis'.[40] On that occasion, Henry IV of France had proposed a meeting with his envoy, the Duc de Biron, and the Queen brought the Court to meet him at Basing.[41] The Duke stayed for four or five days with his entourage nearby at The Vyne. The Queen visited him there, and he visited her at Basing, where he attended her hunting in Basing Park 'and did there see her in such Royalty, and so attended by the Nobility, so costly furnished and mounted, as the like had seldom been seen'.[42]

Although the Old House is ruined, and the New House has disappeared completely above ground level, the original Tudor walled gardens, enclosed by the sixteenth-century brick walls, survive. There are two gardens, side by side, which were made outside the walls of the house, and they are shown on William Brown's 1798 survey.[43] The large rectangular garden would have been the formal pleasure garden, and the survey shows that it had raised terraces on three sides, which would have provided a view of the garden from above. The terraces would probably have been covered with arbours to produce shady green walks. The square sunken garden enclosed by the terraces would have been quartered and decorated with knots in Tudor fashion. In the wall bounding the northwest side of the garden are two octagonal banqueting houses (*11*), known as 'turrets', and evidence of a third, which were later converted to dovecotes.[44] It is probable that Henry VIII walked in this garden with Anne Boleyn in 1535.[45]

The formal garden within this walled enclosure was laid out in 1989.[46] Around the centre, the Paulet motto '*Aymes Loyaulte*', Love Loyalty, is laid out in box, as suggested by Mavis Batey.[47] The garden is planted with flowers and

11 One of the octagonal Turrets in the Walled Garden at Basing House, originally used as a banqueting house and later converted to a dovecote

herbs of the period, including carnations, borage, stocks, pansies and rosemary. The second walled garden was a triangular orchard, and in one corner was another banqueting house.[48] Tudor banqueting houses were frequently associated with orchards in order to enhance the pleasure of eating banqueting delicacies that included marchpane (marzipan) and a wide range of candied fruits, made from the produce of the orchard.

The Marquess of Winchester also owned **Netley Abbey**. Before the Dissolution, Netley was a Cistercian monastery, founded in 1239 at the instigation of Peter des Roches, Bishop of Winchester. Roches died in 1238, before the foundation, and in 1251 Henry III claimed to be the founder.[49] In common with other Cistercian abbeys Netley was built in a remote location by monks who were attempting to recreate the seclusion of desert hermits, in order to rediscover the purity of early monasticism within a self-supporting community. After the Dissolution Netley was developed into a Tudor house and remained occupied until 1704, when it was sold for building materials. Although most of the Tudor building has been demolished, almost all the walls of the thirteenth-century church remain.

On 30 May 1536 the commissioners presented their report on the religious houses of Hampshire. Netley is described in this document as: 'A hedde house of Monkes of thordre of Cisteaux, beinge of large buyldinge and situate upon the Ryvage of the Sees. To the Kinge's Subjects and Strangers travelinge the same Sees great Relief and Comforte'.[50] On the suppression of the smaller monasteries there were only seven monks remaining at Netley.[51] They migrated to the larger Cistercian abbey of Beaulieu, from which their predecessors had originally come.[52] On 3 August the same year, the King gave to Sir William Paulet the site and buildings of the suppressed abbey, together with the grange, mill and lands in Netley. He also received the manor of Hound, lands and a windmill in Hound and Sholing.[53] Paulet set about building himself an impressive new house at Netley, making it one of the largest houses in Hampshire, rivalling Basing.

On the south side of the monastic church was the Cloister, a square of 115 feet with walled alleys covered with wooden pent roofs and enclosed by ranges of buildings.[54] Paulet treated the Cloister as his inner courtyard, the principal court of the Tudor house. To achieve this the Warming-House, Frater, and Kitchen in the southern range were all pulled down except their north wall.[55] The south wall is of sixteenth-century brickwork and had a projecting central gateway flanked by octagonal turrets, and similar turrets at either end of the range, creating a new impressive entrance front, which led into the Fountain Court. The Cloister is now a lawn and at its centre is a mound marking the position of a fountain symbolising Paulet's prestige and power.

Between the church and monastic buildings and the thirteenth-century Abbot's Lodging is a large square area (*colour 6*), enclosed by raised brick terraces, which had a high wall to the north.[56] This was the site of an important new formal garden made in the Tudor period when it would have been known as the 'Great Garden'. Such gardens were a common feature of important Tudor houses, divided into smaller squares, known as 'quarters', and ornamented with symbolic knot patterns made with herbs like hyssop and thyme. On the east side of the Cloister are the south transept, Vestry, Chapter House, inner Parlour, and novices' room; these rooms were retained for use in the Tudor house.[57] Above these rooms on the upper floor was the monastic Great Dorter, which was converted by Paulet into a long gallery overlooking both the Courtyard and his new formal terraced garden. This gallery had two staircase entrances, as well as access from the Great Chamber on the upper floor.[58] Queen Elizabeth would have occupied this suite of rooms when she visited for two days in August 1560.[59] There was a chain of three large fishponds along the coombe to the northeast of the Abbey, filled with water channelled from nearby springs, two of which survive.[60] At the request of Henry VIII, Paulet built in 1542 a small fort, facing directly onto the Solent, within the grounds of Netley Abbey. This was intended to protect the coast and the approach to Southampton.[61] It was later converted to residential use and is now called Netley Castle. After the Abbey buildings were demolished in the early eighteenth century, the romantic ruins became an attractive destination for tourists. Among them was Horace Walpole, who described the place in 1755:

The ruins are vast, and retain fragments of beautiful fretted roof pendent in the air, with all variety of Gothic patterns of windows wrapped round and round with ivy...they are not the ruins of Netley, but of Paradise. – oh! the purple abbots, what a spot they had chosen to slumber in![62]

Like Netley, **Titchfield Abbey**, to the southeast of Southampton, only survives as a ruin. There, the high walls surrounding the site were built in the sixteenth century, enclosing a new Tudor house which replaced the mediaeval

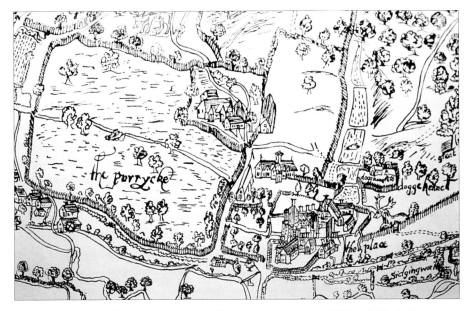

12　A detail of a printed copy of the Earl of Southampton's map of Titchfield, dating to about 1610, showing the house called 'The Place'; the deer park is enclosed by pales and a chain of ponds is marked, which survive today. *Hampshire Record Office: 94M84/68*

Abbey after the Dissolution. The imposing stone Gatehouse with its four-storey castellated octagonal turrets and original doors was built across the nave of the mediaeval church and is virtually intact (*colour 7*). Through the Gatehouse is the central courtyard, which was created from the cloister of the Abbey. To the northwest are large fishponds, shown on an early map, which also records the hunting park and pale (*12*). To the southwest, there is a mediaeval tithe barn, probably built in the fifteenth century, which would have continued in use through the Tudor period.[63]

The Premonstratensian Abbey of Titchfield was founded in 1232 by Bishop Peter des Roches. It was dissolved in December 1537, and the abbot must have had warning, because when the commissioners visited, the church had already been stripped of its valuables.[64] Thomas Wriothesley (pronounced Risley),

later 1st Earl of Southampton and Lord Chancellor, acquired Titchfield immediately after its dissolution.[65] He obtained a grant of the church, the site and
all the possessions of the Abbey, and converted it into a grand courtyard
house, then known as Place House, re-using some of the monastic buildings.
Work was progressing well by April 1538, when John Crayford, one of the
King's Commissioners, wrote to Wriothesley:

> Many do preyse yor worke, som so hieghly that they say/ No man in England
> wtoute exception/ for the quantite of it shall have a stronger more bewtyfull
> nete & pleasaunt house...& I trust yt shall appere to go forward with such spede
> by mydsomer as never no work hath done in so short space wt so Few
> workmen.[66]

Licences were required for crenellation and Wriothesley's alterations were
probably completed by 1542, in which year he received pardon for having fortified his manor house of Titchfield without licence.[67] Marble stones, altars and
the bells from the church were sold, and the tiles of the nave were taken up.[68]
When Leland visited Titchfield he recorded that 'Mr. Wriothesley hath
buildid a right stately House embatelid, and having a goodely Gate, and a
Conducte castelid in the Midle of the Court of it, yn the very same Place wher
the late Monasterie of Premonstratenses stoode caullyd Tichefelde'.[69] To
have a castellated conduit, which suggests that it was a mediaeval-style fountain, in the central courtyard indicates that Tichfield was a house of some
pretension, although nothing now remains of the feature.

Adjacent to the Gatehouse was the porter's lodge, with a principal apart-
ment above, which was subsequently used as a small theatre, perhaps where
some of Shakespeare's plays were performed. The chapter house became the
Chapel and the monastic kitchen was updated as Wriothesley's new kitchen.[70]
When not re-using old materials, the new house was built of Caen stone and
brick. The mason responsible was Thomas Berty from Winchester, who was
also engaged at Winchester Cathedral Priory and in the royal programme of
coastal fortifications at the castles of Calshot, Southsea, Hasilworth and
Hurst.[71] Berty was probably also involved at Netley and Warblington, which
are closely related buildings of similar courtyard design with fortifications.[72]
The house and gardens were impressive, and both Edward VI and Elizabeth I
were entertained there.[73] The house stood until 1781, when it was partially
dismantled for building stone, and has since decayed.[74]

Letters concerning the new Tudor building have been preserved and have
been transcribed by W H St John Hope.[75] On 2 January 1538, immediately after
Wriothesley acquired Titchfield, Crayford and Roland Lathom, the other
Commissioner, wrote jointly to him, suggesting alterations to be made to the
buildings and grounds:

Joynyng to the gardyng & orchard/ soe the kechyng ther & the synk must be alleyed wt you Rosemary and Lavendre &c. so that we allowe yor owne writing wher you say yor phantasie to be sett...for yor dyning plor [parlour] & chaple beneth/& for lodgynge above of two stories if you list/ leaded and battled above/ wt fayer Creste & prospecte west & south upon your gardyng orchard (?) & court/ it was long to write all /to be breve/ you may have wt reasonable charge an house for the Kinge grace to bate & for any baron to kepe his hospitalite in.[76]

The correspondence makes it clear that when Wriothesley acquired the property there were already gardens beside the Abbey buildings. The orchard was inherited from the mediaeval period, and included as part of the design of the newly converted house. The rooms overlooked the gardens, as well as the courtyard with its fountain. A letter from Crayford in April 1538, only three months into the conversion, describes how the gardens were accessed from the building:

An hawte pace [landing], to conveye unto a vice [staircase]/ towarde the garding/ which woll bring up sutors and geste unto your greate chamber galery or dyning plor [parlour] or ells your closset.[77]

The early map illustrates the hunting park and deer, as well as kennels for the hounds. Queen Elizabeth was entertained at some of the great houses of Sussex and Hampshire on her annual progress in summer 1591 and when she stayed at Titchfield two stands were prepared for her to view the hunting in the park. In 1591 Henry Wriothesley, third Earl of Southampton and later Shakespeare's patron, was almost eighteen. He had succeeded to his title on the death of his father ten years earlier, inheriting Titchfield. Shakespeare's *Venus and Adonis*, published in 1593, based on the tale from Ovid's *Metamorphoses,* was dedicated to Wriothesley. The poem describes the love-sick temptress Venus lying on a primrose bank in the heat of the midday sun, the rose-cheeked Adonis fastened in her arms. In contrast to the chaste Diana, Venus is the goddess of love and beauty:

'Fondling', she saith, 'since I have hemmed thee here
Within the circuit of this ivory pale,
I'll be a park, and thou shalt be my deer.
Feed where thou wilt, on mountain or in dale;
Graze on my lips, and if those hills be dry,
Stray lower, where the pleasant fountains lie.[78]

In *Lucrece,* published the following year, and also dedicated to Wriothesley, Shakespeare describes the ill-fated Lucrece: 'As the poor frighted deer, that stands at gaze, /Wildly determining which way to fly'.[79] Might the park at

Titchfield have influenced the poet's verse?

The River Meon flows past the Abbey, and is now a small stream, but in the sixteenth century it was a tidal harbour, and Titchfield was a port.[80] To the northwest of the Abbey is a chain of large fish ponds clearly illustrated on the early map. A letter from Crayford and Lathom describes how they went to view the four ponds, which were 'a mile in length to ford and harbour' and estimated to contain 100,000 'carpes, tenches, breams and pike'.[81] There were 'besides ij fayer pondes at your dore',[82] on the opposite side of the park from the house, which also survive today. The ponds date to soon after the foundation of the Abbey in 1232, and continued in use post-Dissolution.[83] The lower pond acted as the main water supply to the Abbey.[84] They have now been converted into a modern fishery called Carron Row Farm Lakes.

Only the footings of the Tudor hunting lodge can been seen as parch marks in the lawn to the rear of the present **Hursley Park**, which was built in the eighteenth century and is now owned by IBM. Hursley village is on the main road from Winchester to Romsey, and the house is sited in the centre of the park on raised ground to the west of the village. To the north are the ruins of Merdon Castle, which was built by Henry de Blois in 1148 and is now a circular earthwork with a ditch and bank.[85] The Castle was a bishop's palace, but had fallen into decay by the mid fourteenth century; in 1552 John Poynet, Bishop of Winchester, surrendered Merdon to King Edward VI.[86] In the same year Edward granted the Manor of Merdon, together with the park of Hursley, to Sir Philip Hoby, who probably built the hunting lodge called 'The Plase' between 1552 and 1557.[87] In 1559, Merdon was re-granted by Elizabeth to Philip Hoby's half-brother, William Hoby.[88] He died, probably at Hursley, in the late sixteenth century.[89]

A delightfully detailed 1588 map of the estate by Ralph Treswell marks the Tudor house as 'Plase' in the centre of the paled deer park,[90] showing it as a single block with wings projecting into an enclosed entrance court (*colour 8*). There were no formal gardens around the house, so in the Tudor period The Plase was used solely for hunting. The map also marks a small lodge, which was probably for the gamekeeper, and a warren. The park is full of deer and demonstrates that the main value of the Lodge and park was not for agriculture, but for leisure. Sometimes the deer were hunted on horseback, but alternatively, they were enclosed in a paddock, and shot from a stand. Crossbows, lighter for women than those for men, were preferred to firearms for hunting, as they were quieter, easier to use, and the bolt, if it missed its target, could be retrieved. After a deer was wounded with the bow, the hounds would be released to pull it down.[91] The Treswell map shows a fenced enclosure within the park called 'South Launde', between the Lodge and the river. Launde is the same as a lawn, in the sense of a grassy plain extended between woods, and was used for deer coursing.[92] Shakespeare uses the term in *King*

Henry VI, Part III, when two keepers enter a chase:

> Under this thick-grown brake we'll shroud ourselves;
> For through this laund anon the deer will come;
> And in this covert will we make our stand,
> Culling the principal of all the deer.[93]

Elizabeth is not known to have visited Hursley, but **Elvetham Hall**, near Basingstoke, hosted a memorable royal visit in 1591 full of spectacular entertainment and pageantry. A grand Victorian Gothic mansion, now functioning as a hotel, Elvetham Hall was built on the site of an earlier Tudor house that burned down in 1840, and of which nothing survives. However, in the sixteenth century Elvetham was a secondary seat of Edward Seymour, 1st Earl of Hertford. A 300-acre hunting park was enclosed in 1403, and from 1426 the manor was home to the Seymour family.[94] In 1591 Seymour took the opportunity of the Queen's Progress through Hampshire that summer to entertain her in considerable style for four days at Elvetham, and a detailed account of the entertainments is recorded in a contemporary pamphlet.[95] This includes a drawing of the lake (*13*), illustrating how a large number of people attended the event, some on foot, some on horseback. Although little physical evidence of the Queen's visit survives, the site of the crescent-shaped lake on the River Hart, a few hundred metres from the house, can be seen on nineteenth-century maps and on later aerial photographs. The lake has now mostly drained away and the site is overgrown with trees. Another possible sixteenth-century survival is an oak tree in the park, just beyond the present gardens, which is more than 32 feet in circumference. It may well have been planted to commemorate Elizabeth's visit.

The Queen did not travel light. Because she went with the Court, the number of people in her progress retinue was large, and up to 350 people would accompany her on a major journey.[96] The Queen and nobility proceeded in carriages pulled by six horses.[97] Carts full of supplies accompanied the travelling Court, and Elizabeth had as many as 169 for her own use, including thirteen carts for jewels and ten for the wardrobe of the bedchamber.[98] Transport of goods for Privy Councillors, ladies of the court and other household officers meant that up to 300 carts might pass through the countryside.[99]

The park at Elvetham was relatively small, 'but of two miles in compasse or thereabouts',[100] as it was not the Earl's main residence. Nevertheless, he made considerable improvements and immense preparations for Elizabeth's arrival. The crescent-shaped lake, in which there were three islands in the shape of a ship, a fort and a snail mount, was created for her visit. The fort was 20 feet square and 'overgrown with willows', while the snail mount rose to 'four circles of greene privie hedges, the whole in height twentie foot and fortie foot broad

13 The lake at the Elvetham Entertainment from John Nichols's *Progresses and Public Processions of Queen Elizabeth*. The Queen sits beneath a canopy on the left of the crescent-shaped lake, while in front of her tritons sound their trumpets. *University of Bristol Library, Special Collections*

at the bottom.'[101] As well as digging the new lake, the Earl set 300 men to work, 'to inlarge his house with new rooms and offices',[102] and new buildings were erected on a hillside in the park, 'above the ponds head'.[103] These included a room of estate for the nobles with a withdrawing space for the Queen. This was a temporary banqueting house, described in the account of her visit: 'The outsides of the walles were all covered with boughs, and clusters of ripe hasell nuttes, the insides with arras, the roofe of the place with works of ivy leaves, the floore with sweet herbes and greene rushes'.[104] Other rooms hastily constructed in this new entertainment complex included a great kitchen with four ranges, a Pastry with five ovens, a Spicery, Wine-cellar, Ewery, Pantry and cook's lodgings. There was also a large hall for entertaining 'Knights, Ladies and Gentlemen of chiefe account', with tables 23 yards long.[105]

In common with other entertainments given to the Queen on Summer Progress, most of the action took place in the gardens and park. The Queen had previously been staying at Odiham, and the Earl, with a train of 200 men, met her coming out of Odiham Park and escorted her the three miles to Elvetham.[106] As she arrived, she was greeted halfway between the park gate and the house by a poet pronouncing an oration, accompanied by six Virgins, representing the three Graces and 'the other three the Howres...with flowrie

14　This nineteenth-century carving on the chimneypiece in the drawing room at
Elvetham records Queen Elizabeth being greeted on her visit by Lord Hertford;
girls with garlands on their heads strew flowers and herbs before her

garlands on their heads, and baskets full of sweet hearbs and flowers upon their
arms'.[107] They then walked before the Queen towards the house, strewing the
way with flowers and singing a 'dittie' by Thomas Watson.

The drawing room of the Elvetham Hotel has a chimneypiece with a
carving that depicts her visit, showing the Queen arriving on horseback,
greeted by Seymour and with six flower-girls casting petals before her (*14*). The
crescent shape of the new lake symbolised Cynthia, goddess of the moon, and
a pageant was held on the water on the second day of her visit. The Queen was
described as 'her whom all the world adores, Faire Cynthia'.[108] Here Nereus,
Prophet of the Sea, swam ahead of five Tritons 'brest-high in the water'
sounding their trumpets, while three Virgins in a pinnace played Scottish gigs
on cornets.[109] To watch the entertainment, the Queen was seated beside the
pond, beneath a 'canapie of estate', held up by 'foure worthie Knights', while
the musicians played.[110]

On the third day, the gardens were again used extensively to amuse the
Queen. The entertainments began when she 'opened a casement of her
Gallerie window' at nine o'clock in the morning to find three musicians in the
garden below, who greeted her with 'a pleasant song of Coridon and Phyllida'.
Apparently this pleased Elizabeth, as once the song was over, she asked for it

to be sung again. Another of the entertainments provided for the Queen later that day was a game of bord and cord, a variant of handball.[111] After dinner, at about three o'clock, ten of Hertford's men set up lines 'squaring out the forme of a tennis-court, and making a crosse line in the middle', in 'a square greene court before her Majesties windowe'.[112] The men then played five-a-side, and the Queen was clearly amused, because she watched for an hour and a half. As we have seen, the front entrance court to a house was commonly called the green court in the Tudor period, because it was grassed, and frequently used for games; this is likely to have been where the game was played. Later that evening, after supper, there was a display at the lake, with a 'castle of fireworks' at the fort, and on either side 'were many fire-wheeles, pikes of pleasure, and balles of wilde fire'.[113] While the firework display was taking place, the Queen was served a banquet 'in a lowe Gallerie in her Majesties Privie-garden'.[114] The Privy Garden would have been beside the private rooms in the house, and this banquet involved 200 of Hertford's gentlemen carrying dishes down from the new catering buildings 'fourteene score off' on the hillside, their way in the dark lit by 100 torchbearers.[115]

On the final day of her visit, Elizabeth was entertained yet again from the garden, as she watched from the window of her gallery. The account of the entertainments describes how 'there began three Cornets to play certaine fantastike dances, at the measure whereof the Fayery Quene came into the garden, dauncing with her maides about her'.[116] The fairies' song, accompanied by 'an exquisite consort', played on lute, bandora, base-violl, citterne, treble-violl, and flute, praised Elizabeth as 'the fairest Quene' and 'sweet Elisa'.[117] She was so delighted with the performance that 'shee commanded to heare it sung and to be danced three times over, and called for divers lords and Ladies to behold it'.[118] Despite Seymour's considerable efforts to please the Queen, she did not restore his sons to legitimacy, as he had hoped, and they only recovered their titles under James I.

The death of Elizabeth I in 1603 and the accession of James I marked the end of the Tudor dynasty and the coming of the Stuarts. In garden terms, little changed: elaborate, flower-filled compartments continued to be wrapped around the skirts of the house. The greatest Jacobean house in Hampshire is **Bramshill**, built by Edward, 11th Baron Zouche of Harringworth. Indeed, it is one of the finest Jacobean prodigy houses in England, ranking alongside Knole in Kent, Hatfield in Hertfordshire and Audley End in Essex, all raised by Zouche's political rivals. The house was also visited by royalty, in this case James I. Zouche began to build in 1605 on a spur overlooking the valley of the River Hart, and the house is sited in a prominent position above the surrounding landscape. It was still not complete at his death in 1625, making this an unusually long building programme, which was protracted by Zouche's lack of funds.

Surrounded by formal brick-walled gardens aligned with the house, Bramshill has one of the most perfectly preserved garden arrangements of the period. The approach is from the north, along a drive that skirts a large lake, within which there is a square artificial island. This brings the visitor up to the rear of the house, and it is not until walking around to the front that the magnificence of its original entrance can be appreciated. Here, Zouche's drive stretches southwest for around a mile. About halfway along its length the drive crosses the river by an elegant ornamental bridge with double arches. The section between the house and bridge was originally flanked by a double row of elms, now gone.[119] On the far side of the bridge, the drive rises between lines of oaks. Approaching the house the drive climbs a steep ramp to the fore-court, which is enclosed along the sides by brick walls and flanked by two octagonal brick Turrets (15). The entrance front, impressive today, was originally even more so, as it had two wings, now demolished. These, and other

15 Twin Turrets on the approach to Bramshill flank the entrance forecourt; they are likely to have functioned either as porters' lodges, or banqueting houses, or both

elements of the layout, can be seen in a 1699 map by Isaac Justis; they were removed by Sir John Cope, who built new terminating walls in 1703.[120] A stone terrace runs along the east front of the house and it appears that the arches, which are formed as loggias to either end of this terrace, have been moved. It is likely that they were loggias along the courtyard elevation of the missing wings.[121] The 1699 map also marks a wall and gateway between the vanished wings. It is possible that the Postern Gate, which gives access to the walled garden to the northeast of the house, was moved from the entrance court-yard.[122] If so, the elegant triple arches of the Gate would have mirrored the triple arches on the entrance front of the house.

Zouche was brought up by Sir William Cecil, Lord Burghley, as a ward of court, and he was under Cecil's care from 1569, when he was thirteen, until his majority eight years later.[123] He was undoubtedly influenced by Cecil's important gardens at Theobalds and Burghley, which were both in the process of being built when Zouche was under Cecil's guardianship. Cecil was an enthusiastic gardener, and he employed the renowned doctor and botanist, John Gerard, to maintain and develop his gardens. Between 1587 and 1593, Zouche travelled through Europe, both to enrich his education and to qualify for diplomatic service. In Altdorf he met Sir Henry Wotton, with whom he corresponded frequently, and he stayed with Wotton in Vienna in 1591.[124]

Following Cecil's lead, Zouche set out to create a botanic garden at his home in Hackney, which was then a small village favoured for its healthy fresh air. Hackney became a gathering place for plantsmen, and a site for Zouche's collection of exotics, so it is likely that, when he went on to establish the gardens at Bramshill, he created a similar exotic garden. When the eminent Flemish botanist Matthias de L'Obel returned to settle in London in 1585, he won a position as supervisor of Zouche's gardens at Hackney.[125] On his travels, Zouche visited Constantinople, and so saw at first hand the gardens of the Ottomans. The formal Muslim gardens there captivated him, particularly their densely planted beds of tulips, irises and lilies. Other bulbs he had never seen before, such as the early blue-flowered hyacinth, which he brought back with him on his return to England. De L'Obel also records that Zouche came back with two small white tulips, a winter crocus and a *Colchicum*, as well as a number of lilies.[126] Zouche gave seeds of some of the new plants to John Gerard, who was interested in their medicinal properties. Of the 'Thornie Apple' (Jimson weed), Gerard writes:

> There is another kinde heereof altogither greater than the former, whose seeds
> I received of the right Honorable the Lord Edward Zouch; which he brought
> from Constantinople, and of his liberalitie did bestow them upon me, as also
> many other rare & strange seeds; and it is that Thorn apple that I have dispersed
> through this land, whereof at this present I have great use in chirurgerie, as well
> in burnings and scaldings, as also in virulent and maligne ulcers, apostemes, and
> such like.[127]

De L'Obel dedicated the 1605 edition of his *Pharmaceuticam officinam animadversiones* to Zouche. He later became royal botanist to James I, who was entertained at Bramshill in 1620. One of the rooms at Bramshill is decorated with 150 panels, painted with plants taken from woodcuts in de L'Obel's books.[128]

Bramshill is an entirely outward-looking house, as its long, narrow central courtyard has only the east window of the Chapel looking onto it. The Long

16 One of the two loggias on the East Terrace at Bramshill with the Troco Stone.
The loggias were originally on the entrance forecourt, while the terrace doubled as
a vantage point for views out to the deer park and as a bowling alley

Gallery occupies the whole of the first floor of the northeast range and remains
essentially as Zouche would have known it, with windows in either end, as well
as along the outer wall, overlooking formal gardens to the east and west of the
house. In the north loggia on the east terrace is a large 'Troco Stone' carved
into a rhombicosidodecahedron, one of the thirteen Archimedean polyhedra
(16). Such a demonstration of scientific knowledge was an important element
of Renaissance culture. The stone seems to have had a dual purpose, as it has
a sundial on top and round holes in the sides in which Troco balls were kept.
Troco, or lawn billiards, is an Italian game, which was popular in England from
the early seventeenth century. It was a forerunner of croquet, played with large
wooden balls and long handled cues.

Stairs descend from the terrace to a large square garden, now laid to lawn,
which would have been a formal Jacobean garden. The gardens to the west of
the house are also of differing levels because of the sloping site. An inventory
of furnishings made in 1634 describes 'the Corner Chamber by the bowlinge
greene', and the green, which is balustraded, also overlooks the formal garden
below the terrace.[129] The 1699 map also shows ponds, orchards and a maze, all
common features in a grand Jacobean garden. Zouche spent most of his later
years at Bramshill, where, as well as tending his flowering plants, he was an
enthusiastic collector of shrubs and trees. Amongst these he imported Scottish
firs, which were planted in a long avenue extending from the northeast front of

the house.[130] This avenue is marked on the 1699 Justis map, and the firs were described by Charles Kingsley in 1858 as 'James the First's gnarled giants'.[131] After Zouche's death in 1625, the estate changed hands many times before it was bought in 1699 by Sir John Cope, whose family occupied it until 1935.

3

'Prospect and Vista's noble and great' Formal Gardens

Stratfield Saye, Broadlands, Abbotstone, Shawford Park
Breamore House, Herriard Park, Southwick Park
Pylewell Park, Tangier Park, Rotherfield Park, Chawton House
Beaulieu, Hurstbourne Park, Hale Park, Hackwood Park, Westbury House
Lainston House, Tylney Hall, Hursley Park, Cranbury Park
Walhampton House, Warbrook House, Bevois Mount

The lack of both documentary evidence and visual images of great seventeenth-century gardens in any county makes it extremely difficult to retrieve lost landscapes that were obviously of some consequence. Some shires, like Gloucestershire and Hertfordshire, have early eighteenth-century county histories that contain important engravings of formal layouts, while that indefatigable traveller, Celia Fiennes, can be relied upon to inform us of major gardens. However, more often than not, she leaves tantalising glimpses of the places she visited, particularly Broadlands, which must have had important and elaborate formal gardens before the great reshaping by Lancelot Brown. The formal layout at **Stratfield Saye** was similarly swept away by Lord Rivers in a great reshaping after he succeeded to the estate in 1745, to be replaced by a Brown-style park. Fortunately, a manuscript account, written by his steward Mr Brookes in about 1810, records some details of the garden Lord Rivers demolished: 'he levelled the dreary garden walls, regular terraces and square fishponds with clipped hedges and quaint parterres'.[1] Fiennes arrived at **Broadlands** before the gardens were finished and so we have an incomplete account of their form and extent:

> The Gardens are walled in, some with brest walls some higher with flower potts on them, severall places with open grates to look through with stone balls or figures on the pillars each side the gates every way; there is a water house that by a Wheele casts up the water out of the River just by and fills the pipes that serves all the house and to fill the bason designed in the middle of the Garden with a Spout in the middle; the Gardens are not finish'd but will be very fine.[2]

Another house, which gets a more cursory mention in her travel diary, is **Abbotstone** at Alresford, north of Winchester, even though this was an important property, owned by the Duke of Bolton, whose principal seat was at Hackwood. When Fiennes saw Abbotstone in the late 1690s she wrote that it 'stands on the side of a hill where are fine Gardens and much fruite'.[3] The elevated platform on which the 1680 house stood, which itself replaced a sixteenth-century house built by Bolton's ancestor, William Paulet, 1st Marquess of Winchester, overlooks a lower, square area, banked and defined by small shrubs and trees. This is referred to as the 'Great Garden' in Henry Whitear's 1745 lease of Abbotstone Farm.[4] To the southwest are the remains of a substantial brick walled garden, which probably accounts for Fiennes's remark about the fruit; also there seems to have been an orchard, shown on the 1838 tithe map, at the southeast corner of the Great Garden. Writing of Abbotstone in 1719, Pavey remarks that Bolton's 'large noble brick house edged with stone' was built as a 'convenient hawking seat of which sport he was a great admirer, in allusion whereof he caused two vast large hawkes to be fix'd on top of two banqueting houses just before the entrance into the house'.[5] Moreover, Pavey states that the house was 'built after the Italian manner opening a vista from the end of the house to the other', proving that it was central to a garden of axial formality created in the 1680s by the Duke of Bolton.[6]

Banqueting houses were a feature at **Shawford Park**, Twyford, where Sir Henry Mildmay rebuilt the existing Dares House and laid out extensive gardens after 1685. Like those at Abbotstone, they have all disappeared, and the site is now more noted for recent work to restore and re-adapt the early twentieth-century gardens and wider parkland with its water meadows by Kim Wilkie.[7] However, detailed planting lists, general garden work and the construction of the banqueting houses are all documented in the estate accounts.[8] In the disbursements ledger for 1660-1708 there are at least two entries concerning the 'Banquett houses' in 1695, as well as 'Garden Arches', the 'Pond Wall' and grass and gravel walks, while the carpenter Peter Gregory was paid for his work on the 'Pallisadoe Gatio', or palisade fencing, for either the parterres or the garden environs.[9] While it is clear what Mildmay had built at Shawford, it is hard to ascertain what his formal gardens must have looked like, though a much later sale particulars map (*17*) of 1811 shows the remnants of this formal layout, including a canal and rectangular pond, no doubt associated with the 'Pond Wall' mentioned in the accounts.[10]

A similar layout to Abbotstone, though less well defined in terms of surviving earthworks, may have been constructed at **Breamore House**, near Fordingbridge in the New Forest. Fiennes also visited Breamore:

You enter the Garden on a terrass and that by stepps so to severall Walks of Gravel and Grass; here was fine flowers and greens dwarfe trees and oring

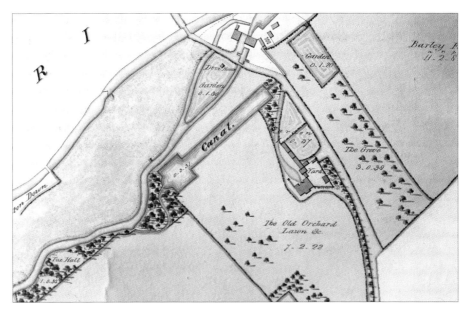

17 This 1811 map of Shawford Park shows the surviving canal of the seventeenth-century formal garden. *Hampshire Record Office: 46M72/E38*

> [orange] and lemon trees in rows with fruite and flowers all at once...here are stately woods and walks. [II]

These terraced gardens must have been laid out to the southeast of the house and will have extended into the fields below to give an elevated prospect of the River Avon; the present terrace is nineteenth-century in date. A sundial dated 1670 above the central doorway on the south front of the Elizabethan house might have been part of the remodelling of the garden that was undertaken by Robert Greville, fourth Lord Brooke, who died in 1676. Or perhaps it was his widow who reshaped the gardens, as Fiennes describes Breamore as the 'Seat of the Lady Brooks', even though by this time she had married Thomas Hoby. She died in 1691, suggesting that Fiennes's visit was made in the late 1680s.

Fiennes's more detailed account of the formalities at Breamore gives a better idea of what may have been laid out within the walls at Broadlands and Abbotstone. Indeed, elaborate parterres of flowers and shrubs threaded with grass and gravel walks were one of the two defining design elements of gardens that were laid out between the Restoration in 1660 and the onset of a more informal style of landscape promoted by Alexander Pope in the 1720s and taken up by William Kent in the 1730s. The other was the wilderness.

Parterres are relatively easy to grasp, being a series of ornamented rectangles, usually bordered by flowers and topiary, with flourishes of plants or coloured gravels at their centres. These decorative sectors were divided into eleven types by George London and Henry Wise in their 1706 book, *The Retir'd Gardener*, which itself was a shortened and improved translation of *Le Jardinier Solitaire* by Sieur Louis Liger. The decoration of these parterres consisted of variations on three themes: 'Cut-work', 'Turfs' and 'Imbroidery'. Cut-work was defined by shaped beds cut into either grass or gravel for the reception of plants; Turfs were shaped areas of grass on either soil or gravel; Imbroidery was described by the two designers as 'Draughts which represent in effect, those we have on our Cloaths'.[12]

Wildernesses are much harder to define and have a longer design history, stretching back to the Tudor period, but essentially they were wooded, shady areas acting as a more naturalistic, even wild, counterpoint to the showy formalities of the parterres.[13] Both 'wilderness' and 'grove' were interchangeable terms in the period, John Evelyn having a 'grove', which had all the characteristics of a 'wilderness', in his garden at Sayes Court, near Deptford, while Thomas Meager offered plans for 'wilderness-worke' in his 1688 *The English Gardner*. While describing the last region of a tripartite garden in his 1700 *Campania Foelix*, Timothy Nourse refers to 'this Third Garden, Grove or Wilderness', but by the 1720s the term wilderness was used consistently, particularly in the garden writings of Batty Langley and Philip Miller.[14] Wildernesses were planted up with forest trees, shrubs and hedges and threaded through with gravel or grass paths. Formal layouts thus displayed a tension between art and nature in the garden, where the parterres, which were open and highly artificial, stood for tamed nature, while the closed wilderness, bounded by tall hedges and trees, offered a contrasting informality more suited to solitude and reflection. In addition, wildernesses encouraged contemplative walking with their meandering paths, which Langley referred to in 1726 as 'arti-natural' lines and walks, while also providing privacy in their open glades.[15] As Philip Miller wrote in 1731: 'there should be some smaller Serpentine Walks through the Middle of the Quarters, where Persons may retire for privacy'.[16]

Though there are few so-called 'Franco-Dutch' formal gardens in Hampshire, either surviving or lost – the only two of significance included in *Britannia Illustrata* and *Vitruvius Britannicus* being Southwick Park and Pylewell Park respectively – of those that were achieved, before the stripping back of formal geometries in the 1720s under Charles Bridgeman, all have parterres or wildernesses, or a typical combination of the two. By far the most important layout in the county, where George London is known to have submitted designs, was at **Herriard Park**, on the A339, south of Basingstoke. Sadly, the blockish parent house, which was probably designed in 1704 by John James, himself a garden writer who would publish in 1712 *The Theory and Practice of Gardening*, a translation of AJ Dézallier d'Argenville's definitive work on Le Nôtre's methods, *La théorie et la pratique du jardinage*, was demolished in 1965, while almost all the formal gardens at Herriard were swept away in a 1790s remodelling under first

Humphry Repton and then John Armstrong.[17] However, most of the family papers have now been deposited in the Hampshire Record Office. Amongst these there is a large-scale plan of the parterre to the south of the house by London, dated 22 May 1699,[18] and a sketch plan, possibly drawn by Thomas Jervoise, of the whole layout.[19] There is also an elevation of the main façade of the 1704 house that shows the proposed garden treatment of the entrance forecourt and the two pools on the south terrace.[20]

Taken together, London's pen-and-ink design for the parterres and Jervoise's sketch of the entire layout give a very clear impression of what was planned for Herriard between 1699 and 1707. It is unclear, however, exactly what was achieved, because the terrace was only built from March 1706, when London and Jervoise were still discussing the parterre design.[21] The intention was to raise the house on a platform and flank it with two rectangular ponds with semicircular ends. Steps were to lead down from the garden front of the house to a terrace walk, bordered by a retaining wall, after which further steps would descend to a grass walk and thence to the parterres, which were to be bisected by a central gravel walk and a cross walk of grass. Judging by the copious inscriptions specifying grass, each parterre was to be bordered and also threaded by green walks, and the southern arm of the central axis was to be punctuated by alternating square and circular clipped topiary.

Thomas Jervoise's sketch plan of the whole layout (*18*) gives a few more details of the planting and areas and includes the wilderness to the east of the house.[22] There is a beech walk bordering the southeast parterre, and between that and the wilderness was the 'Hog Orchard'. The wilderness itself was fairly regular in its pathways and edged on the east by a 'Long Walk'. The circular entrance court had a deep revetment where it connected with the open parkland, while two triangular shrubberies flanking the turning circle were planted with conical and globe-shaped topiary shrubs and edged with flower borders.[23] The only surviving elements of this flowery and shrub-filled garden are the broad terrace on which the present house is sited and a declivity in the field to the east, which may be the site of a pond. It is likely that tree avenues radiated out from the house to the north and south, of which one section of a silver fir avenue, shown on a 1730 estate map, survives to the north. On his arrival in June 1793, Repton was impressed by 'the stupendous double row of large silver firs', but thought it characteristic of the 'false taste of the last century'.[24] Consequently, he advocated the destruction of one half near the house to open up the parkland, 'leaving the other as a magnificent specimen of the ancient style in gardening'.[25] Much of the planting in the north of the park, particularly the combinations of oak and beech, is of Repton's time, but there are some veteran trees, including a sweet chestnut, that must date from the late seventeenth century.

The engraving of **Southwick Park** (*19*) in Kip and Knyff's *Britannia Illustrata* shows Sir Daniel Norton's U-shaped Jacobean house, which had been

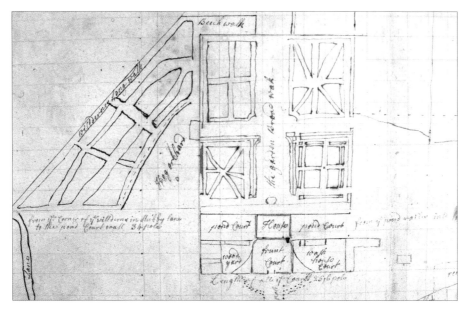

18 Thomas Jervoise's sketch plan for the formal gardens at Herriard Park outlines the
four parterres either side of the Broad Walk, while the Wilderness is separated from
the formalities by an orchard. *Jervoise of Herriard Collection: Hampshire Record Office:
44M69/P1/65*

built onto the ruins of a twelfth-century Augustinian priory. To the east of the
house a fashionable formal garden in the style of London and Wise has been
laid out, presumably for the then owner, Richard Norton, who had inherited
the estate in 1691. By about 1770 the house, offices and greenhouse remained,
but the formal gardens had disappeared. The house was demolished in 1803
and its successor built on a different, higher, site commanding an artificial
lake. This is now at the heart of a golf course, but earthworks of the formal
layout can be traced, marked on Ordnance Survey maps as 'The Slopes', though
they are now lost in fairways. The wilderness wood shown in the Kip & Knyff
view to the north of the gardens also survives between the golf course and
Pinsley Drive.

The Southwick layout must date from about 1700, with its typical Dutch-
style, topiary-edged avenues, simple parterres and angular grove or wilderness.
Most telling is the nine-bay greenhouse with its tall windows, columned
centrepiece and open segmental pediment. It is close in style to several that
William Talman introduced into gardens of the period and which are illustrated by Kip and Knyff, notably at Chatsworth and Bretby in Derbyshire and
Dawley in Middlesex. The Southwick layout had none of the complex water-
works of other gardens of the period, but her familial connection with the

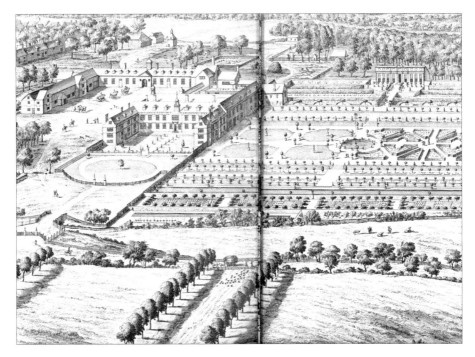

19 Jan Kip & Leonard Knyff's view of Southwick from their 1707 *Britannia Illustrata*
records the extensive Dutch-style gardens laid out on terraces; the site is now a
golf course

Nortons encouraged Celia Fiennes to stop off on one of her tours: 'South-
wicke, Col. Norton's, a good old house capable of being made fine, large
Garden room Woods and Grounds lying well about it and a good Warren
Coppices and the stately'st Timber trees as may be seen'.[26] It was left to
Colonel Richard Norton's son, another Richard, to embellish the 'good old
house' with fashionable formal gardens after his father's death in 1691.

It is frustrating that Daniel Defoe, who visited Southwick on his nation-
wide tour in 1742, while mentioning the furore caused by Norton's will and his
penchant for acting, fails to describe the formal gardens. Apparently, Norton,
who died in December 1732, left his 'Real Estate of about 6000*l. per Ann.* and
a Personal, said to be to the Value of 60,000*l* to the "Poor, Hungry, and
Thirsty, Naked and Strangers, Sick and Wounded, and Prisoners, to the End
of the World"', and made his executors the 'Parliament of *Great Britain*'.[27]
Unsurprisingly, his will was annulled on the grounds of insanity. Norton was
famous for 'acting several Parts in Plays with great Propriety', particularly
Falstaff, 'at a neat Theatre erected by himself, at his house at *Southwick*'.[28]
Defoe describes the parkland rising to 'the highest Point of *Portsdown*' on
which were 'two very large Clumps of *Scots* Fir-trees', planted by Norton,
between which 'that Gentleman intended to have erected a lofty Building'.[29]

This would have commanded Portsmouth and the Isle of Wight on the seaward side and the South Downs on the landward; from the level ground at this spot, Defoe thought that 'this Prospect may be justly esteemed one of the finest in *England*'.[30]

While Southwick's gardens have been levelled, those at **Pylewell Park**, recorded in another early eighteenth-century engraving by Thomas Badeslade (*20*), survive in ghostly form in the balustraded ha-has to the southeast of the house. They were commissioned by William Ingham Whitaker following his marriage in 1903.[31] These were built as an extension to the previous owner's circular parterre, whose southern boundary followed the line of the semicircular exedra, which had defined the northern edge of the wilderness as laid out by Sir Robert Worsley. Badeslade's view of Worsley's layout is particularly interesting in that it depicts a formal garden where the *dulci*, or ornamental, is deftly combined with the *utile,* or practical. To the entrance front there are two canals, possibly the surviving arms of a moat to Baddesley Manor, which once stood on the site, or perhaps the fortifications of a seventeenth-century Jacobean lodge.[32] On either side of the entrance forecourt there is an orchard and vegetable gardens, but also a Union Jack-style parterre with a central statue, which is backed by a pleached and arcaded tree avenue. To the rear, the open lawn, commanded by two intriguing turreted buildings, gives onto a perfectly symmetrical wilderness of close and open areas of shrubs and clipped topiary; thereafter an avenue of double rows of trees extends to the Solent. Whoever designed the garden, and John James has been suggested, as he was working for Sir Robert Worsley at the main family seat of Appuldurcombe on the Isle of Wight, made the best of a very dull and flat terrain.

While the wilderness and grounds at Pylewell must have been laid out in the first decade of the eighteenth century, the Wilderness at **Tangier Park** is much more difficult to date precisely, but it is very close in style to one that John, 2nd Duke of Montagu, devised for Beaulieu before 1718, so may be of the same period.[33] A slightly later layout with rides survives at **Rotherfield Park**, East Tisted, which was remodelled before 1729; a date of between 1725 and 1750 has been suggested for Plash Wood.[34]

There is a similar wilderness to the southeast of **Chawton House**, which survived the eighteenth- and early nineteenth-century improvements in the landscape. It originally formed a geometric sector of a large formal garden stretching across the south front of the house. It is not clear exactly when it was laid out, but perhaps dates from Elizabeth Knight's ownership, or possibly that of her cousin, Thomas Brodnax May Knight, who inherited Chawton from her in 1738.[35] Soon after taking over he instructed his steward Edward Randall to survey the estate and produce a plan (*21*) dated 1741, which shows the Wilderness as an area of grass walks intersected with diagonal paths.[36] At the same time he instructed the artist Mellichamp to paint a view of the

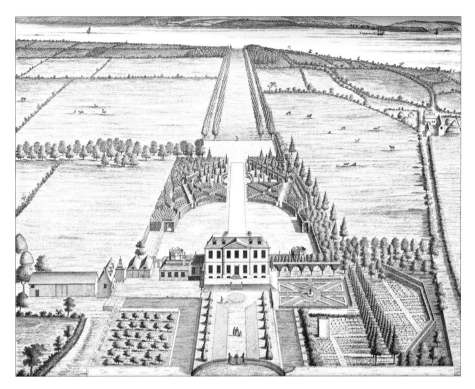

20 In Thomas Badeslade's view of Pylewell Park, from *Vitruvius Britannicus*, a patriotic Union Jack-style parterre fronts the house, while to the rear there is an intensely manicured wilderness. *University of Bristol Library*

entrance front of the house. This depicts a series of walled and gated and fenced compartments between the church and the 1593 stables, with steps and grass terraces punctuated by topiary leading up the slope to the front door. The approach is now open, flanked by trees, but the Wilderness is largely intact and offers framed views of the mellow brick façade of the south front (*colour 9*). Although informal paths were cut through it in the nineteenth century, the stately South Lime Avenue preserves some of its original recti-linear character.

While the Wilderness at Chawton may have been planted as late as 1740, that planted out by the Duke of Montagu at **Beaulieu** was conceived much earlier, in 1718, as just one section of a consciously planned, fortified garden that surrounded Palace House. It is not surprising, in a military age, that earth-works more associated with warfare were to find expression in the houses of the nobility that fought in Marlborough's wars.[37] One such was Montagu, whose character was neatly summarised by his close friend, the antiquary William Stukeley, after the Duke's death in 1749:

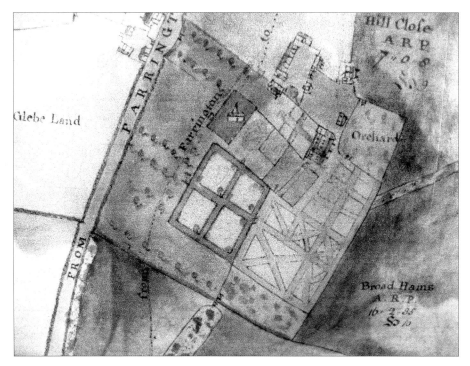

21 Edward Randall's 1741 estate plan of Chawton House shows the geometric
    Wilderness, which survives, though made more informal now with winding paths.
    By kind permission of Chawton House Library

> He had an exact knowledge in military affairs & gunnery, in the management of
> an army. He served under the Duke of Marlborough his father in law, for whom
> he had a great veneratiō, & had he been born to less fortune & taken to arms, I
> am persuaded he wd have been a consummate General. He was very tall in
> stature, of a good shape & symmetry. To sum up all in a few words, he may
> rightly be styled a true English Nobleman.[38]

As well as his interest in military affairs, Montagu was fascinated by mediaeval
castles and drew several schemes to fit up ruined castles on his estates in
Northamptonshire, close to the main family seat at Boughton.[39] His portrait
(*colour 10*) by Charles Jervas depicts him as Master of the Ordnance, with his
hand on a cannon and the Tower of London in the background. It is small
wonder then that, when he decided to remodel the house and grounds at
Beaulieu, he determined on a military garden. According to Stukeley, the two
antiquarian friends had 'exactly the same taste for old family concerns, geneal-
ogys, pictures, furniture, coats of arms, the old way of building, gardening, &
the like'; furthermore, the Duke 'had a very good knack of drawing &
designing'.[40]

22   The Palace House, Beaulieu as seen from the Mill Pool, with its
     mock mediaeval drawbridges spanning the moat and crenellated
     wall edging the water. *By kind permission of Lord Montagu of Beaulieu*

Fortunately the archives at Beaulieu are rich in visual images.[41] There is a
beautiful map of the estate by John Booth of 1718, which shows the moated
enclosure around the house with 'Wilderness' marked above it, and a contemporary view of Palace House seen from the Mill Dam on the Mill Pool, with
its conical corner turrets and drawbridges (*22*). However, the most important
image is a plan drawn by the Duke himself (*23*) of the house and the
surrounding orchards and wilderness, cut through with diagonal paths. Sadly
the Wilderness has disappeared, but reaches of the moat survive with the
conical-roofed turrets at the corners (*colour 11*), while the drawbridges have
been replaced with more mundane but serviceable fixed bridges across the
moat into the house.

Another military campaigner who, after his inheritance in 1707 of the
manor house at Hurstbourne Priors, near Whitchurch, rather than going on
the Grand Tour, which seemed both advisable and prudent for a landowner,
volunteered instead for Marlborough's army. John Wallop, later to become
Viscount Lymington and 1st Earl of Portsmouth, fought at Oudenarde in 1708
and then returned to his estate to remodel the house and grounds. He was
assisted in this restructuring by the architect Thomas Archer, who lived
nearby at Hale Park and who was also in the process of laying out a complex
designed landscape there. Despite **Hurstbourne Park** having been demolished and replaced by another in a more elevated position in the north of the
park, which itself has also disappeared, maps and two beautiful paintings of

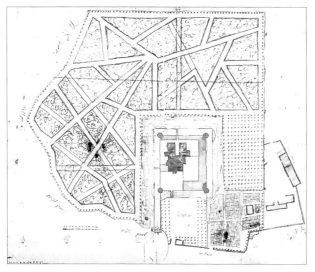

23 The 2nd Duke of Montagu's 1718 plan for the fortified
garden surrounding Palace House at Beaulieu.
By kind permission of Lord Montagu of Beaulieu

1748 by Jan Griffier survive showing the Archer house and its landscape.[42] The
visual and documentary evidence reveal a landscape still clinging on to the last
vestiges of formality, but one in which decorative buildings, more characteristic of the stylistically eclectic gardens of the 1740s, make a significant
aesthetic impact. Two of these survive, while the bricks and flint of one of the
other two lie submerged in the crystal-clear waters of the Bourne Rivulet.

Isaac Taylor's 1759 map of Hampshire shows the house on its manorial site
by the parish church, with the Bourne Rivulet to the east and a canal parallel
to it extending north towards an avenue of trees and, to the northeast, a formal
wilderness of geometric paths paled around.[43] J Netherclift's much later plan
of 1817, prepared after the house had been demolished and replaced in the
1780s by James Wyatt's classical building, also shows the Bourne Rivulet, but
marks a 'Cascade' opposite the church and a 'Mount' on the eastern ridge.[44]
The canal features in both Griffier paintings, one looking south, back to the
north front of the house, in which the gable apex of the Cascade House is just
visible in the backdrop of trees, the other (*colour 12*) of the view up from the
forecourt to the Canal, the Cascade, the mock Folly Castle above it and, in the
Wilderness on the eastern ridge, a domed building surmounted by a figure. In
both views the Canal is flanked by closely-clipped pleached trees, most likely
limes or hornbeam, and in the landscape prospect there are two brick piers
topped by urns close to the house.

1 Robert Adam's recent Garden Pavilion at Crooked Pightle, Crawley, continues the tradition of classical garden buildings. © *ADAM Architecture*

2 This 1730s pastel portrait of Lady Kingsmill by Harriet Lisle, set in its frame of gilded shells, once hung on the trees surrounding the Cruxeaston Grotto. *By kind permission of the Earl and Countess of Carnarvon.* © *Highclere Enterprises*

3 Harriet Lisle's companion pastel portrait of Sir Richard Kingsmill. *By kind permission of the Earl and Countess of Carnarvon.* © *Highclere Enterprises*

4 The monks' refectory in the Cloister at Beaulieu Abbey has been turned into the parish church; the space has been planted up with herbs known to have been grown in the mediaeval period

5 This charming nineteenth-century view of Warblington by CR Cotton shows the remaining octagonal tower of the Tudor Gatehouse. *Portsmouth Museum*

6 This large square green, enclosed by raised brick terraces, beside the ruined monastic buildings of Netley Abbey is where the Tudor Great Garden would have been sited

7 The Gatehouse at Titchfield was built across the nave of the mediaeval abbey church by Thomas Wriothesley between 1538 and 1542. It gave access to a courtyard beyond, which was dramatised by a fountain

8 Ralph Treswell's 1588 map of Hursley Park marks the Tudor hunting
   lodge, called 'Plase', in the centre of the park, and the ruins of
   Merdon Castle to the right. *Courtesy of IBM*

9 The Elizabethan Chawton House, as seen from the early-eighteenth-
   century Wilderness, which was laid out before 1741

10 Charles Jervas's portrait of the 2nd Duke of Montagu as Master of the Ordnance reflects the military obsessions present in his landscape schemes at Beaulieu. *By kind permission of Lord Montagu of Beaulieu*

11 Palace House, Beaulieu, surrounded by the 2nd Duke's early eighteenth-century mock defensive moat and garden turrets

12 Jan Griffier's garden view of Hurstbourne Park with Thomas Archer's Cascade and Folly Castle at the head of the Canal and the Mount in the Wilderness. *E870079 Hurstbourne Priors © Historic England. From the private collection of Lord Braybrooke, on display at Audley End House, Essex*

13 The earthworks of the lost formal gardens at Lainston House are revealed in early morning spring sunshine; the Lainston Avenue beyond stretches for three-quarters of a mile

14 The great avenue at Tylney
Hall, partly canalised,
shown on William
Simpson's 1774 survey, can
still be traced today.
*Hampshire Record Office:
10M48*

15 The 1740 survey of
Cranbury Park by William
Burgess records the Tudor
house surrounded by
compartmented gardens,
while the landscape beyond
retains its early field
pattern.
*Hampshire Record Office:
76M83/1 (purchased with the
support of the Victoria and
Albert Museum Purchase
Grant Fund)*

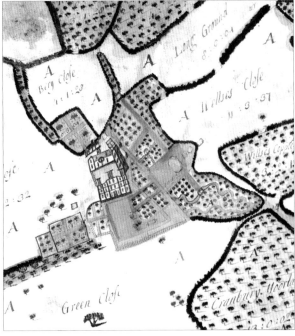

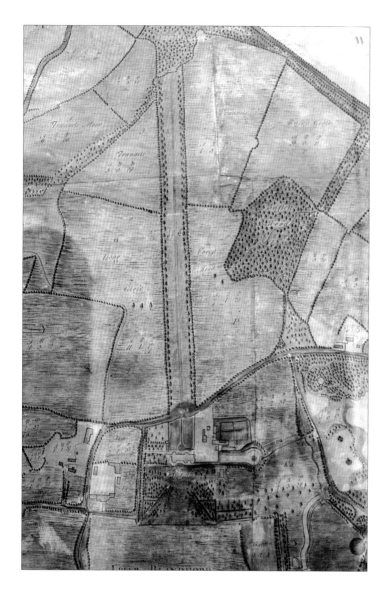

16 A detail of the northern, formal, sector of the landscape at
    Walhampton House from Charles Ley's 1787 survey.
    By kind permission of Walhampton School

24 The tufa and flint-faced Mount at Hurstbourne Park was originally crowned with a statue of Mercury. It provided views over the Wilderness towards the formal Canal, Cascade House and Castle

Walking the site today, much of Archer and Wallop's designed landscape can still be retrieved. The Wilderness survives, though now made less angularly formal in its paths. Although Taylor depicted it notionally with a regular grid of rides and walks, it is shown on the 1842 tithe map as an accurate reflection of the Union flag, created following the Act of Union with Scotland in 1707, the year of Wallop's inheritance. Commanding it is the domed structure present in the Griffier painting and marked as the Mount on the tithe map (24). This is an extraordinary building, unlike any other of its period, built in a consciously rustic style of knobbly stone and tufa, with round-headed niches faced in a chequerboard of squared, knapped flints. Crowning the shallow dome is an imposing statue of a Roman soldier in military dress with a small figure crouching at his feet. If the landscape dates from soon after 1712, the date of Archer's plan for a new house, the Wilderness might symbolise Great Britain and her triumph over the French under Marlborough. The statue may, therefore, represent Marlborough, or perhaps, in a less than self-effacing manner, Wallop himself. 45

The Cascade and Folly Castle appear much closer in style and date to buildings of the 1730s, and the Castle in particular has a stylistic kinship with one of the garden structures at Dogmersfield Park. However, Archer is known to have designed many garden buildings, including a Cascade House at Chatsworth in Derbyshire, and they are likely to be by him. Approaching the Rivulet from the church, the sound of gushing water is almost deafening, with two separate arched channels spouting water from beneath a dam. The central of these two arches may correspond to the main aperture of the Cascade and there are eighteenth-century bricks, shaped flints and sections of moulded stone lying in the water below the cascades, sad remnants of the structure. Stephen Switzer had obviously seen the Cascade at Hurstbourne, for in his *Introduction to a General System of Hydrostaticks and Hydraulicks, Philosophical and Practical* of 1729 he remarked that Wallop's design was based on the Fountain of the Theatre in the gardens of the Villa Aldobrandini at Frascati.[46] Sadly, nothing survives of the Folly Castle, which was also constructed of flints and is close in its round-arched military style to designs by John Vanbrugh, especially the Belvedere at Claremont.[47]

One further building needs to be mentioned, which is on the southern tip of the park by the B3400, and whose architectural features are similar to those on the service ranges of Archer's main house.[48] This is now known as the Bee House, though it is likely to have been conceived as a summerhouse or gazebo when it was first built. This would have offered views to the south which, as the Revd Jeremiah Milles reported, the main house could not: 'the Earl of Portsmouth has a very noble house situated in a very pleasant Park, but it stands too low, & commands very little prospect'.[49] Furthermore, Milles thought the gardens were 'insipid flat, & laid out in ye disagreeable old taste',[50] something which Archer, when he embarked upon a landscape campaign at his own house and grounds at Hale, was keen to avoid.

Hale Park is near Fordingbridge, close to the Wiltshire border in a corner of the New Forest. Archer bought the estate in 1715 and soon after set about rebuilding the house and the parish church in the grounds, while also laying out a new landscape, so the work at Hale is contemporary with Archer's commission at Hurstbourne.[51] The house has undergone several remodellings since Archer's time and bears no resemblance to his original Baroque conception. However, although it was made slightly more informal in the mid eighteenth century, Archer's landscape survived and was recorded in a 1789 survey plan of the estate, drawn by Thomas Richardson for Joseph May, who had bought the house.[52] The plan is an important document because, despite the obvious formalities of the layout, it suggests that Archer was attempting to create at Hale both a *ferme ornée* and an Arcadian grove. The former is indicated by the presence of farm buildings and farmyards between the main house and the parish church, the latter by a planned wilderness to the west of the house extending to the River Avon marked as 'Church Coppice', and later known as 'Shell House Copse', in which a notional *patte d'oie* of paths is bisected with straight and serpentine walks leading to clearings enlivened with garden buildings.

The concept of the ornamented farm, where an estate could be laid out for both aesthetic and practical purposes – the *dulci* and the *utile* – was first outlined by Stephen Switzer in his *Ichnographia Rustica* of 1718. Switzer advocated 'a judicious Mixture and Incorporation of the Pleasures of the Country, with the Profits'; by 'mixing the useful and profitable parts of Gardening with the Pleasurable in the Interior Parts of my *Designs*, and Paddocks, obscure Enclosures, &c. in the Outward: My *Designs* are thereby vastly enlarged, and both Profit and Pleasure may be agreeably mix'd together'.[53] Such ideas had been current in the Commonwealth, but were only just resurfacing after the long interregnum of the Franco-Dutch formal garden. They were to find expression much later in 1725 at Lord Bolingbroke's Dawley Farm and in 1734 at Philip Southcote's celebrated Woburn Farm at Chertsey, both in Surrey.[54] Archer's experiment was, therefore, prescient, as well as practical.

His wilderness, the Church Coppice (*25*), seems less innovative at first glance, but if the 1789 plan is studied closely it is apparent that the various open glades and clearings, or 'Cabinets', as Batty Langley was to term them in his 1728 *New Principles of Gardening*, contain all manner of buildings, seats and statues. Langley asserted that 'these agreeable surprizing Entertainments in the pleasant Passage thro' a Wilderness, must, without doubt, create new Pleasures at every Turn: And more especially when the Whole is so happily situated', as at Hale on its elevated site above the Avon.[55] Langley's advice on the plants and trees suitable for these shady areas gives some idea of how the Hale wilderness might have been planted up:

> To add to the Pleasure of these delightful Meanders, I advise that the Hedge-Rows of the Walks be intermix'd with Cherries, Plumbs, Apples, Pears, Bruxel Apricots, Figs, Goosberries, Currants, Rasberries, &c., and the Borders planted with Strawberries, Violets, &c. The most beautiful Forest-Trees for Hedges, are the English Elm, the Dutch Elm, the Lime-Tree, and Hornbeam: And altho' I have advis'd the Mixing of these hedges of Forest-Trees with the aforesaid Fruits, yet you must not forget a Place for those pleasant and delightful Flowering-Shrubs, the White Jessamine, Honey-Suckle, and Sweet-Brier.[56]

This shady, sweet-smelling sector of the grounds would offer places in which to sit and contemplate, its intersecting paths 'adorn'd with Statues, large open Plains, Groves, Cones of Fruit, of Evergreens...Basons, Fountains, Sun-Dials, and Obelisks', as well as temples.[57]

Archer had already achieved this kind of proto-Arcadian grove before 1710 for the Duke of Shrewsbury at Heythrop Park in Oxfordshire, which Switzer proclaimed was 'the first attempt of this kind, I ever saw', and appears to have pre-dated a similar classical wilderness in Wray Wood at Castle Howard.[58]

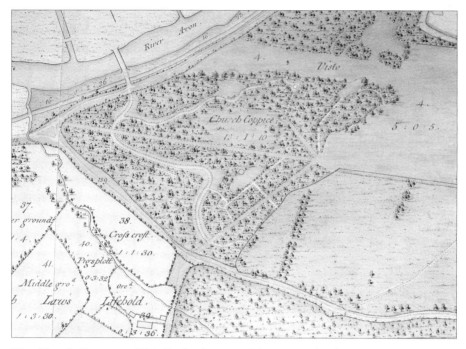

25 The Church Coppice at Hale Park, shown on Thomas Richardson's 1789 survey of
the estate, may well have been an early classical grove designed by Thomas Archer.
By kind permission of Sloan Hickman

Was the Church Coppice at Hale another version of the classical grove that
was to become the essential element of the later Arcadian Garden? There is no
doubt that it contained statues, which are clearly marked on the plan; fragments of sculptures and a bust of Charles Montagu, 1st Earl of Halifax, have
been found on the estate. Halifax was the great uncle of Archer's wife Elizabeth. Certainly Archer's biographer, Helen Lawrence-Beaton, who has pored
over the 1789 plan and discovered no fewer than five garden buildings at the
heart of the Coppice, including a circular building that may well be the Shell
House, is convinced that it 'should be recognised as one of the first Arcadian
Gardens' of the century.59

It is in the light of Archer's early classical experiments at both Hurstbourne
and Hale, that the semi-formal layouts devised in the next decade by Charles
Bridgeman at Hackwood Park and Westbury House should be seen.
Bridgeman was merely developing and perfecting a landscape notion that had
already been expressed on the ground by Archer and conveyed in print by both
Switzer and Langley. At **Hackwood Park**, Bridgeman was working in concert
with the architect James Gibbs, hence the proliferation there of classical
temples and seats.

Until as late as 1652, the park at Hackwood was still largely utilitarian pastureland, but there was a lodge on the site of the present house. This was probably built in the Elizabethan period as a banqueting house for hawking parties. The lodge was possibly favoured particularly for the proximity of Spring Wood, which functioned as its area for leisure pursuits. The house was substantial enough to have a chapel and the 4th Marquess of Winchester died there in 1628. When the 6th Marquess abandoned Abbotstone in favour of Hackwood in 1683 he began a new house on the site of the old hunting lodge and remodelled the gardens. The only feature of the present Spring Wood that survives from the time of the 6th Marquess, later 1st Duke of Bolton, is the Broad Walk, originally called the 'Great Avenue', which still cuts roughly east to west across the Wood. This Great Avenue first appears on Thomas Smith's crudely drawn survey of June 1683.[60] At that time it was only the central section of a much more ambitious double line of trees running right across Hackwood Park, from Park Gate Piece in the east, through Spring Wood and then, after the brief break of the formal parterre immediately in front of the house, continuing on westward to, presumably, the main Basingstoke-Alton road. This was only one of a number of such avenues laid across the park in the years immediately post-1660. East of Spring Wood another avenue crossed it, running north-south, flanked by twelve square plantations spaced out regularly like army battalions parading on each side of it. A second line of trees ran north on a line bisecting the site of the proposed new house, and this cut through two more rectangular plantations. What is significant about all this precise geometry of woodland is that Spring Wood, though sliced through by one avenue, was not itself geometrical at all, but a shapeless mass of older woodland.

The 2nd Duke of Bolton devoted more time to creating formal gardens on the Franco-Dutch pattern north of the new house. The first sector of these ended in an exedra with a complex pattern of scalloped terraces, a design that, after his death in 1722, was to be followed closely in an amphitheatre carved out of the south-eastern quadrant of Spring Wood. This suggests that the great mid-1720s reshaping of Spring Wood by Bridgeman and Gibbs may have been initiated by the 2nd Duke and only carried through by the 3rd.

Bridgeman was faced with a situation similar to that which George London had met in Wray Wood at Castle Howard. London proposed to apply a conventional star pattern of rides to the area of mature woodland, mostly beeches, very close to the house, but Lord Carlisle insisted on retaining the trees and threading them with winding paths leading to various surprise features: statues, urns, seats and summerhouses. To impose some kind of disciplined order, London was allowed to surround the wood with a deep ditch or ha-ha and bastion-like ramparts appropriate to a Britain that was celebrating Marlborough's stunning series of military successes in siege operations and pitched battles against the French. At Spring Wood, Bridgeman compromised skilfully between London's original scheme for Wray Wood and Carlisle's

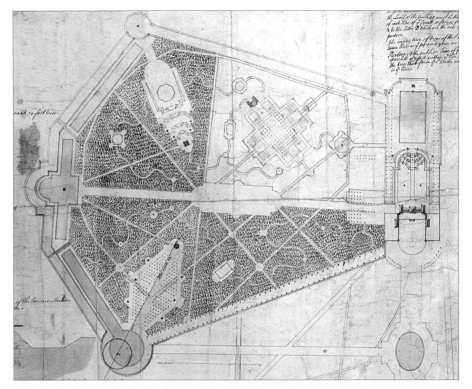

26 Charles Bridgeman's plan for Spring Wood, Hackwood, is close to what was eventually
achieved on the site. The Wood is divided into four quadrants enlivened with walks,
statuary and garden buildings. *The Bodleian Libraries, The University of Oxford, MS.
Gough Drawings a. 4, fol. 34*

preferred solution.

His drawing in the Bodleian Library (26) and a later, badly-damaged, 1725
plan illustrate the same scheme, except that in the later plan the terraced
amphitheatre has been transferred from the southeast to the northeast quadrant of the Wood.[61] The Menagerie area was left unchanged, easily accessible
from the house as an intimate pleasure sector in the southwest quadrant. Over
the wood as a whole Bridgeman imposed the French-style star pattern of rides
that Carlisle had vetoed at Wray Wood. This included a new, major, north-
south, 'Twelve o' Clock Avenue'. Superimposed on this rigid geometry was an
erratic winding trail of minor pathways leading to little clearings with surprise
features: ponds, statues and temples. One survival of these random features is
the 'Cock Pit', which appears on William Brown's 1807 survey in the same
position as an exedral-ended rectangular clearing on the first Bridgeman
plan.[62] Then, to discipline the bulging eastern extremity of Spring Wood,
Bridgeman created a series of three bastions linked by a noble raised walk. The
earth dug out to provide this military-style feature should have left a canal

27 James Gibbs was working in concert with Charles Bridgeman at Spring Wood to
    provide the garden buildings; this is his elegantly austere Menagerie Temple

basin, a moat on the wrong side of the defence system, but in this dry chalk
country there was never enough water to fill it and the depression now holds
the 1908 Wild Garden.[63]

As it was first laid out the Menagerie was a complex geometrical area: a
rectangular pond for the waterfowl set in a cruciform enclosure. A double row
of pyramidal yews surrounded the water; then came eight squares, probably of
clipped yew. At the south end, pulling the composition firmly into a classical
perspective, was Gibbs's Menagerie Temple (27), which Bridgeman's plan
proposed with a projecting portico flanked by two wings. Eight smaller structures, seats perhaps or simply urns, are suggested on the first plan; the two
'Cubs', or classical seats, were built in their place. Gibbs followed Bridgeman's
guidelines for the Menagerie temple very closely. Brick-built and rendered, it
has a slightly projecting Roman Doric portico and a chaste triglyph frieze, with
a pediment carrying the date 1727. The two flanking windows are exactly as illustrated in Gibbs's 1728 *Book of Architecture*, with moulded and eared architraves.
Gibbs's two other temples, both proudly illustrated in his architectural treatise,
have been less fortunate. His French House has gone completely and his Doric
Temple is only a broken circle of columns at the top of the overgrown terraces
of the Amphitheatre. The Wood remains, however, an astonishing survival, an

historic signpost to English garden design and a place of rare enchantment. In complete contrast, nothing at all survives above ground of Bridgeman's contemporary Hampshire layout at Westbury House, East Meon.

Admiral Philip Cavendish bought **Westbury House** from Richard Markes in 1722, after renting the property for several years, and then sought Bridgeman's advice on planting a new garden there once he was in ownership. There is an undated and unsigned plan of the house and gardens in the East Sussex County Record Office, which is clearly in Bridgeman's style, and the inventory states unequivocally that the 'Avenue & Pleasure Garden were laid by Mr Bridgman'.[64] A 1906 house replaced the eighteenth-century Westbury House, but the stables survive of Cavendish's time, along with the pool and water courses to the north of the house that are shown on the plan. There are also the ruins of the thirteenth-century St Nicholas Chapel, which originally flanked a formal, tree-lined avenue leading up to a turning circle in front of the house. On the south side, where Bridgeman designed a bastioned garden, all has gone except the ha-ha dividing the lawns by the house from the fields beyond. Unfortunately, access to the grounds was not permitted for this study, the house being a secure nursing home, but it is clear, from a cursory glance across the landscape and with the aid of aerial views, that the line of the bastioned ha-ha of Bridgeman's garden survives in the field.

Bridgeman's plan (28) has similar features to those he incorporated into his much grander garden at Hackwood, including the bastioned perimeter, axial walks, close-planted shrubberies threaded with serpentine meanders, and garden buildings. The layout extends from a grass terrace with deep revetments, which has a mini amphitheatre at the east end, and thence to a wide central pathway, flanked on either side by the shrubberies. That to the west is bisected by a vista through to another, much more dramatic, grass amphitheatre, while a serpentine water course like that at Rousham in Oxfordshire flows into and out of a rectangular pool. Alongside this, close to the central walk, is an octagonal garden building, mirrored on the other side of the path by a rectangular structure, or perhaps another pool. At the centre of the east sector is an ornamental parterre and what looks like a canal. Looking across the garden from the slightly elevated terrace by the house, the eye would be drawn first into the rising, wooded landscape beyond and then, obliquely, to the amphitheatre at the end of its axial vista. All the other features would be hidden among the shrubberies as places for discovery.

There are Bridgemanesque structural remains – grass banks with steep, military-style revetments – at **Lainston House**, Sparsholt. These are most likely to be coeval with the layout at Westbury and part of the additions made to the property by John Merrill, a wealthy London goldsmith of an Essex family, who bought Lainston in 1721.[65] To the mellow brick, late-seventeenth-century house, Merrill added stately forecourt arcades and a huge hexagonal Walled

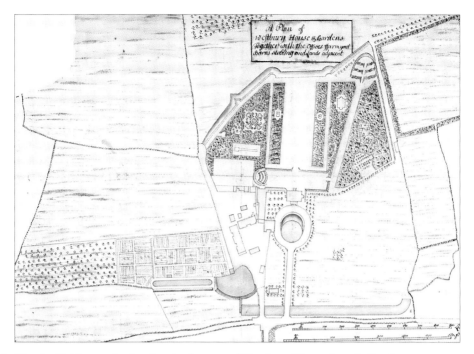

28 Charles Bridgeman's plan for the layout at Westbury House has similar features, including a grassed amphitheatre, to those he designed for Hackwood. *East Sussex Record Office: SAS/G 56/42*

Garden, all of which survive; he may also have built the octagonal Dovecote. His garden layout to the east side of the house (*colour 13*) extended this east-west axial arrangement of features. The angular terraces step downhill to the declivity of a circular pool, after which the axis rises up, flanked by an avenue of mature limes. Seen on a misty February day, with low sunshine casting defining shadows across the earthworks, the ambitious scale and reach of the design can be discerned. John Evelyn, author of *Sylva*, was understandably delighted by the great Lainston Avenue when he visited Sir Philip and Lady Meadowes, describing is as 'a green ascent of near three-quarters of a mile', so it must have been an established feature before Merrill bought the property.[66] The pond acts as a pivot for another avenue that radiates out to the east.

A similar avenue, almost as long and punctuated along its grassy length by a series of rectangular pools, survived at **Tylney Hall**, Rotherwick, as late as 1774, when it was recorded on a survey (*colour 14*) drawn up by William Simpson.[67] Vestiges of this avenue survive to the northeast of the house, along the appropriately named Green Lane, and as a narrow watercourse to either side of the Hook Road. The Lainston Avenue is shown on a 1735 map of Lainston by William Burgess, which also includes a vignette of the neighbouring early eighteenth-century house, known then as Hursley Lodge.[68] As we have seen, **Hursley Park** was originally a paled Elizabethan hunting park with a Great Lodge at its heart and the remains of Merdon Castle to the east. William Heathcote bought the property from the daughter of Richard Cromwell in 1719,[69] and soon after took down the Tudor building and began a new eleven-bay brick house with a central stone portico.[70] Sir William, as he had then become, was advised between 1721 and 1724 by his father-in-law, Sir Thomas Hewett, on the construction of the house and grounds at Hursley.[71] This building, depicted on the Burgess map, survived, substantially unaltered, until Sir George Cooper undertook a rebuilding programme after 1902. *Country Life* articles of 1902, when Joseph Baxendale was in ownership, and 1909, when Cooper had completed his extensions, bracket perfectly the switch from Victorian to Edwardian. Cooper remodelled the Victorian grounds around the house extensively and these are discussed in Chapter 7.

What is significant in the development of the grounds while the house was being built in the 1720s was the rejection by Heathcote of an offer to do the work by Stephen Switzer, who had trained with London and Wise at the Brompton Park nurseries. He was Hampshire born, from the village of East Stratton, a few miles north of Winchester. His *Ichnographia Rustica* had appeared in 1718, illustrated with several designs that might be used by noblemen; Switzer was currently working for the Earl of Cadogan on the Oxfordshire-Berkshire border north of Reading at Caversham Park.[72] John Conduitt, Heathcote's neighbour at Cranbury Park, wrote on 15 December 1720 that 'Mr Switzer' had just left, but 'during his stay in these parts he viewed your situation at Hursley & is very ambitious of serving you, but, as I acquainted him, I presume you will want no body to lay out your gardens since you are so happy as to have the assistance of Sir Thomas Hewett'.[73] As Conduitt predicted, Heathcote decided to work instead alongside his kinsman.[74] Very little survives of their scheme on site today except the south lawn, originally walled and flanked by elm trees, which extends to an exedral termination on the ha-ha. This was a design motif much favoured by Switzer, which would be expanded later in the decade into the Plinyesque 'hippo-dromes' illustrated by Robert Castell in his 1728 *Villas of the Ancients*, the most celebrated and influential being that at Lord Burlington's Chiswick House. The contemporary walled kitchen garden to the east was completely subsumed by IBM's Hursley Park development laboratory, which was built in the 1960s. The pleasure grounds to the west survive, though much altered in the nine-teenth and twentieth centuries. However, a veteran plane tree in this area is likely to be of Sir William's time.

Switzer's presence at **Cranbury Park** is intriguing, for John Conduitt bought the estate in 1720 and must surely have laid out a garden there before he died in 1727. He was a close friend of Sir Isaac Newton, who is thought to have designed a sundial that survives at Cranbury.[75] A beautiful estate survey (*colour 15*), drawn up in 1740 by William Burgess for Thomas Lee Dummer, who was then in possession, shows an agrarian landscape of open fields and woodland, but the area around the house is hedged and fenced in and contains an elaborate series of garden spaces.[76] Some of these are bisected with angular walks, rather like the Wilderness at Chawton House, while others have Switzer's favourite leitmotiv of serpentine paths enlivened with small garden buildings. To the east of the house there was an open lawn terminating in an exedra, which had a series of geometric ponds; the central octagonal pond was on axis with two of the mini wildernesses, each having a garden building at the end of the avenue. It is not easy to make out, but it looks as if the structure to the northeast of the house on this avenue might have been a triumphal arch. This could easily be of the 1720s, for such features had been used to terminate vistas in seventeenth-century French formal gardens, as at Cardinal Richelieu's Rueil, just outside Paris,[77] while Batty Langley gave several designs for them, some of which he advised could be made out of canvas to save money, in his *New Principles*. Conduitt's house and garden have gone, replaced by another designed by George Dance and with pleasure grounds embellished with structures by John Buonarotti Papworth. These are discussed in Chapter 6.

Switzer's influence, if not practical advice, appears at **Walhampton House**, Lyndhurst, now Walhampton School, where there is a beautiful estate map of 1787 showing the grounds in that transitional period from the formal to the natural.[78] As at Lainston, the house is approached from the north by a vast double avenue ending in a turning circle within grass plats (*colour 16*), while to the south are the remains of a wilderness, cut through with avenues to form a *patte d'oie*. To the east of the house, and on alignment with it, is a canal, known as the Banjo Pond from its curious shape, and further rectangular pools. In the wider landscape there are several avenues including a lime walk and a holm oak walk. All this angular formality is undercut by a vast watery landscape to the southeast, enlivened with garden buildings including two mounts and a root house. Two of these are shown as vignettes on the estate map (*29*). This is exactly the kind of design that Switzer was proposing in his 1718 *Ichnographia Rustica*, a '*Rural* and *Extensive Gardening*' suspended between the regularity of the Franco-Dutch formal garden and the emerging informal landscape style.[79]

It is not known precisely when this was achieved, but the formal elements are likely to have been laid out by Paul Burrard, who rebuilt the house in 1711, while the more naturalistic features might be of the 1730s or 1740s. Certainly the serpentine canal, which survives, though bewhiskered with reeds and flag irises, will post-date the Serpentine in Hyde Park, which was dug in 1730. Mounts were a feature of Switzer's designs and the one closest to the house, now replanted with cherry laurel, might be of the 1730s. The dam between the two major sheets of water is also typical of Switzer, who was adept at handling vast water schemes, as would be expected from the author of *Hydrostaticks and*

29 This vignette of the Root House from Charles Ley's 1787 survey of Walhampton is
indicative of the exotic nature of the garden structures added later to the
formal landscape. *By kind permission of Walhampton School*

Hydraulicks. The Walhampton dam is similar to one he planned in the 1730s
for Nostell Priory in Yorkshire.[80] However, it may be that the lakes were
made more irregular in shape after Harry Burrard received his baronetcy in
1769 and enlarged the house with canted bays to take in the landscape. Inside
there is an eighteenth-century chimneypiece with Rococo decoration in one of
the rooms with a canted bay. Perhaps Harry Burrard was responsible for softening the landscape forms and adding the delightfully eclectic buildings. Sybil
Wade's informed report on the grounds suggests that William Gilpin, vicar of
nearby Boldre and a close friend of Sir Harry, may have had some influence on
the naturalistic sector in this later period. Whatever the true dating of the
landscape phases, and there is also important work here by Harold Peto and
Thomas Mawson, the grounds at Walhampton, especially the lily-pad-
encrusted lakes, their edges defined by inspired modern planting, are a
wonderful palimpsest of garden design.

A near contemporary of Hewett's Hursley Lodge, but a house of far more
architectural consequence, was designed and built for himself at Eversley, near
Hook, by the architect John James, who had already worked in the county at
Herriard Park. James is buried in Eversley churchyard and an inscription on his

monument in the north aisle of the church states that 'the said John James built the House called Warbrooks in the Parish Anno 1724'. James's tenure of **Warbrook House** was short lived, however, for, after the tragic death of his wife and son in the 1730s, and financial loss after his brother's printing business failed in 1738, he moved back Greenwich, where he had spent most of his early, formative years.

In typical formal French practice, James's house is set on a central axis, approached via an avenue, mostly of oaks, on the east from the A327 and with a canal to the west. James's east-west axis originally ran for 2.35 kilometres from Eversley Cross, across Eversley Centre, Eversley Chase and an area of common known as the Great A. Another avenue extended north-south for a kilometre from the junction between Eversley Street and Warbrook Lane. Immediately in front of the east façade is a turning circle and semi-circular ha-ha, with a contemporary sundial by William Collier of London on a stone plinth, no doubt designed by James. To the west is a vast open area of grass, most likely the site of complex formal parterres (*30*), which is bounded on three sides by a deep moat from which a canal extends further west.[81] Field evidence suggests that the Canal was the central arm of a *patte d'oie*, the flanking avenues of trees. The Canal terminates in a ruined stone parapet with balustrades and piers under which it passes to flow out into an informal lake. The stonework was rescued from the demolition of Waterloo Bridge and re-used here in the 1930s for Mrs Humphreys-Owen by William Wood of Taplow, under the superintendence of Lord Gerald Wellesley and Trenwith Wills.[82]

It is not known when the parterre garden was grassed over. Certainly it appears as a simple open space on 1870s Ordnance Survey maps. Judging by the principles of design in James's *Theory and Practice of Gardening*, especially those in his second, revised edition of 1728, brought out when he is likely to have been laying out the grounds at Warbrook, the space would have been enriched with 'divers Sorts of Parterres', which James reduces to four: 'Parterres of Embroidery, Parterres of Compartiment, Parterres after the *English* Manner, and Parterres of Cut-work'.[83] It can only be speculation, but the extent of the space to be planted suggests that James would have opted for a garden of quadrants, cut by gravel walks. This was when Bridgeman was striving to simplify formal layouts by banishing the decorative excesses of parterres of embroidery and cut-work, relying instead on plain grass plats, and Alexander Pope was working towards an informal landscape style at his own garden in Twickenham, and through advice in the gardens of his close friends.

One of these kindred spirits was the charismatic Charles Mordaunt, 3rd Earl of Peterborough, whom Pope referred to affectionately as Peterborow. He owned **Bevois Mount**, another lost Hampshire house and garden, which he bought in 1723. It was demolished in the 1940s, its site now subsumed within the northern suburbs of Southampton. The old soldier of the Spanish

30 The formal canals surrounding John James's Warbrook House probably enclosed a vast French-style parterre garden, now laid to lawn

wars with Marlborough was also a close friend of Swift and Gay, and keenly interested in gardening. Pope's letters reveal that Peterborough had assisted their mutual friend, Lady Suffolk, to whom Peterborough was writing love songs in his sixties when she was still Mrs Howard,[84] in designing the gardens at Marble Hill House on the Thames, while there are several references in the correspondence between the two men of the ongoing improvements at Bevois Mount. Pope writes on 24 August 1732: 'I presume you may before this time be returned from the contemplation of many Beauties, animal and vegetable, in Gardens; and possibly some rational, in Ladies; and to the better enjoyment of your own Bevis-Mount'.[85]

Pope spent a blissful six weeks with Peterborough at Bevois Mount between August and September 1734, his descriptions of the holiday evoking the gardens that the Earl had contrived around the little summer retreat he had remodelled. On 2 August, Pope was writing to Dr Arbuthnot 'from the most beautiful Top of a Hill I ever saw, a little house that overlooks the Sea, Southampton, & the Isle of Wight; where I study, write, & have what Leisure I please'.[86] Pope was working on three poems in imitation of Horace, but was also exploring with Peterborough the Hampshire countryside. A later letter of 11 August, written to Martha Blount, describes 'an Adventure and Discovery, made by Lord Peterborow and me' the previous week, when 'he had a mind to a Sea Voyage, and I some curiosity to try if a sea-sickness would be support-able to me, in case I should ever run my country'.[87] The pair sailed around the Isle of Wight, explored the ruins of Netley Abbey, ate their lunch 'using for seats the fallen capitals of two pillars, and for their table, the length of another fallen pillar', sketched the ruins and admired the views.[88] Pope was still at Bevois Mount on 1 September, when he wrote to the Earl of Oxford describing how happy he was at Peterborough's:

> We have the best Sea fish & River fish in the world, much tranquillity, some Reading, no Politiques, admirable Melons, an excellent Bowling-green & Ninepin alley, Besides the amusement of a Witch in the parish. I have an incomparable story to tell you on the last of these, but it would fill 2 sheets of paper. I have been at the Ruins of the finest Abbey & Castle [Netley] I ever saw, within five miles of this place, which I am surprised to find Camden take no notice of. [89]

The gardens were still unfinished on 25 August 1735, when Peterborough was gravely ill, and Pope was writing to Martha Blount to say that he had 'found my Lord Peterborow on his Couch, where he gave me an account of the exces-sive Sufferings he had past thro', with a weak voice, but spirited...he talked of nothing but the great amendments of his condition, & of finishing the Build-ings & Gardens for his best friend [Anastasia Robinson, now his recognised wife] to injoy after him'.[90] Apart from Pope's mention of the bowling green and the elevated site of the house, built on the hill where the local hero, Sir Bevois of Hampton, was supposedly buried, there are no further descriptions of what Peterborough had achieved before his death in Lisbon in October of the same year.

However, almost a decade later, Daniel Defoe visited Bevois Mount in his 1743 tour of the country, as well as the Revd Milles, who was there in the same year, and from their accounts a very clear idea can be formed of this idyllic 50-acre garden. Defoe writes:

> His Lordship purchased it, and converted it into a kind of Wilderness; and as it is full of Trees and Brambles, he has cut through divers circular Walks and Labyrinths, so very intricate, that it is hardly possible to avoid being lost in them...The Mount terminates above, as is feign'd of Parnassus, in a kind of Fork; and between the two Spires is a Bowling-green or Parterre, adorn'd with fine *Italian* Marble Statues, brought by his Lordship from Abroad...On the very summit of the Spire, stands a fine Summer-house, very elegantly built and contrived, with a good Cellar under it, where his Lordship kept his Wines...He intended to rebuild the House, and convert all the Grounds lying between it and the Mount, into Gardens, had he lived a little longer. The Beauty of the

Improvements which his Lordship has made in this Mount, are hardly to be conceived. He has adorn'd it with Statues, Grottoes and Alcoves, and diversify'd it up and down with something new and surprising, at every turn, peculiar to his own fine Taste and Genius in Gardening, wherein no Nobleman excell'd, and few equall'd him in *Europe*. He left this little Seat, and Lands about it, to his Lady, who now enjoys them.[91]

The Revd Milles's description adds little to Defoe's, apart from 'an open Corinthian Temple, which is built in a tolerable taste' near the road.[92] This is likely to have been an addition by Anastasia, 'his lady who is sd to have rather a better taste than her husband had, and takes great delight in this place, & is continually making some new improvements to it'.[93] At this time the gardens were on that stylistic cusp between the demise of formal geometries, laid out by Peterborough, and the emergent eclecticism of the 1740s, embraced by his wife, with its emphasis on more intricate serpentine walks leading to garden buildings of every conceivable architectural style.

4

'The Hermit appear'd to great advantage'
The Eclectic Garden

Headley Park, Paultons Park, Highclere Castle
Dogmersfield Park, The Wakes, The Vyne, Old Alresford House
The Grange

Thomas Archer's proto-eclectic landscape at Hurstbourne Park features prominently on Isaac Taylor's magnificent map of the county, published on 20 August 1759, just before Lancelot Brown's minimalist revolution was to render eclectic mid eighteenth-century layouts old-fashioned and ripe for reshaping. Taylor records the house at 'Husbands Prior' on its site by the church, with the formal Canal extending from it, which develops into a tree avenue, with the Wilderness on the hill to the northeast cut through with rides, the whole park paled round. Intriguingly, the map marks another building to the rear of Hurstbourne by the main road, and a further tree avenue striding out across the fields to the south. Bridgeman's Spring Wood at Hackwood receives the same detailed treatment, with its ha-ha and bastions clearly visible. These are unquestionably true records of the county's mid-century parks, Taylor's cartouche proudly claiming that the '*Estates* are accurately Survey'd and Maps of them neatly drawn at the Customary Prices'. Mediaeval deer parks, usually paled like that at Hurstbourne, can be traced, with their attendant lodges, as can warrens. Barrows and Iron Age hill forts like that at Barksbury Camp, near Andover, and the camp at Beacon Hill south-east of Highclere, are all drawn, as well as racecourses. It is a remarkable record of the Hampshire landscape as it looked in 1759.

For that reason Taylor's map repays close scrutiny from the garden historian because there are so many excitements to be found. Just southwest of Hurstbourne, at the edge of Harewood Forest, high on a ridge, there is a circular structure marked 'The Folley'. Might this have been associated with Hurstbourne? At 'Farley', to the west of Winchester, there is a vast woodland cut through with geometric rides, at the centre of which is a tall, domed summerhouse.[1] At **Headley Park**, south-east of Alton close to the border with Surrey, the deer park is paled and in its centre there is a stepped, conical 'Ariosto Temple'.

William Huggins is given as the owner in Taylor's key to the estates. He inherited Headley Park in 1745 and published a translation of Ariosto's epic poem *Orlando Furioso* in 1755; the temple is likely to have been built as memorial to that literary work. He was also the first Englishman to translate Dante's *Divine Comedy* and was well enough connected in cultural circles to have had his portrait painted by William Hogarth in 1759.

At 'Poltons', near Romsey, now home to Peppa Pig at Paultons Theme Park, two vast avenues of trees converge upon a huge pyramid, set right in the middle of the park (*31*). **Paultons Park** was owned by Hans Stanley who, although he had come of age in 1742, spent most of the 1740s in literary pursuits and travelling extensively in France, where he lived for two years. As a consequence, he had no political foothold in his home county until he was returned as MP for Southampton in 1754. Thereafter, he sought political

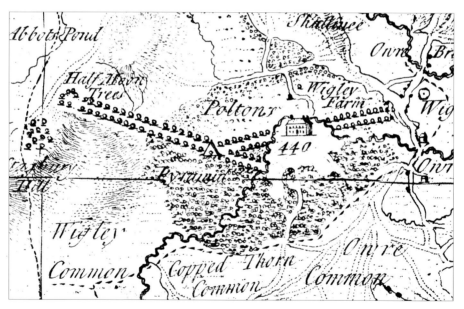

31 This vignette of the landscape at 'Poltons' from Taylor's 1759 county map is the only known image of the 1750s Pyramid in the park. *Hampshire Record Office: 110M89/P67*

favour and was eventually appointed a Lord of the Admiralty in 1757; so the pyramid is likely to date from between 1754 and 1757. It may have disappeared in the 1772 reshaping by Brown, or after Stanley's suicide on a visit to Earl Spencer at Althorp in January 1780; its site is now the golf course. The same fate awaited many of Paulet St John's exotic garden buildings, which are shown on the map at Dogmersfield, southwest of Fleet, when they were demolished in a remodelling of the estate in 1790 by William Emes. However, there is one eighteenth-century park in Hampshire that, due to the careful conservatism of the family, retains its eclectic buildings, some of which are shown on Taylor's map, even though it was reshaped in typical Brownian fashion after 1770. That is the park of Highclere Castle, seat of the Carnarvon earls.

Highclere Castle is sited at the heart of the most beautiful landscape park in the entire county. Its environs are dramatised by embracing hills: Sidown Hill to the south and Beacon Hill to the southeast. To the north there are three tracts of mature woodland: Duns Wood, Clere Wood and Great Pen Wood, while its extensive demesne is enhanced by two sinuous stretches of water: Dunsmere to the northeast, and Milford Lake further north. Yet mystery surrounds the creator of this matchless eighteenth-century environment. There is no adult portrait of Robert Sawyer Herbert at Highclere and no detailed visitor account of the landscape he achieved before his death in 1769. Furthermore, many of the eclectic buildings he must have commissioned have either been altered or have disappeared. While there are many archival sources for the great rebuilding of his successor's late eighteenth-century house by Charles Barry in the 1840s, precious little is known about Robert Herbert's house or the precise genesis of his garden improvements. As regards cartography of the landscape, we have a 1739 map by Thomas Blandy of the estate in Highclere and Burghclere parishes, surveyed before many of Robert Herbert's garden buildings were constructed, and a retrospective survey done in 1794, but purporting to be of the estate in 1768, by Major William Bull, made just before he died.[2]

The Sawyers came to High Clere, as it was called throughout the seventeenth and eighteenth centuries, in 1679, when Sir Robert Sawyer bought a half-share of the manors of Highclere and Burghclere from the Lucy family of Warwickshire.[3] Sawyer had made his money as a successful lawyer and Attorney General under Charles II and James II. On his death in 1692, Sawyer entailed his estates on his daughter Margaret, who had married Thomas Herbert, 8th Earl of Pembroke in 1684. On her and Lord Pembroke's deaths, Wilton and the Wiltshire estates were inherited by the 9th Earl, but Highclere was reserved for Margaret's second son, Robert Sawyer Herbert. He was born in 1697 and, after coming of age, became MP for Wilton in Wiltshire and then held minor government posts for the next thirty years. At Highclere he rebuilt the main house, the parish church having been remodelled earlier by Sir Robert, and, according to the 4th Earl of Carnarvon, 'laid the foundation of the collection of pictures'.[4] Although the 4th Earl could not give 'many details of him or of his life' in his history of the Herberts, he confirms that Robert Herbert 'built the greater part of the house at Milford, the Arch on Siddon Hill [Heaven's Gate], the Temple in the garden [immediately opposite the house, now known as Jackdaw's Castle], the one in the Park [now known as the Rotunda, sited above Dunsmere], and he began the long course of improvements in the place which have been steadily pursued since his time by successive generations'.5 As for Herbert's house, the Revd Jeremiah Milles saw it on a tour of Hampshire and Sussex he undertook in 1743 and described it as 'a very good one in ye antient taste [which] has been so much altered and improved by the present Posessor yt is for its size one of ye most beautifull and elegant homes in England. It has besides one good old Gothic front, which faces the stables, two other modern ones'.6

It is clear from the survey of the estate taken by Thomas Blandy in 1739, when Herbert was forty-two and had already embarked upon his 'long course of improvements' in the park, that he had achieved an elaborate layout to the northeast of his house around a walled garden.7 The vast plan is centred by a faintly coloured area, which records a semi-formal design (*colour 17*), inter-woven with serpentine paths in the manner of Batty Langley's 'artinatural' style, as popularised in his *New Principles of Gardening* of 1728. The ground plan of Herbert's house reveals that the 'good old Gothic front' was likely to have fronted a U-shaped Tudor house, to which Herbert added a new block with show façades. That to the east gave on to a parterre from which radiated an approximation of a *patte d'oie*, one tree-lined avenue focusing on an indetermi-nate circular feature, a central grassy axis of the 'Long Walk' and a further arm, which ended abruptly, confined by a driveway. It is not clear what kind of garden Herbert inherited from his mother, but the 4th Earl records that he had 'heard that the lime avenue at the foot of the garden was planted by her', which might account for this southern arm of the goose foot.8 Shrubberies, cut through with winding paths, two of which terminated in an open circular glade, or 'variety', as Langley would have described it, flanked the northern avenue. Another open area in the shrubbery was centred by a statue on a plinth. There appears to have been a hexagonal basin alongside the walled garden, from which extended a small canal. On the other side of the main approach driveway there was an open lawn, which led to the 'Temple in the garden' on its revetment flanked by regiments of trees. Further out in the park there were no designed features, merely fields and meadows. Significantly, the Long Walk up to 'Siddon' Hill ended without incident or terminal feature; the Arch was yet to be constructed.

Milles's account of the estate is the only record that has come to light thus far of Herbert's eclectic landscape. Unfortunately, that inveterate traveller Bishop Pococke, who has left us long and detailed descriptions of these ephemeral parks, including a particularly good commentary on Dogmersfield, got as far as the 'three leg'd cross, near Cruxeaston' in 1754 and then went 'by Hawcleer and Penwood', without leaving a record of what he saw, on his way to Newtown.9 It seems that he missed the celebrated Grotto at Cruxeaston, at the southwestern tip of Grotto Copse, which is contiguous with the planta-

32 Robert Herbert's Heaven's Gate, an eye-catcher crowning Sidown Hill on the Highclere estate, collapsed soon after its construction in 1739 and had to be rebuilt

tion on Sidown Hill, though he obviously knew Robert Herbert's nephew and successor Henry Herbert, later to become 1st Earl of Carnarvon.[10]

The Arch on Sidown Hill was sited at a point known as Heaven's Gate (32), in 'a little scrubby wood of whitethorns and oaks'. It consisted of 'one large arch in ye middle, & a small one on each side, which opens into a square room, which is pavd with stone, and ye walls stucco'd, & in which the family some times drink Tea'.[11] Behind the Arch was 'a circular seat, from whence you have ye most beautifull prospect of ye country thro ye great arch, which by confining it each side serves as frame to that beautifull picture'.[12] Heaven's Gate was built in 1739, just after Blandy made his survey, at the end of a half-mile long avenue of beeches extending from the house. It was run up hastily 'in one summer', as it collapsed later that year and had to be rebuilt. Milles had been dining with Herbert on the fateful day and hurried up the hill in time to see it 'cleave from ye foundation, & it fell with such a noise that it was heard at 3 or 4 miles distance'.[13]

It is possible that Herbert was inspired by his brother, the 'builder' 9th Earl of Pembroke, who was a prime mover in the early eighteenth-century revival of Palladianism. He had also raised an arch at Wilton,[14] and might well have advised Herbert on the Garden Temple (*colour 18*), a roofless structure which has walls with Palladian-style features. Milles remarks that the Garden Temple was 'lately erected', and also describes a wooden 'Tuscan Temple' sited on the brink of a chalk pit within a small copse.[15] This must refer to the temple (*33*) that is now close to the house; its original position must have been in what is now the Rookery. It is likely that Herbert's Tuscan Temple was re-sited closer to the house either by the 1st or the 2nd Earl and given a spirited plaster frieze inspired by the Panathenaic procession from the lately arrived Elgin Marbles. In a letter of 1756 to Sanderson Miller, Charles Lyttelton of Hagley reported that the Corinthian columns of the Garden Temple 'were saved out of ye ruins of Devonshire House in Piccadilly when it was accidentally burnt'.[16] This refers to Hugh May's 1665 Berkeley House, which was replaced by William Kent's Devonshire House after a fire of 1733. It is likely, therefore, that the Garden Temple was raised in or about that year, long before Heaven's Gate.

Finally, Milles does not mention either the Milford Lake House or the circular Temple in the Park, now overlooking Dunsmere, which suggests that they had not been built by 1743. Both underwent alterations when Barry was reshaping the house for the 3rd Earl of Carnarvon after 1838, and documentary evidence survives to prove that Robert Herbert built the Lake House.

The Temple in the Park, or Rotunda, now known as the Temple of Diana, is another matter entirely. It is presumed by Mark Girouard to have been one of Robert Herbert's structures and confirmed as such by the 4th Earl in his history of the family. It is not present on John Spyers's map of Capability Brown's suggested improvements for the park, preserved at the Castle, but the map does not identify existing structures, only ones to be added.[17] The Rotunda (*colour 19*) was originally a much simpler structure without a drum to the dome, with no decorative urns and with a colonnade of more tightly spaced Ionic columns. On the lower floor there was a kitchen, as well as a bedroom, closets and a WC, while above there was a grand 'Belvedere Room'. These were all sited in the central and eastern sections of the building; the west-facing section had an open colonnade on both the ground and first floors, to take in views across Milford Lake to the Lake House and beyond. Fortunately, drawings of the Rotunda dated July 1838 'as at present', and showing Barry's proposed alterations, survive to record the differences.[18] Essentially, Barry heightened the structure by adding the drum, and evenly spaced the columns in creating a continuous open colonnade on the first floor. A bundle of papers in the Hampshire Record Office relates to the rebuilding of the Temple between 1839 and 1842 and again between 1851 and 1852.[19] Sited on the slope of Tent Hill, it would have been a dramatic feature to be viewed from the water-side terrace of the Lake House to the northwest. Sadly, these sightlines have

33   The Tuscan Temple, now re-sited closer to the house, is another survivor
of Robert Herbert's eclectic landscape

now been lost in the sprawling growth of trees and rhododendrons between
the two buildings.

The date and original form of the Milford Lake House, a beautiful lakeside
fishing pavilion and summerhouse, are more difficult to determine. Indeed,
several authorities, including Nikolaus Pevsner, have taken it to be a building
by Barry or Thomas Allom, who were both busily remodelling the Castle in the
1840s.[20] However, as we have seen, the 4th Earl was quite clear about Robert
Herbert having built the 'greater part of the house at Milford'. It is drawn as a
tripartite building with only a corridor linking the wings on Bull's estate map
of 1794 and as a vignette on the frontispiece of an early nineteenth-century
book detailing the contents of a collection of Highclere and Burghclere estate
maps at the house.[21] Although its interiors have some Palladian elements
installed from Henry Herbert's house, when it was also extended to the rear,
the exterior of the building remained substantially unaltered from the three-
part pavilion that Robert Herbert had created as a retreat in the park. This has
a Palladian feel, its grey-green stock brick enlivened with chequer patterning
similar to designs by William Kent, or perhaps that other Burlington protégé,
John Vardy, who provided lodges at Hackwood Park, now lost, chequered with
dark flint and light stone, for the Duke of Bolton in 1761.[22] Through his close
contact with his brother at Wilton, Robert Herbert will have been conversant
with the latest architectural fashions.

Perhaps the clearest evidence of the exact function of the pavilion lies in the character of Robert Herbert. He is caught most vividly in the letters of his close friend the Earl of Chesterfield, from which he emerges as a 45-year-old philanderer in the fashionable circuits of Bath.[23] He was part of Chesterfield's social circle at the spa during October and November 1734. Chesterfield gave him the nickname of Amoretto because he was always hopelessly and help-lessly in love. He describes Herbert walking 'upon Lansdowne to evaporate his grief for the loss of his Parthenissa [Pope's friend Martha Blount] in memory of whom (and the wind being very cold into the bargain) he tied his handker-chief over his hat and looked very sadly'.[24] For Beau Nash's ball at Lyndsey's Rooms three days later 'he wore his gold laced clothes on the occasion, and looked so fine, that, standing by chance in the middle of the dancers, he was taken by many at a distance for a gilt garland. He concluded his evening, as usual, with basset and blasphemy'.[25] Some days later Chesterfield wrote: 'Amoretto took a vomit in the morning, and then with a clear and excellent stomach dined with me, and went to the ball at night, where Mrs Hamilton chiefly engrossed him'.[26] Chesterfield summed up his friend's gadfly behaviour in a letter from Bath of 14 November to the Countess of Suffolk:

> You will, I am sure, expect from me *l'histoire amoureuse et galante* of Mr Herbert; but I am very sorry, both for our sake and his, that it makes but a very small volume this year. He lies in bed till between ten and eleven, where he eats two breakfasts of strong broth; then rides till one or two; after which he dines commonly pretty plentifully with me, and concludes the evening at billiards and whist. He sometimes laughs with the girls, but with moderate success.[27]

It is in the light of these episodes that the Milford Lake House in its first form needs to be reconstructed: a pleasure house by a lonely lake, perfect for fun, fishing and flirtation. Clearly the place was created for a roisterer with a sense of style and very little reserve. Who knows what he might have got up to in the Cruxeaston Grotto, in Pope's absence, with the nine attendant Lisle sisters.

When Robert Herbert died in 1769 he had achieved a small pleasure ground of eclectic incidents close to the house, had extended tree avenues into the wider parkland and built at least three structures of scenic quality: the Arch, the Temple in the Park, and the Milford Lake House. Without an heir to carry on the improvements to the estate, Highclere was left to his brother William's son, Henry, who became Lord Porchester in 1780 and 1st Earl of Carnarvon in 1793. It was Henry who would call in Lancelot Brown to assess the capabilities of Robert Herbert's existing landscape, but who would carry out Brown's suggested improvements in his own time and, seemingly, without the guiding hand of the great practitioner.

Highclere has been fortunate in retaining many of the early eighteenth-century features with which Robert Herbert enriched his landscape, even after its reshaping into a Brown-style park. Sadly, this was not the case at nearby **Dogmersfield Park**, where the captivating landscape that Paulet St John laid out after 1736 and before 1747 has almost all disappeared. Its ornamental buildings, apart from King John's Hunting Lodge, were ruthlessly demolished in 1790 to make way for open parkland devised by William Emes. This, in turn, has been stripped of most of its trees, giving the estate a bare, soulless appearance. Unsurprisingly, given its close proximity to Highclere, Paulet St John's layout also included a Gothick arch and a temple commanding views of the landscape from elevated points of vantage to the north and south. These, and his other garden structures, are shown in two early eighteenth-century paintings

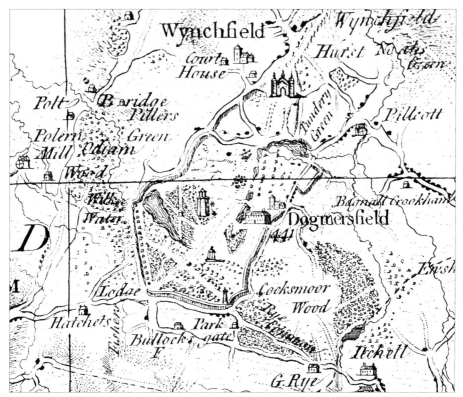

34 Almost all the garden buildings of the Eclectic layout at Dogmersfield Park are marked as vignettes on Taylor's 1759 map of the county. *Hampshire Record Office: 110M89/P67*

of the estate by an unknown artist, possibly in the circle of John Wootton.[28] They are also drawn on Taylor's map (*34*) and described in generous detail by Bishop Pococke, who had seen them in 1754:

A long mile from Odiham is Dogmansfield, Mr. St. John's...The ground, water, the park and plantations, are very beautiful...From the house there is a view of seven ponds, which appear like a serpentine river and of a Gothick arch on an advanced ground half a mile further, it is built of brick and flints in squares. There is an imitation of a British or Druid avenue to it of large stones set up on end for half a mile, which are found on the sandy heaths. On the other side of the house is a small round hill well planted, with a colonnade in the front of it, call'd the Temple; beyond this on a more advanced ground is another plantation and an octagon turret, on the summit which commands a fine view of the country...they call it the Belvidere. Below this in a wood is a thatch'd house, further down a large piece of water of thirty acres, in the middle of which is a small low turret on four Gothick arches, called the Chinese building, but it is rather defective in the execution, and near the water is a cottage built to resemble a Gothick chapel.[29]

The two landscape paintings – a wide panorama of the park taken from just below the Belvedere, and another bird's eye view from above the Belvedere – show many of the garden buildings described by Pococke set within a beautifully wooded and expansive park. The southernmost pond of the chain of pools in front of the house is drawn as a formal canal and this water sequence leads northwards to what is now the Tundry Pond, around which were clustered the village cottages that were swept away in the 1790s. There is also a copy of the 9th Earl of Pembroke's celebrated Palladian Bridge across one of the tributaries, though whether this was actually built is uncertain. What the presence of the bridge does suggest is that the Earl's pre-1746 'Rococo' garden at Wilton in the next county may have exerted a strong influence on Paulet St John.[30] High above the Tundry Pond is the Gothic Arch, a toy fort structure with a sharply pointed opening in the centre and wings with canted bays, all decorated with Gothick windows and quatrefoils and topped by battlements and crocketed pinnacles. Just perceptible in the detail of the painting is the curving path leading up to the Arch, which, as Pococke mentions, was flanked by stones imitating a Druid avenue. In his 1743 book on Avebury, William Stukeley congratulated the Earl of Pembroke on his preparation of a 'fine and costly model of *Stonehenge*' for his gardens at Wilton.[31] It seems that this was never realised, but Paulet St John managed to catch the prevailing antiquarian fascination with Britain's pre-history with his Druidic avenue. Needless to say, this was also razed to the ground in the later improvements.

Walking the park today, particularly from its access driveway between two lodges on the A287 near Odiham, the contours of the park can be appreciated. The bridleway and footpath threads through woodland and then opens out at the edge of Dogmersfield Lake, now commanded by a grand modern house called Aragon Hall, where once stood on stilts the Gothick-Chinese Building. The pathway then snakes up the ridge and at the crest the base of the Belvedere has been recreated so that its panoramic views can be appreciated again. The house is in the park below to the right, while in the dip behind the revetment, in the centre of a woodland cut with rides now gone, was the Thatched House; the site of the Temple is just out of view to the right, but would have been visible from the lantern of the four-storey Belvedere. Arch Plantation can be made out on the far horizon to the left. The one Paulet St John building that does survive, but is not shown on the Taylor map, is that described by Pococke as the 'cottage built to resemble a Gothick chapel'. This is sited outside the park wall, as it is marked on early sheets of the Ordnance Survey, at the northern extremity of Dogmersfield Lake, commanding another pool known as Wilts Water. It can be found at the end of a track off Bagwell Lane, its attenuated shaped gables and ogee-cusped windows giving it a curiously startled appearance. King John's Hunting Lodge (*colour 20*) is close in style to the Gothick Arch and has traces of whitewash on the russet brickwork, suggesting that it was originally painted white, like the Belvedere and the Arch, to act as an eye-catcher from the main house. An elegant modern garden with more Gothick features, which are in perfect harmony with the Lodge, was laid out by John Fowler after he bought the house in 1947; this has been enriched by the present tenants.[32]

Sadly, an entry in the estate accounts records 'Pulling down ornamental buildings in Park £300'.[33] If Paulet St John's Eclectic park dates from the 1740s, as is likely, then it might also have been inspired by a similar landscape at Halswell House, near Bridgwater in Somerset. Paulet St John's first wife died in 1733 and he married Mary, widow of Sir Halswell Tynte, in 1736. Her brother-in-law, Sir John Kemys Tynte, with the help of the architect and landscape gardener Thomas Wright, created an evocative park at Halswell, which featured a varied range of Gothick and classical buildings, as well as a Druid's Temple.[34] Wright's Halswell temple was not a stone circle, avenue or cromlech, but a thatched summerhouse. His 1755 book, *Six Original Designs for Arbours*, did much to popularise this cult for rustic buildings with a numinous air, their thatched and mossy roofs supported on twisted tree trunks. The names of these garden buildings were interchangeable; they were often called root houses, or moss houses, but most usually hermitages or hermits' cells, inhabited by pseudo-holy men when required to entertain guests or even, as at Hawkstone in Shropshire, salaried hermits. Robert Drummond of Cadland Manor was approached by an anonymous would-be hermit who asked for a hermitage to be built for him 'Near your honers house in a wood', where he would live for seven years 'with out seing any human Creature' to see what 'Nature would turn [him] to in that time'.[35] The letter contained a drawing of the proposed hermitage – a blockish, primitive Gothick structure with a trefoil in the gable and a cross on its apex – with annotations suggesting that it could be built of old wood in a fortnight. Unlike the root house at Walhampton, mentioned in the previous chapter, it was never realised, but the most famous eighteenth-century hermitage in Hampshire, which was achieved but is now lost, was sited on the edge of Selborne Common at the top of the mazy Zig-Zag Path that climbs up the beech Hanger overshadowing the village below.

The Zig-Zag Path is accessed via a footpath marked to Selborne Common in the car park to the rear of the Selborne Arms. This path skirts open fields at **The Wakes** to the right, where the naturalist Gilbert White set up in 1754 a painted wooden statue of Hercules close to his own private gate to the Hanger, an entirely appropriate gesture for a labour to be endured.[36] White and his brother Henry constructed the Path between 1752 and 1753, and at the top they sited the Hermitage to take in the view of the village below and as a place in which to take alfresco refreshment. It features on the frontispiece of White's celebrated 1789 *Natural History of Selborne*. Samuel Hieronymus Grimm's engraving (35) shows the 'straw-clad cell' surrounded by shrubs and rocks, while close by is a Rococo-style seat made of tortuous wooden branches. A bearded hermit, dressed in a voluminous cloak, a crook in one hand and a rosary in the other, surveys the scene. Quotations from Homer: 'A harsh place, but a good nurse to youth/For my part, I cannot think of anything sweeter than one's native land', and from Cicero: 'At last that kingdom – harsh, rugged, plain, unchanging, nurse of our fellow men – and our own' give the rather fanciful image some intellectual gravitas.[37] The cliff edge at the top of the Zig-Zag Path offers a matchless view of White's sweet 'native land', his beloved Selborne, with his own house and garden at The Wakes in the middle ground. *Natural History* also contains another engraving, taken from the other side of the valley, with White standing proudly in front of a specially erected tent set up for refreshment, with the Zig-Zag Path prominent on the Hanger in the far distance (36).

The Wakes has been taken over by the heritage industry, but this has meant that money has been generated for a landscape management plan, prepared by Kim Wilkie, the implementation of which began in 1995. Consequently the grounds around the house have been meticulously restored using White's gardening diary, the *Garden Kalendar,* which he kept between 1751 and 1771. Essentially, in White's day the garden was a small holding of about seven acres, consisting of orchards, vegetable plots, flower gardens and a miniature landscape garden.[38] Lawns in front of the house extend to a ha-ha on which is sited a sundial, and, to the left, a small classical Alcove (37), backed by a yew and a cedar of Lebanon, that gives views across open fields to a Conical Mount on which there is a seat – the revolving Wine Pipe – carved out of a barrel. All these features were in place by 1762. Further on, to the left, there is a series of compartmented gardens: the Kitchen Garden, 'The Field and Basons', the Field Garden with a Melon Ground House and an enclosure for cutting beds. On the other side of the central lawn there are more enclosed gardens: the Six Quarters, the Wild Garden, the Herb Garden and the Annual Garden.

As well as White's own letters and garden diary, there is another valuable

35 Samuel Hieronymus Grimm's drawing of the Hermitage above the Hanger at The
    Wakes was used as the frontispiece to Gilbert White's *Natural History of Selborne*.
    The hermit shown in the engraving is White's brother Henry.
    University of Bristol Library, Special Collections

36 An engraved view of the village of Selborne from White's *Natural History*, with the
    Zig-Zag path climbing up the Hanger in the distance.
    University of Bristol Library, Special Collections

37 The ha-ha at The Wakes, Selborne, is enlivened with a classical Alcove and a sundial

record of how the pleasure grounds were enjoyed when White was in ownership at The Wakes. In June 1763, the three Battie sisters – Anne, Catherine
(Kitty) and Philadelphia (Delphy) – daughters of Dr Battie, President of the
Royal College of Physicians, arrived to stay for two months at Selborne
vicarage.[39] Kitty kept a diary of her summer holiday at Selborne, 'A Little
Journal of some of the happiest days I have had in the happy Valley in the year
1763', and she records with obvious delight her visits to see White and his
circle of family and friends.[40] The following November, White himself evoked
this summer scene of alfresco dining in his poem, 'The Invitation to Selborne':

> Oft on some evening, sunny, soft, and still,
> The Muse shall lead thee to the beech-grown hill,
> To spend in tea the cool, refreshing hour,
> Where nods in air the pensile, nest-like bower;
> Or where the Hermit hangs the straw-clad cell,
> Emerging gently for the leafy dell;
> By Fancy plann'd...[41]

On 24 June, Gilbert, his brother Henry (Harry) and the three Battie sisters
climbed the Zig-Zag Path and had tea in the Hermitage at the top. In the
middle of the party Harry appeared, dressed as the hermit, and gave Kitty a
delightful shock. Thereafter, they walked around the High Wood until dusk,

returning to the Hermitage, which was now lit by lamps. Kitty wrote passionately: 'Never shall I forget the happiness of this day, which exceeded any I ever had in all my life'.[42] On 20 July, Harry's friend Thomas Mulso gave the sisters 'a discourse upon natural Phylosophy & Astronomy', and he read them 'some of Thomson's Seasons', after which they walked in the woods.[43] On the following day Kitty went out into the 'Hay field [and] toss'd the hay about a little', walked to The Wakes, 'sat in the Alcove [and] spent the morn most delightfully', returned home for dinner, walked back again to The Wakes and 'went up to the sweet Hermitage sat viewing its beauteous views some time then walk[ed] round the wood back to the Hermitage'.[44]

It was not long before the sisters and the three young bachelor clerics – Harry White, Ned Mulso (Thomas Mulso's brother) and Basil Cane (Gilbert's cousin) began to act out the pastoral Arcadia that they were caught up in during that unforgettable warm summer. They took to calling each other after characters from pastoral poetry and, at times, dressing up like them. Kitty was Daphne; Harry, Ned and Basil were, respectively, Strephon, Corydon and Collin, shepherds taken from Virgil and Spenser.[45] On 28 July the entire party had a picnic on the Hanger, which Gilbert recorded in his *Garden Kalendar*:

> Drank tea 20 of us at the Hermitage: the Miss Batties, & the Mulso family contributed much to our pleasures by their singing, & being dress'd as shepherds, sheperdesses. It was a most elegant evening; and all the parties appear'd highly satisfy'd. The Hermit appear'd to great advantage.[46]

The Battie sisters left Selborne on 3 August, Kitty reminiscing soulfully:

> Adieu happy Vale enchanting Hermitage much loved stump beauteous Hanger sweet Lythe...here the scene closes the play is done the pleasing dream is oer & tomorrow I must awake and find myself in London.[47]

Not surprisingly, given their closeness over the summer, Harry wrote her a personal elegy of many stanzas entitled 'Daphne's Departure' and signed it 'Strephon'.[48]

Not all mid-century landscapes were remodelled wholesale in the newly fashionable Eclectic style; indeed, some retained elements from earlier campaigns and were updated by the simple addition of one or two buildings and some ornamental shrubberies. This was the case at **The Vyne**, near Basingstoke, where John Chute's focus in the 1750s was on aggrandising his sixteenth-century house in a mix of Gothick and classical detail rather than creating a contemporary landscape. A map by William Moss of 1776 shows the house commanding a 'Pleasure Ground' of lawns and regimented trees, while a shrubbery snakes out between the road and the Old Orchard.[49] The canal-like pool in front of the house was given a Chinese bridge, shown in a view of 1756 by Johann Heinrich Müntz,[50] and one of the two brick Summerhouses is marked, tucked alongside the road. The other, by this time extended, is further out at a bend in the road, while on the other side of the water the landscape still retained its field patterns, including an enclosed 'Pheasant Ground'.

One landscape that underwent a complete transformation was that at **Old Alresford House**, where Admiral Lord Rodney used his prize money from the War of the Austrian Succession to purchase an estate and build a house. He chose Alresford, five miles from Avington Park, the home of his godfather, George Bridges. The house was rebuilt between 1749 and 1751 by the architect William Jones in an austere Palladian style, but with Rococo interiors.[51] Rodney married in 1753 and continued to expand his estate by buying up farms and, being fond of animals, Alresford Pond to protect the wildlife. However, this tranquil period of family life was shattered in 1757 by the outbreak of the Seven Years War, when Rodney was called to sea again, and the death, after childbirth, of his wife Jenny. On his return to Alresford in 1763, and after his second marriage in 1764, he set about more improvements to the house and the landscape, a plan for which was obtained from the landscape designer Richard Woods.[52] The plan (38) accords with the landscape today, with an open lawn in front of the house leading to a ha-ha and flanking walks on the perimeter threaded through beech and yew, which frame the view across Bighton Lane to the south of Alresford Pond. The plantations are thickened to mask the kitchen garden to the east of the house and further planting screens the churchyard to the west. The circular clearing on the east was intended for a bowling green or 'saloon', enriched with an urn or statue. This minimalist, almost Brownian landscape does not admit of any of Woods's usual garden buildings or other embellishments except 'Various kinds of Benches to the different Prospects'.[53]

The same year, 1764, saw the creation of a similar proto-Brownian park in the county, laid out by Robert Henley after he was made first Earl of Northington. Henley inherited the house that had been built between 1664 and 1673 by William Samwell for an earlier Robert Henley, the brick west front of which can still be seen today, encased in the great Greek Revival house that Henry Drummond commissioned from William Wilkins in 1809.[54] Most authorities on **The Grange** have, unsurprisingly, written about the Greek house and its terraced gardens, set on its high revetment above the south-flowing Candover Brook, a tributary of the River Itchen.[55] Fortunately, English Heritage, who care for the site, have provided a useful map of the estate on their signage (39) and this, together with contemporary accounts and some documents, make it possible to retrieve what they call 'the lost landscape of Grange Park'. It only requires a cursory glance of the map to see that the landscape has all the attributes of a Brownian park, but the great practitioner

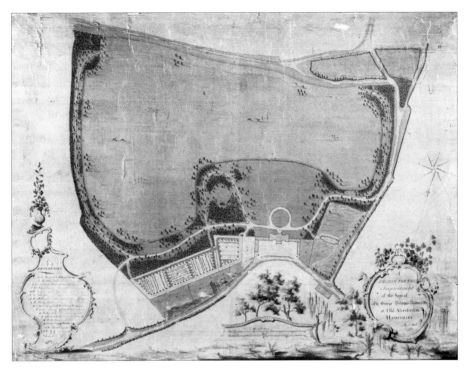

38 Richard Woods's 1764 plan of the improvements at Old Alresford reveals his intention to introduce lateral shrubberies for framing views across the open lawn in front
of the house to Alresford Pond on the other side of the road. *Hampshire Record Office:
116M88/B17. Photograph by Paul Carter*

is not recorded as having worked here. Indeed, his earliest commission in the
county was at Broadlands in the following year. Tantalisingly, and somewhat
confusingly, the sign records that Alexander Baring, who bought The Grange
in 1817, 'increased the size of the park' and 'added waterfalls' to the lake and 'a
bridge designed by Robert Adam'. The syntax is unfortunate, for although
Baring may have remodelled the existing landscape that he had purchased from
Henry Drummond, he could hardly have commissioned Adam to design a
bridge, as the architect had died in 1792.

What appears to have happened is that, on his elevation to the earldom in
1764, the 1st Earl set about creating an ornamental landscape dramatised by a
series of artificial lakes, produced by damming the Candover Brook. He
commissioned Robert Adam to prepare drawings for new domestic offices for
the house and a bridge to take one of the drives over the lakes.[56] The bridge
design was composed of a single segmental arch, with enclosed lion masks in
the spandrels, while the rusticated piers had decorative swags and urns set
within niches. We can be fairly certain that Adam's plans remained unexecuted, but a slightly later contemporary account of the grounds, which

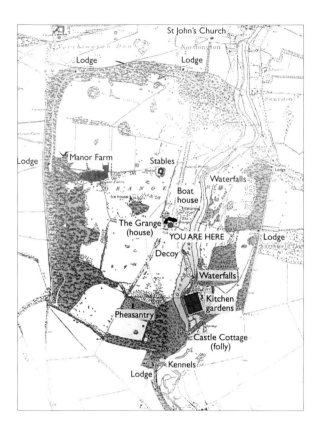

39 An English Heritage sign at The Grange shows the extent of the eighteenth-century park ringed by shelter-belts, with the Candover Brook snaking through the middle of the landscape. Might this be a layout by Robert Adam, who designed a bridge for the lake?

appeared in the *Gentleman's Magazine* of 1788, described them as 'beautifully laid out and not deficient in wood though it seems principally of modern growth', and that their boundaries were 'well planted'.57 The pleasure grounds by the house were much improved by Alexander Baring, who commissioned Charles Robert Cockerell to add the templar Conservatory and Italianate Garden, which will feature in a later chapter of this study. Baring, as we have seen, also remodelled the parkland, encircling it with a series of entrance lodges, adding two flint and brick bridges, a battlemented Folly Tower (*colour 21*), also of flint, a boathouse and a pheasantry. However, the form of the lakes, the shelterbelt plantations threaded with walks and rides, and the combination of scattered tree clumps and open greensward must be of the 1st Earl's campaign. They anticipate the design aesthetic that was to become synony-mous for the next two decades with Lancelot Brown and his acolytes.

5

'Let nothing appear with ostentation, or parade' Brownian landscapes

Broadlands, Highclere Castle, Paultons Park, Exbury, Warnford Park
South Stoneham House, North Stoneham Park, Cadland House
Eaglehurst, Cuffnells Park, Elvetham Hall, Dogmersfield Park
Brockenhurst Park

Lancelot 'Capability' Brown's professional life was one continuous journey, taking him the length and breadth of England in the creation of parks designed for leisure, to offer opportunities for sport, and, above all, to provide profit for the landowner. At his death, no fewer than 200 estates had been shaped by his personal design,[1] while over 4,000 landscape parks had been created by a new generation of landscapers inspired by him,[2] including men like William Emes, whose work features in Hampshire at Brockenhurst Park, Elvetham Hall and Dogmersfield Park. These followers continued his legacy well into the nineteenth century, while Brown's self-styled successor, Humphry Repton, started his design career contriving small Brownian parks for the emergent *nouveaux riches* who were his client base. That is, until the aficionados of Picturesque theory – Richard Payne Knight and Uvedale Price – pressured Repton into modifying Brown's idealised landscapes and embracing instead the rougher charms of unadorned nature. Never at ease with this shift away from the artificial, Repton was seduced eventually by the dubious charms of the shrubbery and the basket-edged flowerbed to develop a new style of ornamental gardening for the next century.

Hampshire has an important place in garden history for many reasons, not least because it was home to the originator of Picturesque theory, even if his somewhat literal definition of the phrase: 'a term expressive of that peculiar kind of beauty, which is agreeable in a picture', differed from that of the later writers.[3] This is, of course, the Revd William Gilpin, who first coined the term in his 1768 *Essay upon Prints*, and who developed it in relation to landscape with his 1782 *Observations of the River Wye and several parts of South Wales, etc. relative chiefly to Picturesque Beauty*, based on tours he had made back in 1770. Born in

Cumberland, where the rugged scenery must have made an impact on him as a young man, he was educated at Oxford and then pursued a career in education and the church. In 1777 he became vicar of Boldre, near Lymington in the New Forest, and would later write about the topography and particular scenic qualities of that woodland in his 1791 *Forest Scenery*. The full title of the book explains clearly his aim: *Remarks on Forest Scenery, and other Woodland Views, (Relative chiefly to Picturesque Beauty) Illustrated by the Scenes of NEW-FOREST in Hampshire*.

The publication date was timely, as Brown had died in 1783, after which Repton set up in business as his successor in 1789. A re-evaluation was, therefore, long overdue, and the book gave Gilpin the chance to assess Brown's contribution on his home turf. Among the detailed sections on the creation of the forest, its laws, specific trees and their qualities, Gilpin took every opportunity to visit important estates, some of which had been designed by Brown, and to convey to the reader their relative merits. In so doing he gave an accurate account of how a Brownian park was constructed, relying for its overall impact upon several design elements, repeated at each site. It is fair to say that at this point, though still more attracted to the 'savage' landscapes he had highlighted in the paintings of Salvator Rosa, and which Payne Knight and Price would adopt in the 1790s as perfect exemplars for the new Picturesque fashion in landscape, Gilpin had an informed appreciation of Brown's design revolution.

After a section on clumps of trees in *Forest Scenery*, Gilpin moved on to '*park-scenery*, which is generally composed of *combinations of clumps*, interspersed with lawns'.[4] He saw the park as 'one of the noblest appendages of a great house', which should stand nearly in the centre of the park', the '*exact spot* depends intirely on the ground', while the lawn should be 'varied with clumps of different forms, receding behind each other, in so pleasing a manner, as to make an agreeable scene'.[5] There were always situations where such artificial remedies would be difficult to apply, but Gilpin suggested that they are rare in nature and that 'the variety of landscape is such, that it may almost always be brought in one form, or other, to serve the purposes of beauty'.[6] All of this sounds like a template for a typical Brownian parkscape; indeed, Gilpin asserted: 'the many improvements of the ingenious Mr. Brown, in various parts of England, bear witness to the truth of these observations'.[7]

Like Brown before him, Gilpin saw the park as a 'scene either planted by art, or, if naturally woody, artificially improved [where] we expect a beauty, and contrast in its *clumps*, which we do not look for in the wild scenes of nature'.[8] This distinguishes Brown's idealised landscapes from the Picturesque theoreticians' preferred advocacy of raw, unadorned nature. Gilpin continued:

In the wild scenes of nature we have grander exhibitions, but greater deformities, than are generally met with in the polished works of art. As we seldom meet with these *sublime* passages in improved landscape; it would be unpardon-able if any thing *disgusting* should appear.[9]

Unsurprisingly, given such a minimalist aesthetic, 'expensive ornament', including 'Temples, Chinese-bridges, obelisks, and all the laboured works of art', was deemed '*disgusting*', and suggested 'inharmonious ideas'.[10] Banished then, were to be all the whimsical confections that had characterised the mid-century landscapes – the 'Rococo', or more accurately, the Eclectic gardens – in favour of an artificially 'polished' scene. If any building was required, it needed a specific function and should be 'as simple, as its use...let nothing appear with ostentation, or parade'.[11] Small wonder then that his later critics, especially Payne Knight and Price, castigated Brown after his death for his dull, boring landscape parks:

> Our modern taste, alas! No limit knows: -
> O'er hill, oe'r dale, through woods and fields it flows;
> Spreading o'er all its unprolific spawn,
> In never-ending sheets of vapid lawn.[12]

Interestingly, this posthumous criticism of Brown's vapid, identikit landscapes had begun much earlier, while he was still alive and busily changing the face of the country's landed estates. He appears as 'Mr Layout' in Joseph Craddock's *Village Memoirs* of 1775, an epistolary book of letters written between a cler-gyman and his family. One letter discusses the improvements at a country estate where Mr Massem and Mr Layout 'talk of taste as if it was to be brought down in a broad-wheeled wagon, and they had nothing to do but to scatter it at random – Mr Layout thinks there should be a clump, and there is one; the squire thinks it would look pretty to cut a vista through it, and it is cut'.[13] The demise of the Eclectic landscape and its replacement by Brown's formulaic designs is summed up neatly in the grove at Marleston. There 'the rustic seat was, with the Horatian motto of *Hae latebrae dulces & si jam credis, amoenae*', which is 'condemned to be cut down, as well as the large one, which Mr Arlington had used to call Shenstone's Grove, for the urn to his memory was prettily executed, and the placing of the statue of the Sibyl in front of it, which seemed to exclaim, *Procul O procul este profani*! was in my opinion a very happy thought'.[14] They are all to be swept away, and as for the 'intended alterations to the water, - it is destined to take any course but its own, for the merit of everything seems to consist only in the sum it is to cost'.[15] As we know, Brown charged extortionate fees for his landscape proposals.

Returning to Gilpin's strictures against 'expensive ornament', he was happy to allow for a practical park gate at the entrance to the estate and a carriage drive that should be 'spacious, or moderate, like the house it approaches...to have the convenience of winding along a valley' to pass 'obstacles' – a bridge, a wood or a piece of water – which would divert the traveller; 'Mr. Brown was often happy in creating these artificial obstructions'.[16] Brown's favoured shelterbelts at the extremities of his parks were also cited: 'From every part of the approach, and from the ridings, and favourite walks about the park, let all the boundaries be secreted'.[17] However, Brown's experiments with water, something for which he has since become noted, came in for heavy criticism from Gilpin:

> Mr. Brown, I think, has failed more in river-making than in any of his attempts. An artificial lake has sometimes a good effect; but neither propriety, nor beauty can arise from it, unless the heads and extremities of it are perfectly well managed, and concealed: and after all, the success is hazardous. You must always suppose it a portion of a larger piece of water; and it is not easy to carry on the imposition. If the house be magnificent, it seldom receives much benefit from an artificial production of this kind. Grandeur is rarely produced.[18]

Although Gilpin mentions 'Blenheim-castle' in 'Woodstock-park', one wonders if he had ever visited it to see Brown's lake, brilliantly developed from the infant Glyme and Colonel Armstrong's canals, which dramatises Vanbrugh's Grand Bridge and provides a perfect reflecting mirror to Blenheim Palace.[19] It will be instructive, therefore, to assess Brown's improvements in Hampshire to gauge whether they would have satisfied the discerning vicar of Boldre.

Brown's first commission in the county seems to have been at **Broadlands**, near Eastleigh, where, before his death in 1757, the 1st Viscount Palmerston had already begun to de-formalise the gardens, 'giving away all the fine pyramid greens to those that will fetch them, of which many cartloads have gone'.[20] However, it was his successor, the 2nd Viscount, who called Brown in to remodel the landscape and provide new designs for the house. Brown's architectural work has received little detailed attention thus far, but the parent house was always an integral part of his carefully composed landscapes. Much of Brown's architectural work was executed by Henry Holland, a master builder from Fulham, and later by Holland's eldest son, also Henry. In 1771 Brown went into an informal partnership with the younger Holland, handing over to him the architectural side of his practice; and in 1773 Holland married Brown's daughter Bridget. As Humphry Repton was to write much later in 1803, in his assessment of Brown's architectural career, 'the many good houses built under his direction, prove him to have been no mean proficient in an art, the practice of which he found, from experience, to be inseparable from landscape gardening'.[21] William Mason offered a more contemporary view of Brown's architectural work, in a letter written to Repton, which was subsequently published by him in his *Sketches and Hints* of 1795:

I am uniformly of the opinion, that where a place is to be formed, he who disposes the ground and arranges the plantations ought to fix the situation at least, if not to determine the shape and size of the ornamental buildings. Brown, I know, was ridiculed for turning architect, but I always thought he did from a kind of necessity having found the great difficulty which must frequently have occurred to him in forming a picturesque whole, where the previous building has been ill-placed, or of improper dimensions.[22]

At Broadlands, Brown was commissioned to form a new suite of reception rooms and a portico on the west, garden side of the existing house. While there may have been earlier entries in one of Brown's lost account books, his surviving ledger shows that in 1765 he was arranging to carry out work on the house with the mason, John Devall, and the carpenter, John Hobcroft.[23] Nothing is known of these works, though an unsigned drawing, probably in Brown's hand, records a very plain nine-bay south front with a three-bay centrepiece topped by a pediment.[24] Brown re-cased the house in white brick, while the south front duly received its four-columned Ionic portico. Acting like a classical garden building, this provided a sheltered viewpoint from which to survey the remodelled landscape, its flat terrain enlivened by the River Test, which sweeps in an arc past the south front (*colour 22*). As well as forming new lawns and plantations, in 1768 Brown made alterations to an existing orangery (*40*), which he extended at the back.[25] Dorothy Stroud records a succession of payments to Brown between 1766 and 1779 for the work at Broadlands, which amounts to the enormous sum of £20,750.[26]

Of similar consequence, even though he was not responsible for its execution, was Brown's design work for the 1st Earl of Carnarvon at **Highclere**. As we have seen, Robert Sawyer Herbert had already developed a designed landscape around the house and garden that he had inherited from his mother. When he died childless in 1769, he left Highclere to a nephew, Henry Herbert, later Baron Porchester and 1st Earl of Carnarvon.[27] The new owner promptly called Brown in to suggest improvements to the park, and Brown sent his assistant John Spyers in November 1770 to make surveys of both the grounds and the house. Brown made drawings based on these surveys and submitted a general plan for the alterations of the grounds, for which he charged £40, a separate plan for the intended water, charged at £10, and 'many plans for the alteration of the house and offices'.[28] These last, for which he charged £25, had given him 'a great deal of trouble'.[29] In addition, Spyers's expenses were put at £52.10s, which covered the copying of an old survey.[30]

What was actually achieved of Brown's plans for the grounds at Highclere is unclear, because he was not contracted to carry out the work, the park being reshaped by Herbert's own workforce, but the 4th Earl's history of his family gives some clues.[31]

40 Lancelot Brown added an Ionic portico to both the main house and an existing Orangery at Broadlands, to offer views out across the lawns and the remodelled River Test below

As for the house, if indeed Brown's designs were implemented, it was altered considerably by the 2nd Earl in the 1820s,[32] and almost entirely rebuilt by Sir Charles Barry for the 3rd Earl after 1842. The eighteenth-century remodelling took place between 1774 and 1777, producing a blockish brick house in late Palladian style, with an attached, columned portico and double corner pilasters.[33] In his biography of his father, Alfred Barry described this house disparagingly as an example of the 'comparative flatness and insipidity of bare classicism', which is a fair judgement on its undecorated façades and bald outline.[34] This is in stark contrast to the parkland that surrounded it, where sensitive new plantations had enhanced the natural beauty of the existing topography.

Fortunately, Brown's general plan for the grounds survives, and is now at Highclere.[35] This, together with a 1794 survey of Milford by Major Bull,[36] helps to identify the eighteenth-century elements, which have been subsumed in parts by a later growth of rhododendrons and trees.[37] Brown's suggested improvements were predictable, practical and eminently achievable. He proposed a continuous shelterbelt of trees around the environs of the estate, leaving only one section of the perimeter, in Sidown Vale to the southwest of the house, interrupted for views out of the park. A carriage drive was proposed to thread through or march alongside the belt, while further drives were planned to enter the park from the east and meander across to Dunsmere and Milford Lake. The shrubberies between these two stretches of water were to

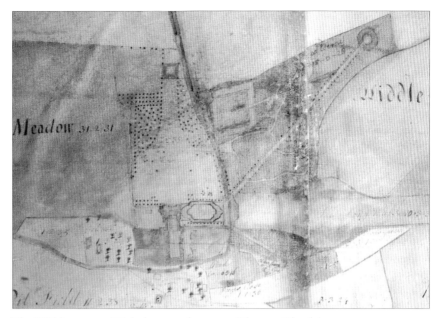

17   The Wilderness at Highclere, as shown on Thomas Blandy's 1739 estate map,
      records Robert Herbert's first improvements of the landscape, including
      'artinatural' paths derived from Batty Langley. *Hampshire Record Office: 52M88/2.*
      By kind permission of the Earl and Countess of Carnarvon

18   Robert Herbert's Garden Temple on the lawn at Highclere incorporates
      seventeenth-century Corinthian columns salvaged from the demolition in 1733
      of Berkeley House, Piccadilly. It is now known as Jackdaw's Castle

19 The Rotunda overlooking Dunsmere Lake at Highclere. A garden building of indeterminate date, which might have been added to the landscape by Robert Herbert before 1769, or it may be a scenic device of Lancelot Brown's contrivance for the 1st Earl of Carnarvon. Charles Barry altered it in the 1840s

20 King John's Hunting Lodge is a rare survivor of the 1740s Eclectic landscape at Dogmersfield Park, which was originally littered with exotic garden buildings

21 Alexander Baring added this Folly Tower, after his purchase of The Grange in 1817, to the 1760s Brownian landscape laid out by the 1st Earl of Northington

22 The serpentine river at Broadlands, a signature feature by Lancelot Brown, is commanded by the portico Brown designed for the south front of the house, and also the portico on the end wall of the Conservatory, which he altered

23 The cedars of Lebanon surrounding the Castle at Highclere, essential elements of the Brownian park, were grown from cones brought back by Bishop Pococke and presented to the 1st Earl of Carnarvon

24 Lancelot Brown's plan for the miniature landscape at Cadland has an inscription urging that the planting of the shelterbelt should not interrupt any views out across the Solent and towards the Isle of Wight. *Courtesy of the Cadland Trustees*

25 This delightful ornamental cottage on the edge of the park at Cuffnells may be a survivor of William Emes's 1790s improvements for Sir Thomas Tancred

26 These elegant twin bridges that span the Tundry Pond at Dogmersfield, built in the 1780s when William Emes was reshaping the water, once gave access to an earlier Druid avenue, at the top of which was a Gothic Arch

27 A Brownian-style park adapted in the 1770s by John Morant from an earlier landscape of fields
    dotted with veteran oaks at Brockenhurst

28 Houghton Lodge, possibly designed in the 1790s by John Plaw, is the epitome
    of the *cottage ornée*. The rotunda of its drawing room has French windows giving
    access to the grounds and providing views across the River Test below

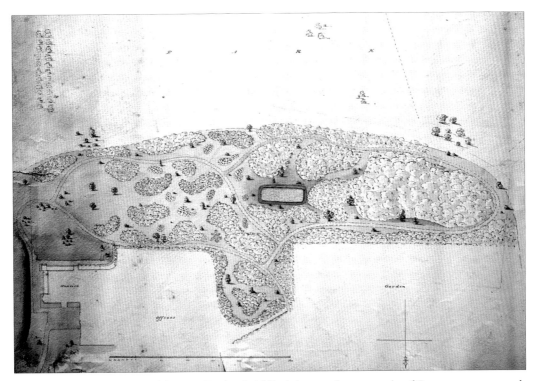

29 This design for the shrubbery at Rotherfield Park is a perfect example of Regency ornamental planting with open and closed walks. *By kind permission of Sir James & Lady Scott*

30 William Wilkins's great Doric portico at The Grange acts as a giant garden temple from which to view the eighteenth-century landscape in the valley below

31 William Garrett's Regency house at Leigh Park with its garden verandah and attached conservatory as depicted by JF Gilbert. Ornamental shrubberies frame the house, while gardeners tend the flowery island beds. *Portsmouth Museum*

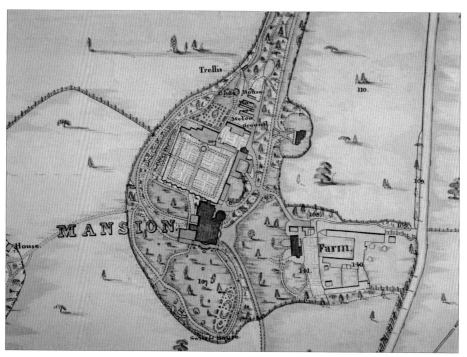

32 This detail from Charles Lewis's 1842 map of Leigh Park shows the productive walled garden George Thomas Staunton inherited on his purchase of the estate from William Garrett, and the Dutch Garden with its Swiss House. *Hampshire Record Office: 76M78/E/P6*

be laid out with woodland walks. Almost all vestiges of Robert's avenues were to be broken up – the existing avenues are shown as dotted lines on the plan – and the parkland enlivened with tree clumps, though the eastern approach was to be tree-lined along most of its extent. Some buildings were to be demolished, including, it would seem, the Garden Temple, now known as Jackdaw's Castle: 'the other dotted lines are Buildings, to be taken away and Hedges'. The shape of Milford Lake was to be improved and there was to be a new piece of water – Dunsmere – with three arms, their terminations hidden from view.

Henry Herbert set about transforming the landscape on his own and his great-grandson, the 4th Earl, gives a good account of the progress of the work. The Earl's narrative is worth quoting at length as it describes in some detail how a Brownian park was constructed. One of the first things to be done was to open up the landscape so that uninterrupted views could be achieved from the house:

> At the foot of the hill on which the Castle stands, over that part of the Park which is now clear and which stretches away towards Milford, there was a large wood of oak which my great-grand-father swept down almost entirely, thereby obtaining, I believe, eight hundred valuable trees and opening up the Park.[38]

Then he turned his attention to the old rabbit warren beyond, 'which he broke up and planted in different places'.[39] Apparently, an account of the 'Character of the Park and the Cedars' had been handed down in the 'Library of Useful Knowledge, Useful and Ornamental Planting' in which the 'size and dates of the cedars raised from cones brought by Bishop Pococke from the Lebanon' were given.[40] This is a fascinating insight into how seeds were shared in the period and proves that, even though Pococke left no description of Robert Herbert's landscape when he was there in 1754, he was on close friendly terms with Herbert's successor, his nephew Henry. The surviving cedars by the house and others out in the park must, therefore, date from this late eighteenth-century reshaping (*colour 23*). Of the original trees, the 4th Earl continues:

> One of these trees, which stood near the conservatory and the flower-garden, was snapped in two one night in a violent gale, some six or seven years since – 1865. Two of the cedars now on the lawn were raised from Bishop Pococke's cones: the third was destroyed by snow. [41]

Not all the tree clumps, as would be expected, date from Henry Herbert's campaign. Those planted in threes with two aligned and the other projecting centrally, were the work of 'my grand-father, the second Lord', who was also responsible for the specimen trees, but his great-grandfather Henry, later the 1st Earl, 'planted the beech, and is said to have done so purposely, lest his great-grandson should be a spendthrift and cut them down'.[42]

By far the most interesting part of the 4th Earl's account of his great-grand-father's improvements was the digging of Dunsmere:

> It was originally a very marshy, wet piece of ground, supposed to be worthless, and covered with a copse. The water had been penned back in what was then called the River Wye, but broke out one night when the work was only half completed, and partially flooded the enclosure. The trees and the underwood in the copse had not even been grubbed, and the bottom of the Lake is to this day quite rough with them.[43]

As if that were not enough, the estate workers had difficulty in making the head: 'I have heard that in one night it would sink two or three feet, being swallowed up in the morass upon which it was formed. When, indeed, it was made, it slipped bodily backwards many feet, and entirely destroyed the sluices which had been built into it. The head of those sluices can be distinctly seen above the water now some fifty feet in the lake'.[44] Perhaps the 1st Earl should have retained Brown, as he would never have countenanced such ineptitude from his contractors. This is not to say that the Earl was lax in his overseeing of the works: 'he would tire out two horses in the day riding backwards and forwards, and...would be down on the spot sometimes at six in the morning, to see with his own eyes how the work went on'.[45] But the men he employed 'came over from Kintbury, and as they were paid by the day, used occasionally to shirk their work'.[46]

Could it be that the rotunda, known originally as the Temple in the Park and now as Diana's Temple (*colour 19*), was part of the reshaping of this sector of the landscape? As we have seen, it is not present on the Spyers-Brown map, though that is not proof of its existence, or otherwise, in 1770. Certainly the 4th Earl was sure that Robert Herbert had raised it prior to his death in 1769. It is certainly a most scenic device, rising dramatically above the waters of the new lake on the drive out to the London Lodge. This last was not built until 1793, to commemorate Henry Herbert's creation as 1st Earl of Carnarvon, but there was a drive into the estate at this point throughout the eighteenth century. Brown favoured rotundas as Claudeian features to enrich his otherwise uncluttered landscapes; there is an early one at Croome Court in Worcester and he planned another for Trentham in Staffordshire. A survey drawing of the original by Barry shows it to have had a much shallower dome, not unlike the rotunda at Croome before it too was altered.[47]

One of the contemporary criticisms of Brown's revolution in design is that tenants on the estate were often banished to the park environs, their dwellings wilfully destroyed in the improvements. It seems as if this happened at High-clere where, although some cottages still clustered around the west side of the house in the 1st Earl's day, the 4th Earl asserts that in Robert Herbert's time this 'must have been a little village'; on the north side he noted that there were 'the buildings of the Farm, the foundations of which could be traced in the grass' in 1908.[48]

There is no better description of what the 1st Earl had achieved at his death in 1811 than William Cobbett's winter rhapsody of 1821, published in book form in his later *Rural Rides*:

> I came from Burghclere on an early November morning, through Lord Carnarvon's park. The oaks are still covered, the beeches in their best dress, the elms yet pretty green, and the beautiful ashes only beginning to turn off. This is, according to my fancy, the prettiest park that I have ever seen: a great variety of hill and dell; a good deal of water…The great beauty of this place is the lofty downs, as steep in some places as the roof of a house, which form a sort of boundary in the form of a part of a crescent to about a third of the Park and then slope off, and get more distant for about half another third. A part of these downs is covered with trees, chiefly beech; the colour of which forms a most beautiful contrast with that of the downs itself, which is so green and smooth.[49]

Although Brown missed out on the Highclere commission, his next recorded work in the county, carried out between 1772 and 1774, and for which he charged £640, was for Hans Stanley at **Paultons Park** near Romsey.[50] The cost suggests that this would have been a considerable undertaking, however it is hard to assess what was achieved, as the house was demolished in 1955 and the landscape is now Paultons Theme Park – Home of Peppa Pig World. Fortunately, we have another account by Gilpin that helps with the assessment. He was under the impression that it was one of Brown's first works in the county and, as such, 'deserves the attention of the curious'.[51] The house was set low, like an abbey, 'sheltered, and sequestered. It is contained within a paled boundary of about five miles in circumference: but the whole is so woody, that the boundary is no where visible. When Mr. Brown first undertook this place, it was full of ancient timber; and nothing was wanting, but to open the area judiciously into ample lawns, screened with wood'.[52] Many of Brown's commissions involved either the breaking up of formal avenues of trees into informal clumps, or the thinning out of existing woodland to create glades and lawns. This is exactly what was happening at nearby **Exbury**, near Beaulieu, where William Mitford, acting as his own designer and with the aid of his estate workforce, was busy reshaping his ancestor's formal gardens:

> In laying out this inner circle [of a woodland ride], Mr. Mitford had his greatest difficulties to contend with: for here he had all his grandfather's formal groves to encounter: and it was no easy matter to break their formalities; to make judi-

cious inroads through them; and unite them in one plan. He often lamented – what other improvers have lamented before him – the injudicious sufferance of the growth of trees.[53]

According to Gilpin, Mitford had exercised true taste, that of harmonious simplicity, in contriving his Brownian park:

> To an injudicious person, or one who delights in temples, and Chinese bridges, very little would appear executed in the scenes I have described at Exbury. There is scarce a gravel-walk made: no pavilion raised: nor even a white-seat fixed. And yet in fact, more is done, than if all these decorations and a hundred more, had been added, unaccompanied with what has been done.[54]

Mindful of Brown's perceived lack of judgement when it came to contriving water features, Gilpin found fault at Paultons with Brown's 'attempt to improve a little forest-stream (by forming a head) into a river. Attempts of this kind seldom answer'.[55] It did not help that Brown had compounded his error by constructing a glaring, 'great, white, Chinese bridge [which] stands every where in sight to remind us of it'.[56] Ever the puritan when it came to ornament, Gilpin wished for 'simple ornaments on all occasions – ornaments which the eye is not *obliged to notice*. Here the ornament was particularly out of place; as it was not only a fault in itself: but led the eye to the detection of other faults'.[57] Quite what those 'other faults' were he does not specify. A watercolour, purported to be by Brown, showing the house in its new landscape, certainly suggests that he had achieved a typical ideal parkscape.[58] The ridge behind the house was defined by a shelterbelt; the house itself was framed by tree clumps; a sinuous watercourse snaked in front of the house to provide reflections, and the wooden Chinese bridge arched gracefully over the water to give access to the park from the lawns by the house. The watercolour is, in fact, uncannily close to the engraving of an improved estate made by Thomas Hearne to illustrate Payne Knight's polemical poem, even down to the Chinese bridge. Both engraved view and Brown's achieved landscape at Paultons are synonymous with Payne Knight's despised 'dull, vapid, smooth, unvaried scene'; they are both what he would have expected from the 'meagre genius of the bare and bald'.[59]

A corrective to this assessment is George Frederick Prosser's later comment, made in 1833, praising Stanley, who had 'much improved this estate, having planted considerably under the superintendence of Brown, the celebrated landscape gardener; and also formed from a small stream or branch of the river Test, which intersected the park, the extensive piece of water that now contributes so much to the beauty of the grounds'.[60] By Prosser's time, after the estate had been inherited by William Sloane Stanley, the Chinese bridge had been replaced by 'a handsome bridge of three arches, over the beautiful artificial river that forms so pleasing an object in the approach'.[61] Charles Heathcote Tatham designed this new bridge when he was carrying out alterations to the main house in 1828. Despite the encroachment of the theme park, the U-shaped lake survives, still crossed by Tatham's elegant structure.

There are several sites in Hampshire where Brown is documented as having had some contact, but his input is not always clear. One is the Brown-style landscape at **Warnford Park**, south-east of Winchester, which was originally known as Belmont. Brown made an undated journey there, a survey was noted, and a letter from the owner, the Earl of Clanricarde, to Brown of 13 April 1773 asked if he could arrange for Lord and Lady Wandesford to have a 'view of Kew Gardens'.[62] Quite what this means is obscure, but it does at least prove that Brown was in touch with the Earl. That is all we know, so Brown's possible authorship of the park has to be tested against the surviving fragments left at the estate, the house having been demolished in 1958.[63] Fortunately, two garden buildings survived the demolition and they are very close in style to other documented works by Brown. There is also the presence of a serpentine water, developed from the River Meon to the west of the house site, but any skilled practitioner might have achieved this. Of more consequence are the Grotto, on the east perimeter of the pleasure grounds and the Bath House, also known as the Dower House or Lady Mary's Bath House, on the southern edge of the grounds.

The flint-faced Grotto originally comprised a central arched opening, flanked by niches. The one to the left is hanging on perilously, while the right-hand niche has disappeared completely. Above the central arch is a keystone with *Memento Mori* carved in Gothic lettering. The structure is built against the revetment of a channel that once carried water from this point along the eastern edge of the shrubbery to an octagonal pool, which survives at the south-eastern corner, after which the water course was directed right to flow beneath the Bath House. A structure added for meditation and memorial, the Grotto is similar to a 'grotto bridge' that Brown devised in 1765 for Rothley in Northumberland.[64] But it is the Gothick-style Bath House (*41*), a delightfully playful structure also constructed of local flints, which seems most like Brown's work. He had already produced a Gothick bath house for Paul Methuen at Corsham Court, which was built in 1760, and had submitted designs for a Gothick bath to be built on top of Rosamund's Well at Blenheim in 1763, which remained unrealised.[65] The Warnford Bath House is almost identical to another unexecuted design, this time for a lakeside lodge at Rothley.[66] Both have simple pointed-arched windows, a prominent canted bay in the centre and a row of quatrefoils below the cornice. The only difference is that the Rothley design has crenellations, but those at Warnford may well have been taken down when the building was given a new roof, including tall

41 Lady Mary's Bath House at Warnford Park may have been designed by Lancelot Brown in the spirit of his contemporary work at Rothley in Northumberland. There is also a Grotto at Warnford, which might be attributed to him

chimneys, most likely after Henry Woods purchased the estate in 1865. He was responsible for the Italianate garden to the northeast of the house, which is in decay, and also the south terrace, which has a parapet to the boundary wall that matches the profile of the chimneys. The *Morning Post* described the grounds in 1789 and implied that the scheme had been completed by the 7th Earl's death in 1782.[67] The newspaper mentioned a 'Hermitage', so the layout must have been more complex than that which survives. Certainly, the flinty ruins of St John's House by the parish church were retained as an evocative feature in the landscape to be viewed from the house.[68]

We are on much surer ground as regards Brown's involvement at **South Stoneham**, now subsumed within the suburbs of Southampton and part of the campus of Southampton University. This is a fascinating yet bizarre site, with the red-brick parent house, possibly designed by Nicholas Hawksmoor for Edmund Dummer between 1705 and 1708,[69] dwarfed by a tottering tower block, which is ripe for demolition. The estate was bought in 1740 by William Sloane, brother of Sir Hans Sloane, and his son, Hans Sloane, inherited in 1767. Brown's first payment for work carried out here was in May 1772, but payments continued until 1780; the total spend was £1,050.[70] Almost the entire landscape has been built over, although a vestige of Brown's planned water survives alongside the River Itchen, now fenced off, and there are a few specimen trees, but these are mostly Victorian.

The 1883 Ordnance Survey map suggests that Brown's work might have been confined to managing the water on this modest site by creating a spade-shaped pool to the southeast of the house on the opposite side of the river, enlivened by two curving islands, and a further pool, with circular islands, due south of the house, again on the other side of the river. The larger pool was lined with trees along its banks, so as to be out of sight of the main house; access to it was via a bridge across the Itchen and along a walk, which bordered the churchyard next to the house. There was a weir between the Itchen and the smaller of the two pools that was at the highest point to which the ordinary tides flowed; it must always have been a watery site, liable to flooding. The rest of the landscape comprised open lawns, as it does today, with a mixture of evergreen and deciduous trees.

The South Stoneham site is recorded as comprising only 177 acres, whereas the estate at **North Stoneham**, at over 1,000 acres, was a far more impressive landscape. However, it is now one of the saddest sites in Hampshire's garden history. The parent house has gone, while the lyrical Temple Lodge, with its four-columed Ionic portico that welcomed visitors at the entrance by the parish church, has been reduced to rubble, scattered amongst the snowdrops in Spring, its green driveway curving off into woodland. Further up, the stables have been forced into new service as a farm with ramshackle additions, their back courtyard littered with decaying vehicles, and the walled garden is derelict, choked by bramble growth.

Plans for alterations were made in 1775 for the owner John Fleming and were carried out by Brown's foremen, Alexander Knox and Andrew Gardiner, though nothing survives of the documentation. The work was completed in 1778, when Brown was paid £1,400.[71] It is likely, however, that Brown informalised the landscape by breaking up the tree avenues and replacing them with tree clumps and modified the existing ponds.[72] When the 'Conductor', John Claudius Loudon, visited the estate in the summer of 1833, a 'fine avenue of sweet chestnuts which led to the old house' by the church still remained.[73] The Deer Park to the south was retained as open parkland, as was Avenue Park to the north. These were contrasted with Home Wood to the northwest and an area on higher ground to the southwest known as Rough Park. Charles Tomkins saw the estate in its maturity in 1796 and wrote: 'At North Stoneham, John Fleming, esq. has a handsome house, and extensive park, well stocked with deer. Judiciously placed, on an eminence at the extremity of the latter, stands a summer-house, from which the view is extensive, and well contrasted'.[74] Brown was not responsible for the summerhouse at the southwest corner of the park, as it was seen by Jeremiah Milles in 1743. He described it as consisting 'of one room most beautifully & richly adorned with stucco both on ye sides, & the roof: & is one of the compleatest rooms of the kind yet I ever saw. In the front of it is an Ionick Portico of 4 pillars, in a very good taste: & underneath is a Kitchen, Larder, & other conveniences for dressing a dinner'.[75] By 1819, after the architect Thomas Hopper had been called in to design a huge Greek mansion for the Willis Fleming family, the summerhouse, or Belvedere as it was then called, was remodelled as a triumphal arch to serve as the principal entrance to the park. Hopper also added a replica of part of the Parthenon frieze to give it extra authenticity. There is a fine view of it by George Prosser;[76] it was largely demolished around 1900.

John Willis Fleming inherited the estate in 1813 and Hopper's new Grecian mansion was begun in 1818, taking the next 26 years to materialise, and even then it was not finished.[77] Indeed, when Loudon saw it in 1834 he was disparaging: 'A new house has been lately built, which we went over; and many alterations have been made in the grounds: but the whole, though it contains many fine features by nature, appears to a stranger sadly bungled'.[78] A serpentine drive led from the Belvedere Lodge in the Rough Park along the valley and skirted the sinuous Park Pond to arrive at the west front of the house (42). The drive from the east at Temple Lodge was threaded between Shrubbery Pond and the walled garden, passing an icehouse on its way to the rear of the house. Loudon found fault with the approach drive from Belvedere Lodge: 'the road is so exceedingly steep, that, in many parts of it, a carriage could not stand still, either in ascending or descending, without a stone being put under the wheel'[79] and, like Gilpin before him, he was critical of Brown's water management, if, in fact, Brown had actually included the reshaping of the ponds in his modest fee:

> The water consists of a number of pools, on different levels, one being placed below another down the slope of the ground; whereas, had the water been carried across the declivity, one grand lake might have been formed all on the same level; and the effect from the lawn front of the house would have been magnificent.[80]

All the landscape features were still in place in 1867, when the Ordnance Survey mapped the estate, though by that time Park Pond had been enlarged, suggesting that Brown had little to do with the water.[81] As a postscript to this essentially flawed Greek vision, the mansion was demolished in 1939 and the park disappeared after its sale in separate lots in 1953; it now hosts a golf course and a number of sports facilities. The southern and western sectors of the estate were sacrificed for the M27 in 1983 and the M3 in 1991.

In the mid 1770s, Brown was working concurrently on three other Hampshire estates: Highcliffe Castle for Lord Bute, Cuffnells Park, near Lymington, for Sir Thomas Tancred and at Cadland, Fawley, for Robert Drummond.[82]

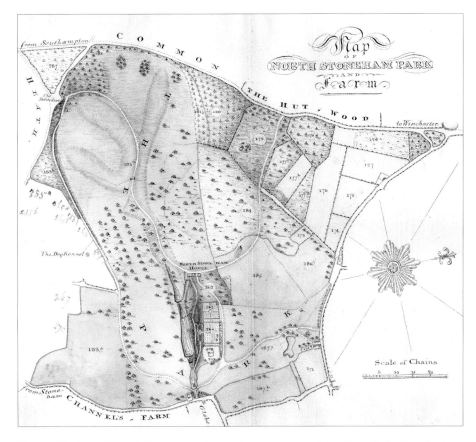

42 This 1818 plan of North Stoneham shows the serpentine drive from Belvedere Lodge
to the west front of the eighteenth-century house before it was remodelled by
Thomas Hopper. *Southampton Archives D/Z 639*

Highcliffe is now in Dorset,[83] while Brown's vestigial work at Cuffnells was
subsequently re-worked by William Emes, and so will feature later in this
chapter. At **Cadland** Brown was working in partnership with his son-in-law,
Henry Holland, to build a new house and provide a landscape for Robert
Drummond who, after the death at Culloden of his father, Lord Strathallan,
left Scotland and settled in Hampshire. Both Brown and Holland were clients
of Drummond's Bank. Drummond had chosen a perfect site on a hill overlooking the Solent. Understandably, Gilpin was in raptures over the setting:

> It stands on a gentle eminence on the banks of Southampton-bay, with a great
> variety of ground playing beautifully around it; which is every where adorned,
> and in some places profusely covered, with ancient wood. The whole country
> indeed was so well wooded, that no addition of wood was any where necessary;
> in many parts it was redundant. This abundance of old timber gives the house,

tho lately built, so much the air and dignity of an ancient mansion, that Mr. Brown, the ingenious improver of it, used to say, 'It was the oldest new place he knew in England'.[84]

Holland devised a simple, two-storey marine villa of classical understatement, which was estimated to cost £3,050, but with the decoration and the garden work, the bill came to more than £12,500, with an unspecified balance to be paid in January 1779.[85] Ever scrupulous in his financial dealings with clients, however, Brown repaid Drummond £100 for an overcharge on the 'Out of Doors work'.[86]

Plans for the house and Brown's plan for the landscape are preserved at Cadland in a bound book dated 1775.[87] These include drawings for Cadland House, a double octagon fishing lodge (43) set in the grounds to the south known as 'The Sea Cottage' and then 'Boam Hill Cottage', and a design for the layout of the grounds around both. In 1785 the fishing lodge was burned to the ground and rebuilt on the same foundations in 1786. Two small wings were added after 1803; thereafter, Sir Jeffry Wyatville enlarged it between 1837 and 1838. Cadland House was requisitioned by the army during the Second World War, acquired for an oil refinery and then demolished in 1953. So the present house at Cadland is a remodelling of Holland's original fishing lodge for Robert Drummond.

Brown produced one of his typical landscape plans but in miniature, with his usual repertoire of tree clumps, shrubberies, gravel paths, and a woodland walk (colour 24). Rather than enclose the landscape, his shelterbelt is broken up to take advantage of the views, the plan being annotated: 'None of the Views must be interrupted by Planting'. To complement the 'combinations of ash, and other trees' on the site Brown chose a mixed palette of deciduous oaks, beech and sweet chestnut, and for evergreen contrast, ilex, yew and Scots pines.[88] These last are not typical of his planting regimes and Clive Aslet surmises that they may have been chosen by Brown to remind Drummond of his boyhood home in Perthshire.[89] It may also be that they were symbols of the family's Jacobite sympathies.[90] The understorey comprised Portuguese laurel entwined with roses, lilacs, broom and other flowering shrubs.

Brown's circuit walk heads off east from the house through woodland and then turns south through more woodland to develop into a terraced walk cut into the bank, which commands the beach. This is marked A on the plan as 'The Sea Bank with a Path of Gravell amongst the Furze Bushes etc.' It then proceeds west through more woodland, giving glimpses of the sea; one view is aligned on the tower of Ryde church on the Isle of Wight. A Zoffany painting of Drummond, his wife and seven of their children has one of the boys holding a telescope and gesturing at the ships in the Solent, while Mrs Drummond, no doubt a keen gardener, drops rose petals in her daughter's lap.[91]

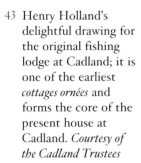

43 Henry Holland's delightful drawing for the original fishing lodge at Cadland; it is one of the earliest *cottages ornées* and forms the core of the present house at Cadland. *Courtesy of the Cadland Trustees*

The walk then turns back towards the house, looping again through woodland. This sector is marked B: 'A Path or Walk under the hedge with Shrubs and Plants that will Grow', that is plants that could cope with the sandy soil and the salt air. This northern section of the walk has two openings into the central lawn, which is contoured and has a large clump of trees and shrubs. The walled garden at Cadland, built in the 1820s, is to the west of the house, so what appears to be a walled garden on the plan is, in fact, a hedged and quartered flower garden.

From 1833 onwards, Andrew Robert Drummond extended the grounds to the east by acquiring the neighbouring **Eaglehurst** estate and linking Cadland with Luttrell's Tower in a series of ornamental drives and lodges.[92] The Tower was built in about 1780 for Temple Simon Luttrell and designed by Thomas Sandby. Even though the Tower had not been raised when Brown was designing his new layout for Cadland, it must soon have become a focus of at least one of his contrived views from the pleasure grounds. We have Gilpin to thank again for a contemporary account of the building. He saw it just before 1791 and gives an intriguing description of the Tower in his *Forest Scenery*:

> Near this part of the coast stands *Luttrell's tower*; built as the station of a view: but as it is intended for a habitable house likewise, the offices, which it could not contain, are constructed of canvas around it. It is finished in the highest stile of expence; and if it were not for the oddness, and singularity of the conception, and contrivance, it is not intirely destitute of some kind of taste. But the building is so whimsical, and the end so inadequate to the expence, that

we considered it on the whole, as a glaring contrast to those pleasant scenes, we had just examined at Exbury. In which true taste had furnished us with a delightful entertainment at a trifling expence.[93]

Gilpin mentions the 'great storm in February 1781', which blew down 'nineteen of [the] ornamental trees' at Cadland,[94] but Brown's vision remained relatively intact, though much overgrown, until the early 1980s, when the rediscovery of his plan in the Cadland papers enabled Gilly Drummond and Hal Moggridge to restore the landscape with historically accurate plants that would have been available in 1780, and re-instate the contrived views. The trees suffered damage in the storms of 1987 and 1990, after which there was a substantial programme of replanting under the expert guidance of Mark Laird. Brown's detailed list of plants in the Wilderness at Petworth was used as a prime archival source for this replanting.

There remain two other tantalising references to Brown's involvement in the county: at Testwood, near Totton, and at Cuffnells Park, on the edge of the New Forest. All we have for Testwood is an undated letter from Mr Serle inviting Brown to stay with him at Testwood when on his way to North Stoneham. Serle adds: 'Mrs Serle flatters herself Mr Brown will not for ever pass by Testwood without taking any notice of his friends there', suggesting a closeness between Brown and the family.[95] A Georgian house was built along-side the Elizabethan manor house and a park contrived around it, but there is no evidence to prove that Brown was responsible.

It is also unclear as to what Brown might have done at **Cuffnells Park** on the edge of the New Forest, south of Lyndhurst. He received £165 from Sir Thomas Tancred for 'Work done at Cuffnells before it was sold to George Rose',[96] which also suggests little more than an initial survey and perhaps some tree management. However, when Brayley & Britton came to write their *Beauties of England and Wales* they stated that 'when the late Mr Emes was called in to exercise his art of landscape gardening on this spot, he found that Nature had nearly superseded his intended operations, and was obliged to confine himself to a few plantations and walks in the vicinity of the House: these, however, are disposed with taste, and are creditable to his professional judgement'.[97] It is unlikely that Tancred would have commissioned Emes so soon after settling the account for Brown's work, so Emes must have been working for George Rose, presumably in concert with the architect Sir John Soane, with whom he was acquainted, between 1794 and 1795. To confuse the narra-tive even further, it appears from Gilpin's slightly earlier, 1791, account of Cuffnells, that George Rose had already been improving his landscape without the help of a landscape practitioner:

It is not placed exactly as might be wished. High-ground rises immediately in front, which is always a circumstance to be avoided. But Mr. Rose has happily managed an inconvenience, which he found, and could not remove. He has laid out a very handsome approach, which winds to the house under the rising ground; and makes of it much less consequence, than when the road was carried abruptly down the slope to the house. His chief improvements he has thrown to the back front, where a pleasant forest-scene opens; along the skirts of which he is leading a beautiful walk among various combinations of old oak. – But his improvements are yet incomplete.[98]

Soon after, Soane was called in to remodel the south front of the house and construct an adjoining conservatory: 'the south front is formed by a Drawing Room, thirty-six feet by twenty-four; the Library, forty-two feet by twenty-four; a handsome Vestibule, and the *Conservatory*: the latter filled with a choice assemblage of indigenous and exotic plants, and, from its size, is much admired. It communicates, by large folding doors, with the *Library*'.[99] This is the house shown in an engraving in the *Beauties*. Rose was a keen gardener and raised many newly introduced exotics in the conservatory at Cuffnells. The house was demolished after being requisitioned during the Second World War and little remains of the eighteenth-century estate, which is now farmed, apart from the cuboid East Lodge and a delightful ornamental cottage on the edge of the estate where it connects with the New Forest (*colour 25*).

Emes's work has not fared much better at **Elvetham**, the site of the great Elizabethan entertainment of 1591. Brayley and Britton record that the vast park, which originally included 'an area of about two miles in circumference, [was] much improved by Mr Emes, the landscape gardener, who had a lease of this estate for twenty-one years: several of his alterations have since been obliterated'.[100] Today the park has been overlaid with Victorian planting, as befits SS Teulon's extraordinary Hall of 1859-62, including a magisterial avenue of Wellingtonias, which marches across the fields close to the crescent-shaped lake that was the focus of the Elizabethan festivities. Similarly, at **Dogmersfield**, the 'Shrubbery and Pleasure Grounds', which Brayley and Britton remark were 'laid out by Emes', between 1780 and 1790, survive in vestigial form to the south of the house, but the landscape is almost entirely bare of trees, though a landscape restoration was underway in 2015.[101] What do survive are two elegant bridges (*colour 26*), spanning in three graceful arches, watery fingers of the Tundry Pond that Emes must have extended when his client, Henry Paulet St John Mildmay, swept away the village that surrounded it.

Much of Emes's work in the county is, therefore, vestigial, unexecuted or obliterated, but for **Brockenhurst Park** in the New Forest we have at least a 1793 plan of the 'demesne lands' with 'some alterations', from which his suggested improvements can be deduced.[102] Emes was working for John Morant, who had inherited the property from his father Edward, who in the

44 John Plaw's design for a classical Bath House for Brockenhurst Park, from his *Ferme Ornée* of 1796; its bathing pool was decorated with stylised trees. *University of Bristol Library, Special Collections*

1770s had already removed all the agricultural hedges, but retained the hedgerow trees, which were mostly oaks, thereby creating instant parkland.[103] Veteran oaks still dramatise the landscape (*colour 27*), while around the terraces and canal of the lost house, replaced by a modern building in 1965, which was designed by Harry Graham, majestic cedars still spread their great boughs. Gilpin thought that the contrast Edward Morant had produced 'between the open, and woody parts of the distance, and the grandeur of each part, [were] in the highest stile of picturesque beauty'.[104] John Morant commissioned Emes, who was working in partnership with John Webb, to prepare a series of proposals for the existing landscape, and the pattern book architect, John Plaw, to design picturesque buildings. Brockenhurst is a perfect example, therefore, of how an eighteenth-century Brownian park could be adapted to the newly emergent ornamental gardening of the Regency.

Sadly, Morant died in 1794, before Emes and Webb's master plan, including the widening of the Lymington River on the east boundary of the estate and their proposal to create a 'new river supplied from the forest brook' could be implemented.[105] However, Morant's heir, another John Morant, did carry out some of the proposals, while Plaw published many of his designs for Brockenhurst, including a domed bath house and a 'Fishing Lodge *and* Keeper's

Dwelling', in his *Ferme Ornée* of 1796. The bath house (*44*) was situated 'a small distance from the brew-house and reservoir, by which it [was] supplied with hot and cold water, sufficient to make a full tepid bath'.[106] It had 'provisions also for a shower bath occasionally' and its dressing room was 'furnished with a couch and stove'.[107] The interior of the bathing pool was decorated with stylised trees, their branches arching up into the dome.

Plaw's Fishing Lodge may never have been executed, because he comments that the design was made for the 'late John Morant', and that it was 'intended to have been executed with roots and trunks of trees, near the river in his park'.[108] This early *cottage ornée* would have promoted the alfresco life so enjoyed by Regency landowners, as its front would have contained 'accommodation for Tea-drinking parties'.[109] Plaw's most bizarre building for Morant was his 'Cottager's Lodge', designed ostensibly to stand guard at the entrance gates to the park, but 'if properly built on wheels, might be moved at pleasure'.[110] Whether this was intended as a tongue-in-cheek remark, or was meant as a serious concept is unclear, but it does signal a harking back to the more whimsical, eclectic landscapes of the mid century and anticipates eagerly the ornamental gardening that characterised the next forty years.

6

'The glorious strife of Art and Nature'
Regency Gardens

▼

Captain Rainier's Villa, Houghton Lodge, Chawton Cottage
Rotherfield Park, Herriard Park, Stratton Park, Norman Court
Somerley Park, The Grange, Rookesbury Park, Bishopstoke Rectory
Leigh Park, Langstone, Cranbury Park

With the dual 200-year anniversaries coming up of Jane Austen's death in 1817 and Humphry Repton's in 1818, it seems entirely appropriate that the Historic Gardens of England series has reached Hampshire, Austen's home county and where she is buried, and where Repton carried out several landscape schemes, even if much of his work has now disappeared. These two giants of the Regency must be the catalysts for an overview of the garden history of the period, which has been long overdue. It remains woefully under-researched by garden historians and is consequently misunderstood, a time characterised by the garden chronicler and encyclopaedist John Claudius Loudon's own, oddly confusing, portmanteau term the 'Gardenesque', when, in reality, several land-scape styles were fashionable.[1] These included the Cottage Garden, Swiss Picturesque, Old English and Italianate. In many ways, this was a return to the 'Rococo' gardens of the mid eighteenth century, which had delighted in colourful shrubberies enriched with garden buildings of riotous eclecticism. Hampshire had perhaps the most important, but least well known, of these Rococo Revival gardens, a bizarre mixture of exotic structures with a strong Chinese theme, set around an artificial sheet of water at Havant.

Regency gardens themselves were characterised by exuberant formal parterres, jewelled island beds of graduated flowers, frothy basket-work borders, shrubberies and over-arching trellises covered with rambling roses, jasmine and clematis. Their lawns were enamelled with spring bulbs, enlivened with elegant vases, strewn with Chinese barrels for casual alfresco seating, cut with reflecting oval pools backed by specimen shrubs and dramatised by deep-delved grottoes. Every pleasure ground had its meshed aviary and pheasantry; there were fountains with writhing dolphins, rustic garden seats, thatched and pebbled-floored, Swiss-style bridges and glasshouses overflowing with exotics.

These flowery paradises were readily accessed from the house via ground-length sash windows, tree-trunked verandahs entwined with climbers and conservatories arcing out from the house into the garden. By day they were ablaze with colour and by night, lit by coloured lamps hanging from the trellises and the trees, they sparkled and glittered.

The Regency, in stylistic terms the four decades between the mid 1790s and the early 1830s, was a period of vibrant, often vulgar, excess, when architect and garden writer John Buonarotti Papworth could urge that a garden alcove hung with brightly coloured Chinese pendants 'should be so decorated as to become highly ornamental, and be in splendid harmony with its accompanying parterres, and flower-beds'.[2] More so than Repton's several books on landscape gardening, which were over-laden with aesthetic theory, Papworth's popular *Hints on Ornamental Gardening* of 1823 was the key text, offering practical advice on how to lay out a garden or a wider landscape, with twenty-eight plates of highly decorative garden buildings ranging from an aviary to a cenotaph. Moreover, Papworth's introduction to the book, charting the development of the pleasure ground, urged an owner to 'apply the pictures of his fancy' in substitution for the 'simple excellencies' of nature.[3] Papworth's major work in Hampshire would be for Thomas Chamberlayne in the 1830s at Cranbury Park. Humphry Repton had, of course, been encouraging owners to develop the grounds close to their houses in this ornamental fashion since he had freed himself in the mid 1790s from the shackles of the Picturesque.[4] However, Papworth's accessible book did much to reinvigorate this decorative, if ephemeral, style of gardening after Repton's death in 1818. It remained fashionable throughout the 1820s and well into the 1830s before the overweening architectural layouts of the Italianate supplanted it, heralding the arid historicism of the Victorians.

Several of these ornamental gardens were laid out around marine villas, which were cottages sited on the coast serving as weekend retreats from the bustle of the city. JC Loudon saw one of these – **Captain Rainier's Villa** – on his regular perambulations around the country in 1835 and gave a detailed description of it in his *Gardener's Magazine*:

Captain Rainier's Villa and Garden, about a mile from Southampton, are well worth visiting, as a specimen of how much may be got into a little compass. In front of the house there is a small lawn, tastefully varied by groups of flowers and shrubs, with a fountain and some other architectural ornaments. Among the finer plants are camellias and myrtles as standards, the New Zealand hemp, and a species of bamboo, and also the common *Arùndo Dònax*, growing luxuriantly...There is a green-house, containing the celebrated banyan tree...An adjoining hot-house contains a magnificent bananaplant...There are two hot-houses for pines, grapes, and stove plants. On the whole, there is an immense number of excellent things crowded together in little space; which are as well managed as, under these circumstances, they can be, by the gardener, Mr Dawson. A detached building contains a museum of Egyptian antiquities, highly spoken of; which, owing to Captain Rainier's absence, we did not see.[5]

This has all the elements of a typical ornamental garden on a small scale, particularly the growing interest in cultivating exotics, but with the added bonus of an archaeological collection housed in a purpose-built structure.

As we have seen one of the exponents of ornamental buildings for these mini paradises was John Plaw, whose 1796 *Ferme Ornée* pattern book of architectural designs includes a 'Poultry House *and* Aviary' made for 'a Lady in the New Forest and intended to be erected on a lawn in front of a neat cottage villa'.[6] Plaw had spent most of his formative years in Westminster, but moved to Southampton in 1795 and may, therefore, have designed the beautiful Houghton Lodge, sited romantically on the banks of the River Test, south of Stockbridge. Certainly the early core of the building with its pointed-arched windows and quatrefoils above is very close in style to several of his pattern book designs, and he records the construction of a *cottage ornée* near Lymington in his 1800 *Sketches for Country Houses, Villas and Rural Dwellings*.[7]

Dates for the building of **Houghton Lodge** (*colour 28*) are vague, but in an advertisement posted in *The Morning Chronicle* for 27 November 1799, a Mr Smith offered the freehold cottage and its paddock of 30 acres for sale, 'to be viewed by tickets only'. The particulars mention the 'Drawing-room and superb Rotunda, finished in the highest style of Gothic Architecture, with Windows to the floors, variegated Glass, beautiful Landscape tablets and Sky Ceiling'. A recurring feature of the period is this attempt to connect interiors with exteriors, as here at Houghton in terms of interior décor. Papworth was to advocate the same much later in 1818, when he wrote that a *cottage ornée*, which he had 'designed for the neighbourhood of the lakes', had a hall decorated with 'trellising, composed of light lath and wicket basket-work, very neatly executed, and painted a dark green', while 'flower-stands and brackets are attached at various parts, from the bottom to the top of the staircase'.[8] To complete this garden-like atmosphere, 'the most elegantly beautiful flowering plants are selected as embellishments', so that the walls were 'every where adorned with them, and some are trained over the trellis of the ceilings, whence they hang in festoons and unite their branches'.[9] Papworth's description recalls Jane Austen's Uppercross Cottage in *Persuasion*, the 'compact, tight parsonage, enclosed in its own neat garden', which had 'received the improvement of a farm-house elevated into a cottage...with its viranda, French windows and other prettinesses'.[10] Much earlier, Mary Ann Hanway's Duke of Southernwood, who is passionately in love with Ellinor, the eponymous heroine of Hanway's novel, vows to provide her with a 'superb town house immediately fitted for your reception; a charming *cottage ornée* in all the *studied simplicity* of fashionable elegance, to retire from the battle of public admiration', if only she will consent to be his, and his alone.[11]

Jane Austen's own house, **Chawton Cottage**, where she lived from 1809 to her death in 1817, is not so much a vernacular cottage, more a neat little brick house, which was originally a farmhouse and then, for a short period, an alehouse. However, in its twentieth-century reincarnation as a shrine to the great writer, it has been reinvented as a Regency country cottage surrounded by a cottage-style garden (*45*). Although the signage states that 'the garden, as it is now planted, is quite different from that in the Austens' time', the recreation of a 'typical country cottage garden' is justified by the their love of flowers. The text of one sign quotes a letter Jane wrote in 1811 from Chawton

45 The grounds at Jane Austen's Chawton Cottage have been restored as a Regency-style country cottage garden. In Austen's day there would have been more productive areas to complement the ornamental

to her sister Cassandra: 'the whole of the Shrubbery Border will soon be very gay with Pinks and Sweet Williams, in addition to the columbines already in bloom'. Jane's brother, Edward Austen Knight, planted hedges and a shrubbery walk for the four women – Jane, Cassandra, their mother and their friend Martha Lloyd – who lived happily together here. As well as the ornamental areas, there was a kitchen garden and an orchard. It is described fondly by James Edward Austen-Leigh, in his memoir of Jane Austen: 'There was a pleasant irregular mixture of hedgerow, and gravel walk, and orchard, and long grass for mowing, arising from two or three little enclosures having been thrown together'.[12]

If parterres and wildernesses are the main features to be found in the formal gardens of the Franco-Dutch period, then ornamental shrubberies threaded with shaded paths are the key to the Regency, not just as horticultural design elements, but also as places for assignations and trysts. Indeed, many of Jane Austen's most romantic and dramatic exchanges between her characters take place in the landscape. In *Pride and Prejudice*, Darcy proposes a second time to Elizabeth Bennet when they are walking to a neighbouring house, and in *Mansfield Park*, Fanny Price and Edmund Bertram fall in love 'wandering about and sitting under trees...all the summer evenings'. Emma escapes her needy father by retreating to the garden: 'Emma resolved to be out of doors as soon as possible. Never had the exquisite sight, smell, sensation of nature, tranquil, warm, and brilliant after a storm, been more attractive to her... She longed for the serenity they might gradually induce...she lost no time in hurrying to the shrubbery'.[13] There she would have found gravel paths, usually wide enough to accommodate three walkers abreast, flanked by borders of graduated planting, with flowers at the front, bushes in the middle and trees at the back. If the planting was on one side only, it was an 'open shrubbery', if on both, then a 'closed shrubbery'. Directions on planting and design were given in several garden books of the period, especially Henry Phillips's 1823 *Sylva Florifera*:

> In extensive shrubberies, each walk should lead to some particular Object; to the orchard, kitchen garden, botanical borders, green-house, dairy, ice-house, mushroom-hut, aviary, poultry-yard, or stables. The intention of the plantation should seem to be, to conduct the walker in the most agreeable manner to each outlet and building of utility or pleasure.[14]

A typical pleasure ground of the period was laid out at **Rotherfield Park**, East Tisted, after the Tudor Gothic house been built in 1818-22 for James Scott. The design for the shrubbery (*colour 29*) reveals both open and closed sections of the gravel walks which encircle and thread the shrubberies, while at the centre is a rectangular pool and, at the southwest edge, a seat to take in the wider parkland.[15] Some of this planting, as well as the pool, survives on the site, but has been augmented by later campaigns.

Jane Austen was well aware of the latest fashions in landscape gardening, particularly Humphry Repton's sales gimmick of the 'before' and 'after' watercolours in his Red Books showing the improvements he proposed. She made frequent visits to her elderly cousin's estate at Stoneleigh Abbey in Warwickshire, for which Repton had prepared a Red Book in 1809,[16] and Mr Rushworth's Sotherton in *Mansfield Park* is obviously modelled on Stoneleigh.

When Rushworth is considering improvements to the estate he has just inherited, Miss Bertram advises: 'Your best friend upon such an occasion…would be Mr Repton, I imagine'. Rushworth agrees: 'That is what I was thinking of. As he has done so well by Smith, I think I had better have him at once. His terms are five guineas a day'.[17] There follows a lively discussion, led by Mrs Norris, on the rewards of improvements, and Rushworth determines to commission Repton: 'Smith's place is the admiration of all the country; and it was a mere nothing before Repton took it in hand'.[18] Lady Bertram, to whom Rushworth is attempting to defer in matters of taste, is adamant about what should be the main feature of the improvements: 'if I were you, I would have a shrubbery. One likes to get out into a shrubbery in fine weather'.[19]

A fascinating correspondence between Repton and George Purefoy Jervoise of **Herriard Park** survives, which proves that this fictional account is very close to the truth, both in matters of contemporary garden taste and, indeed, as regards Repton's costs.[20] Repton's letters begin in June 1793 and end in April 1801. They chart his attempts to return to Herriard to see the progress being made on his recommendations, which were outlined in a Red Book he sent to Jervoise on 9 October 1793. However, it soon becomes clear that Jervoise intends to take the work in hand himself, for in a letter of 25 October, in which Repton complains of a 'nervous disorder' that prevents him coming to Herriard, he requests tentatively that Jervoise explains 'by letter the nature of the Departure from the plan'. This was not the only departure from Repton's original intentions for Herriard's pleasure grounds. His letter of 1 January 1794 begins: 'I hope you recd safe in London the plan for the Kitchen Garden & Plantations which I sent on the 9th December. I did not then trouble you with the inclosed because that is a disagreeable task which I always reserve to the 1st day of every new year'. The 'disagreeable task' was, of course, his account for the work done. Repton's bill for his advice at Herriard is given on the verso of the letter and itemises his daily attendance rate of five guineas, costs of three and five guineas for travel, the provision of a Red Book of proposals for £21 and an extra guinea for the revised plan and planting instructions for the Kitchen Garden.

Thereafter, the correspondence makes melancholy reading, as Repton tries again and again, without much success, to visit Herriard to see how the garden works are progressing. This must have been due, in part, to Jervoise wanting to avoid any further expense – a Repton letter of 1 February 1799 mentions visits he made in 1795 and 1796 for which he had not yet been paid – and also because in September of that year Jervoise had appointed John Armstrong to complete the work. Armstrong was a nurseryman from North Warnborough, so he would have been well placed to supply plants for his 'Proposed Alterations for a Pleasure Garden and Orchard' at Herriard.[21] Poor Repton was still hopeful that he might call at Herriard on 13 April 1801 if he could be of any use 'to finish the plans of improvement begun under my directions', while a subscription notice for his forthcoming *Observations on the Theory and Practice of Landscape Gardening* in the Herriard archive suggests that he was still trying to curry favour with Jervoise as late as December of that year.

Sadly, the Herriard Red Book is lost, but Repton's begging letters make it clear that his suggested improvements were primarily confined to the new, octagonal Kitchen Garden and the shrubberies surrounding it. Today, half of the Kitchen Garden, which has two date stones recording its construction in 1796, is mostly given over to modern buildings and parking, while the other, closer to the main house, retains a sylvan atmosphere, with a simple formal garden of urns and fountain on axis flanked on the west wall by sensitively designed structures replacing the glasshouses. However, the Regency commission can be retrieved through the survival of an 1818 plan of the gardens and shrubberies (*46*) by John Pearce, a surveyor, or perhaps even a landscape gardener, of Upton Grey.[22] A serpentine path led from the house to circumvent the Kitchen Garden, which was surrounded by a deep border of shrub planting; there were further island beds of shrubs on the approach. As with most Repton commissions, the service buildings to the west of the house were shielded from the pleasure grounds by more deep shrubbery planting, while the Kitchen Garden had a hothouse and greenhouse, a melon ground and a flower garden. How much of this layout is by Repton, or Armstrong, or perhaps even by Pearce, is not clear. The Pearce plan may simply be a survey of the grounds in 1818, but another plan of the same year (*47*), which he made for J H Beaufoy of Upton Grey, might have been a proposal rather than a mere record.[23] Certainly both plans show similar features, as would be expected at this time.

Repton lists **Stratton Park** at East Stratton, Micheldever, in his *Observations* 'as one of the places' where he 'gave general plans for the *whole*, with the assistance of my son only in the architectural department'.[24] These plans were for Sir Francis Baring, an eminent London merchant, director of the East India Company and founder of Barings Bank. He had bought the Stratton estate in 1790 from Francis Russell, 5th Duke of Bedford, with only a part of the original Palladian building still standing.[25] Repton's plans seem to have been submitted at the same time that Baring was seeking advice from the architect George Dance. In the event, John Adey Repton's design for the house was passed over in favour of Dance's severe essay in primitive Greek Doric (*48*), with a 'Paestum-proportioned, unfluted Doric portico', which was built between 1803 and 1806.[26] Undeterred by losing out on the architectural commission for his son, Repton delivered his Red Book for the Stratton landscape in December 1803. This survives in a private collection, but a summary of Repton's remarks from the proposals suggests that his main focus was his attempt to remove the turnpike road from the grounds.[27]

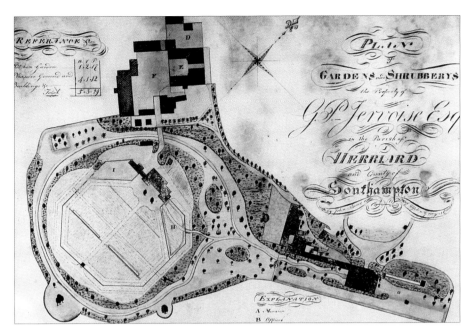

46 John Pearce's 1818 plan of the gardens and shrubberies at Herriard Park record the layout around the octagonal Kitchen Garden much as it exists today. *Jervoise of Herriard Collection: Hampshire Record Office: 44M69/P/1/76*

47 Open and closed walks threading the shrubberies are shown on John Pearce's 1818 plan of the pleasure grounds at Upton Grey. *Jervoise of Herriard Collection: Hampshire Record Office: 44M69/P/1/77*

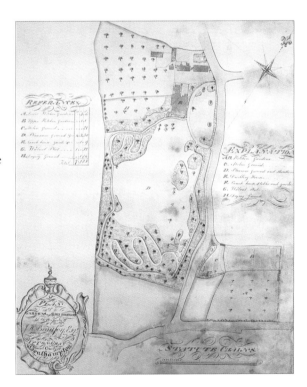

48 George Dance's great 1805 Doric portico left beached in front of the incongruous and dysfunctional 1960s house at Stratton Park

This is understandable given the oddity of the landscape he found at Stratton. The parkland was bordered on the east by the village road and on the west, much closer to the house, by the ruler-straight line of a Roman Road, and a little further west and parallel to it, the turnpike. This left a very narrow sliver of a park, which extended to the north and south, but which was constrained about its east-west axis. Repton rightly concluded that, in its present form, the site was 'unadvisable for a larger house', and that a site for a replacement depended upon the removal of the turnpike. This expedient would be 'equally necessary to the privacy and enjoyment of the great avenue, which is doubtless one of the first features of the place'. The avenue, running from the northeast corner of the front lawn northwards, is visible on nine-teenth-century Ordnance Survey maps and can still be made out today. Repton's other idea was to bring the plantations together on the western side of the road to give coherence to the whole and, thereby, mitigate the severing effect of the highway. In other parts of the park, especially in front of the proposed new house, he advocated that 'the vast extent of open fields could be lessened, and the ground sub-divided by live hedges, instead of the present unsightly dead ones'. By these means the 'general character of the country might be improved in appearance, as well as in real value, both to the landlord and the tenant'.

Although Baring opted for Dance's designs for the new house, he does seem to have heeded at least some of Repton's advice. He attempted to extend the park to the east and west and the turnpike was moved a little further west, but it still remained very close to the pleasure grounds and is now the A33. As a

33 The Chinoiserie features around Leigh Water in an evocative watercolour by C R
Cotton. The three-arched bridge has been repaired, but it has lost its fretwork
balustrade. *Portsmouth Museum*

34 The Canal at Brockenhurst Park, beyond which is a double set of rising steps that
lead to hedged garden compartments; the mature topiary trees were originally in pots

35 Obelisks proliferate on the terracing that encloses RS Wornum's Italian Garden at Tylney Hall; the ogee-roofed Summerhouses at is outer corners are based on Jacobean banqueting houses at Montacute, Somerset

36 The Water Garden at Tylney Hall, formed by two ponds linked by a series of pools running through rockwork, was created by Robert Weir Schultz in 1906 from a formal eighteenth-century canal; it was originally planted by Gertrude Jekyll

37 The Canal at Rhinefield was the centrepiece of extensive 1890s pleasure grounds

38 William Lethaby's terrace at Avon Tyrell features robust balustrading and circular stone planters built into the steps, while the retaining wall has supporting brick piers which double as garden seats

39 Edwin Lutyens's brilliant improvisation on circular geometric forms, carried out in local materials, in the oak-arched Pergola at Marsh Court

40 Even though the 1920s water garden at Amport House was a collaboration
between Edwin Lutyens and Gertrude Jekyll, it has a Victorian rather than
an Arts and Crafts impact

41 The Sunken Garden at Townhill Park is one of the greatest historic
restorations in the entire county

42 Lady Swaythling's Seat, set close to the Loggia at Townhill Park, provides a perfect vantage point from which to view the restored planting of the Sunken Garden

43 Topiary proliferates in the Sunken Garden at Weir's Barn. Robert Weir Schultz's enclosing trellises have gone, as has his sundial, which has been replaced by an urn

44 The 'puzzle-stream' at Ashford Chace was probably designed by William Unsworth and inspired by the Alhambra in Granada. It conducts water from a fountain down to a tank decorated with mosaics featuring fish

45 The Pergola at Hinton Admiral may be part of Harold Peto's early twentieth-century remodelling of the grounds for Sir George Meyrick. Pergolas are ubiquitous features in Peto's designs, especially in his own garden at Iford Manor, Wiltshire

46 These two herms at Walhampton House might be the clue to the designer of the Italian Terrace. Their bodies appear to be antique, whereas the heads are modern. Harold Peto often adapted antique sculpture for display in his gardens

49 George Dance in hybrid architectural mood – classical and Moorish – at his London
Lodge to Stratton Park; the M3 motorway thunders below

consequence, Dance's house has never commanded an extensive park. The
house was demolished in 1961, and a new one built to incorporate Dance's
surviving south portico, but this house was, in turn, compromised in 1985 by the
construction of the M3 motorway, built between it and the A33, roughly on the
line of the Roman Road. Dance's ancillary buildings have fared better. He
designed nine pairs of estate cottages for East Stratton village in 1806, five of
which are still standing, remodelled Micheldever parish church, and contrived a
pair of classical lodges with an oriental-style gateway in between (49), derived
from his London Guildhall, which survives as the London Lodge.[28]

Repton's work at **Norman Court**, West Tytherley, for another of the
Baring dynasty fares little better, having almost all disappeared and, like his
commission at Herriard, the Red Book, if indeed one was prepared, is lost.
What does survive is a ground floor plan and elevation with a *porte cochère* for
the main house by Repton, 'correctly of the date of Henry VIII & Queen Elizabeth's House Gothic'.[29] Repton's Tudor-Gothic house would have provided
that internal connection with the exterior he favoured through an open enfilade
of rooms on the south side – Drawing Room, Library, Breakfast Room, Lobby
– leading on axis to a Conservatory, while his Billiard Room on the west was to
lead, via a lobby, to the 'Flower Garden'. As with his attempt to get the architectural commission at Stratton Park, his plans were not implemented.

The mid eighteenth-century house built by Robert Thistlethwaite of
Southwick Park as a hunting box – hence the towered profile on the entrance
front – had been bought in 1807 by Sir Francis Baring's son-in-law Charles
Wall. He had married Harriet Baring in 1790 and had been a partner and

general manager of the firm, retiring with 'as many thousands as there are days in the year'.[30] Charles Wall called on George Dance, who was staying at Stratton when he made his first visit to Norman Court, and he produced several Gothic and classical alternatives.[31] It is likely that Repton was also approached at this time and, always with an eye to providing work for his architect sons John Adey and George Stanley, offered designs for the house as well as the grounds. The death of Sir Francis in September 1810 and the suicide of John Baring, Mrs Wall's cousin, after visiting the vault in which his uncle's remains were interred, delayed the start of works, though some modest schemes may have been carried out in the next couple of years.

Another tragedy hit the family in 1815 when Charles Wall, who was staying at another of his properties, Albury Park in Surrey, had a fatal fall from his horse while out riding by his wife's carriage.[32] Thereafter, the estate passed to Charles Baring Wall, who employed Thomas Harrison to complete the works. The two major building campaigns make for an odd, Janus-like house, with Georgian brick on one side and Regency cement on the other. Harrison's Greek Revival remodelling (50) dates from between 1818 and 1820, so anything Repton might have achieved at Norman Court would have been around the grounds of the Georgian house. Intriguingly, there is a tantalising later account of the house and grounds in George Prosser's *Select Illustrations of Hampshire* of 1833, which suggests that he did, in fact, make improvements.

Unsurprisingly, given Prosser's particular interest in architecture, his Norman Court account describes the sumptuous Greek Revival interiors in lavish detail, as well as the 'elegant conservatory, connected with the west wing', which was accessed from the Drawing Room via 'glazed folding doors, opening to a glazed passage'.[33] On the other, Georgian, side of the house, the entrance front was 'now nearly screened from view by trees and shrubs', its courtyard enclosed by gates.[34] This greenery is now lost and the courtyard, opened up to the parkland, is a car park. Also gone is the 'flower-garden' to the southeast, but the 'pleasure grounds...formed on the termination of the ridge of hill on which the mansion is situate, commanding a view over a small deep valley to the opposing eminences, which are clothed with stately beech wood', praised by William Hazlitt, survive west of the stable court.[35] Hazlitt may well have been extolling the beauties of Repton's planting when he wrote: 'Ye woods that crown the clear lone brow of Norman Court, why do I revisit ye so oft, and feel a soothing consciousness of your presence, but that your high tops, waving in the wind, recall to me the hours and years that are for ever fled'.[36]

Prosser continues his account of the landscape:

The land in the vicinity of the mansion, though not wholly thrown open as a park, presents much of that character, being ornamented by fine timber; the green rides and drives are also extensive. In several situations are remarkably

50 House and Conservatory in perfect architectural accord at Thomas Harrison's Greek Revival Norman Court

> neat rustic cottages, erected from the designs of H Repton, Esq., and at about half a mile south of the mansion, towards the village of Tytherley, is the site of the old house, now the kitchen garden...There are two carriage approaches, one from the side towards Salisbury, the other, the Stockbridge or London approach, commences about three miles from the mansion; its course diversified by passing through woods and groves of beech trees.[37]

This is a perfect template for a Reptonian park, with its ornamental planting, rides and drives threaded through groves of trees and flower garden 'detached and distinct from the general scenery of the place',[38] while the kitchen garden is sited some way off. It must surely be an accurate description of what he had achieved for Charles Wall between 1807 and 1810. The intriguing detail is the mention of 'neat rustic cottages', which are a feature of John Nash's contemporary practice, particularly when he was working in partnership with Repton in the 1790s, but also of Repton's own collaboration with his architect sons.[39] It seems that the cottages have all disappeared, but an octagonal timber Game Larder set on staddle stones, overshadowed by an old yew tree, survives, now set between modern buildings near the former stable court. This is mentioned in sales particulars of 1906,[40] and although it has been suggested that it was brought to Norman Court, it is just as likely to be one of Repton's rustic buildings.

Repton is to be found again at **Somerley Park**, near Ringwood, working for another of the great banking dynasty, Henry Baring, the third son of Sir Francis. He bought the house, which had been designed between 1791 and 1795 for Daniel Hobson by Samuel Wyatt, in 1814, before it had been completed, and then added an Ionic colonnade to the south front while finishing the interior.[41] According to drawings preserved, he also carried out or projected various works in the gardens. When writing about the house in 1958 in *Country Life*, Christopher Hussey stated: 'There are plans by Humphry and John Adey Repton, introducing a rustic pergola centred on a circular thatched pigeon house; for a conservatory (1813); and another for a trellis pergola by CA Busby'.[42] It is likely that these were actually built, for Loudon visited Somerley in 1835 and recorded:

> On the platform behind the house is some pleasure-ground scenery, with aviaries, and other ornamental buildings, very neatly kept; but the buildings are in bad taste, being finished with half columns, and having, in the intercolumniations, doors and windows with circular heads, and of different heights, even under the same pediments; than which nothing can be more contrary to unity of system and effect.[43]

All the fripperies of this 'pleasure-ground scenery' must have been swept away between 1868 and 1870 when the 3rd Earl of Normanton commissioned William Burn to enlarge the house, as well as lay out formal terraces on the east and south side.

Easily the most impressive Greek Revival house in the county is **The Grange** at Northington, another Baring property, with its thunderous Doric portico flanked by the Ionic façade of the Conservatory, all set on a massive revetment like a Hampshire acropolis (*colour 30*). As we have seen, the house belonged to the Henley family throughout the eighteenth century until 1787 when Robert Henley, 1st Earl of Northington, died and his sisters, as co-heiresses, sold it to the Drummond family of Drummond's Bank. The house was at first leased out as a hunting box, but in 1804, when Henry Drummond came of age on returning from a Grand Tour of Greece and the Mediterranean, the decision was taken to rebuild The Grange in Greek Revival style. Drummond commissioned William Wilkins to draw up plans for a complete re-casing in Roman cement of the seventeenth-century brick house.[44] It was no coincidence that Sir Francis Baring had, just one year earlier, employed Dance to add the first strictly Greek Doric portico to a country house at Stratton. Starting with such grandiose aims, Drummond soon tired of the lengthy process – it took the best part of ten years to complete – fell out with his architect and regretted his extravagance. In 1817, 'satiated with the frivolities of the fashionable world', Drummond sold up and set out for the Holy Land to begin a new career as a mystic.[45]

The Grange was bought by Alexander, second son of Sir Francis Baring, who had succeeded his father as head of the family banking concerns. Not only

51 The Conservatory of 1824 at The Grange, with its cast-iron, sheet-iron and glass construction, was a revolutionary deployment by Charles Robert Cockerell of prefabrication long before Joseph Paxton's Great Conservatory at Chatsworth, or his Crystal Palace

did Baring find the house inconvenient, but by this time the Greek style had gone out of fashion, so Robert Smirke was called in to remedy the deficiencies. He built a single-storey wing to the west of the house, but still the house was not big enough for Baring, so in 1823 Charles Robert Cockerell was commissioned to extend Smirke's wing and add a conservatory. This last was due to Baring's passion for exotics; he was a fellow of the Royal Horticultural Society. Cockerell had travelled extensively and had undertaken several archaeological excavations and made surveys at Greek sites. He determined to have an Ionic portico for the Conservatory and used the order from the Temple of Apollo at Bassae. The Conservatory was completed in 1824, having been created at the works of Jones & Clark, Metallic Hothouse Manufacturers, of Birmingham, taken to pieces, transported, and then re-assembled on site at Northington (*51*). The iron and glass construction provided parallel walks and beds divided by cast-iron columns, the beds being roofed with metal rafters and glazing, while the walks had arched coverings of double plates of sheet-iron.

The Conservatory is approached by a flight of steps leading to the portico, under which is a large reservoir to catch the rainwater for its re-use as the water supply for the house. The building was described in some detail in the *Gardener's Magazine* for 1827, accompanied by an engraving of the interior.[46] Interestingly, the proprietors of Jones & Clark, who sent in the article, end their piece: 'in the autumn of 1825, we put up a very beautiful conservatory for C. Baring Wall, Esq. M.P., at Norman Court'.[47] An earlier article in the same magazine describes the 'Mode of preparing the Soil, Planting &c. with a List of the Plants in the Conservatory at the Grange'.[48] The plants were 'all planted out in the beds, and grow luxuriantly, with scarcely an exception, although consisting of a collection of our best green-house plants and some generally thought too tender for the conservatory'.[49] There was also a vestibule in which 'stand plants in boxes or pots; being fine specimens, or fine flowering plants, of Orange-trees, Camellias, Proteas, the Chinese magnolias, Buonapartea juncea, Croweas Gardenias in flower, and Erythrina cristagalli (which last, when cut down and forced a little, will flower three times in the season)'.[50]

Prosser gives an evocative account of the building and mentions the terraced gardens:

> the CONSERVATORY, one hundred feet in length by fifty in breadth, is approached on the exterior, from the lower terrace, by broad flights of stone steps, ornamented in the ascent, on each side, with stone vases, conducting to this area of perpetual spring, under a deep Ionic portico, the floor of which is on a level with the upper terrace, and beside the columns stand large Sculptured stone and marble vases. A promenade, under an opaque roof, occupies the central division, which is embellished by a small jet d'eau. Before the south side is a beautiful flower-garden, on a level with the lower terrace, ornamented and enclosed by a stone balustrade, and also decorated with numerous vases.[51]

The *Gardener's Magazine* article of 1826 gives a plan of the gardens (52), which at that time were still being planted: 'the ornamental scenery, immediately surrounding the garden, fronting the house, partakes of the symmetry of its architecture; it is not entirely finished, but will be heightened with all the care and taste for which the liberal possessor is so distinguished'.[52] These comprised a vast circular flower garden to the southwest of the Conservatory, to be viewed from the terrace above, and two small enclosures to the rear of the building. Ordnance Survey maps of the 1870s suggest that when it was eventually planted the flower garden comprised two separate sectors, both with fountains, and that the rear garden was also centred by a fountain, most likely the one that survives today.[53] David Watkin has argued that these 'formal Italianate gardens' were as revolutionary as Cockerell's employment of prefabrication in the Conservatory, anticipating the Italian revival of William Andrews Nesfield and Charles Barry.[54]

Returning to Loudon's description of the Reptonian pleasure grounds at Somerley, it is reminiscent of J Hewetson's more measured account of a similar layout at **Rookesbury Park**, near Fareham. In the eighteenth century this had been the home of Dr George Garnier, Apothecary General to the Army

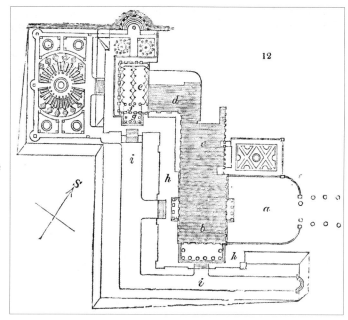

52 The layout of the lost Italianate flower gardens around The Grange from *The Gardener's Magazine* of 1826

and personal physician to the Duke of Cumberland. He was a close friend of Lord Chesterfield and regularly entertained the leading celebrities of the age including John Hume, William Hogarth, Edward Gibbon, the poet Charles Churchill and the actor David Garrick. Garnier's third son William inherited in 1796, eventually demolished the old house, and in 1824 commissioned Charles Heathcote Tatham to design a new one in Greek Revival style. Hewetson described this house in his 1830 *Architectural and Picturesque Views of Noble Mansions in Hampshire*:

> The building stands on rising ground backed by exceeding fine woods; and commands a most cheerful prospect over the pleasure grounds...the windows open to a most delightful flower garden, arranged under the direction of Mrs Garnier...In the flower garden is a beautiful grotto, communicating with a romantically wooded glen, where secluded paths wind, as they rise, to the opposite height, upon which an elevated Tower is now building.[55]

Prosser saw the estate three years later and gives a more detailed account of the flower garden, which was accessed from the Boudoir: 'The flower-garden before the east front is enclosed by a dwarf wall, with piers surmounted by stone vases; in the centre is a small fountain, and in the north wall a grotto formed by Lady Harriett Garnier, the daughter of the late Hon. and Right Rev. the Lord Bishop of Winchester, and widow of the Rev. William Garnier'.[56] Prosser also walked the ravine to the 'Observatory or Tower commanding extensive views over the Bere Forest to Chichester Chase, the Isle of Wight, &c'.[57] This was not all, as Prosser ends his account with a tantalising glimpse of another ornamental garden on the estate: 'On the property, and within the south boundary of the park, is the retired and pleasant residence of the Miss Garniers, whose taste has led them to form, and promote the cultivation of one of the most beautiful and well designed Bower gardens, for its extent, in the county'.[58] Sadly, nothing survives of the gardens on the site today; even the tower has gone, demolished in 1973.

The Garniers, like the Barings, feature prominently in the Hampshire gardens of this period. Their most important figure is, without doubt, the Revd Thomas Garnier, Rector of Bishopstoke, Eastleigh, from 1808 and later Dean of Winchester, who was a noted collector of plants. On accepting the living of **Bishopstoke**, Garnier demolished the old house, built a new Regency house with a tented verandah, set about acquiring more land and then laid out an arboretum of trees and shrubs. He travelled frequently to Kew to see the latest importations and to discuss planting regimes and the cultivation of exotics with Sir William Hooker. Loudon visited the Rectory in August 1833, and published his glowing account of the place in 1834, illustrated with an image of the house and a plan of the gardens with a numbered key to the plants, both engraved from Garnier's own drawings.[59] Loudon was in no doubt that this was a significant garden; hence the number of pages devoted to its description:

> This is a place of an acre or two, on a bank facing the south, remarkable for its wall, covered with choice half-hardy plants, and its lawn, ornamented with the finest American shrubs and most select trees. It is a perfect gem of botanical beauty in the foreground, heightened in effect by interesting gleams of distant scenery, seen between and over fine oaks and elms, on the lower part of the declivity.[60]

The accompanying plan shows the entire layout, its circuit walk bordered by a shelterbelt of trees, its lawns studded with island beds, shrubs and single specimen trees. The eastern sector was dominated by a circular rose garden of diminishing circles planted with 'tree roses and dwarf georginas', its outer edge a 'collection of herbaceous plants of the brightest colours'.[61] There was a conservatory, 'designed by Mr. Page, and placed on a plinth of three steps, which forms a termination to the terrace walk. The outer border of this walk is ornamented with vases, placed at regular distances'.[62]

It is not easy to envisage how all this busy horticulture would have looked on the ground but, fortunately, Loudon analysed Garnier's 'general principles' of planting, which gives the plan a sharper focus: 'first, he arranges all his flowers and shrubs in masses of one kind...by which he produces brilliant masses of the same colour; secondly, all his groups and masses are of plain forms, such as circles, ovals, squares, and parallelograms....thirdly, he transplants the azaleas, rhododendrons, and other American shrubs every year, and at any season of the year, so as to keep every individual plant detached from the rest'.[63] Garnier gardened at Bishopstoke until 1865 when he sold the property to Alfred Barton, who incorporated it into the neighbouring Longmead estate. Today, most of the grounds have been built over, but the walled garden, peach house and some of Dean Garnier's specimen trees survive in a private garden.

As with the Bishopstoke Rectory garden, time has not been kind to **Leigh Park**, the present outskirts of which, to the north of Havant, could not be less like the approach to what was once one of the most delightfully ornamental gardens of the entire Regency. The road threads through a drab 1950s housing estate to reach a sign directing visitors to the Staunton Country Park, which is now a public open space, created in 1987 out of the northwest quadrant of the original parkland. It is named after Sir George Thomas Staunton, who bought the estate in 1819. Visitors are first directed right, to the plant shop and animal farm around the original walled garden complex and ornamental farm of Staunton's house, now demolished except for his Gothic library, rather than left, to the other side of the road, where the park proper begins. There is an entrance fee for the farm, while the park is free to visitors. Both sites are important in reconstructing Staunton's vision for the estate, but it is the parkland that captures most poignantly the mini Rococo Revival landscape of exotic buildings that Staunton created after his purchase.

Until recent scholarship by local historian Derek Gladwyn and archaeologist Chris Currie, it was thought that Staunton was responsible for the entire Eclectic layout at Leigh Park, but Staunton's letters and an 1817 description by William Butler prove that the previous owner, William Garrett, not only rebuilt the eighteenth-century house on the site but also laid out his own ornamental garden around it.[64] Staunton inherited this complex, centred by the Walled Garden, around the skirts of the house close to the village street, and then proceeded to expand his landholdings and extend the pleasure grounds into the more private areas north and west. He did this by creating a small lake – Leigh Water – which he enriched with garden buildings of various exotic styles, but mostly Chinese. This lakeside garden was essentially complete by 1836, when Staunton wrote a guidebook to the estate and commissioned Joseph Frederick Gilbert to record the layout.[65] His creation was also the subject of a somewhat unctuous poem by James King which, despite its laboured verse, is valuable in that it describes many of the buildings and their decorations.[66]

George Thomas Staunton had been searching for a country estate for some time after returning from China, where he had been one of the commissioners in the embassy at Canton. He had made no fewer than five trips to China and several to the Continent, but by 1819 was ready to settle down in London and serve as an MP and to 'have what is called "a stake in the hedge"…a respectable country residence and estate' which, he felt, would give him '(what no man can posses if confined to the metropolis,) a sphere of action peculiarly my own, which when suitably taken advantage of, would be calculated to extend and improve my social position, and proportionably add to my happiness'.[67] After looking at several properties, he wrote to his mother from Petersfield in Sussex on 22 July 1819:

> I am just returned from seeing Leigh Place, and in time to give you a line by the Post. As Mr. Garrett the Owner was at home…He was very obliging in shewing me the House and grounds, and prevailed on me to stay [to] dinner…It is not in all respects what I could wish; but as it possesses several sterling good points, I am inclined to be satisfied with it, and not harass myself with any further search – The place is a good-deal in the style of Hall's at Totteridge, and has the same defect of a bad approach – The views are beautiful though not equal to those at Heathfield – and it is an excellent moderate house.[68]

Garrett had bought the estate in 1801 and in the following year commissioned the Southampton architect, John Kent to rebuild the existing eighteenth-century house sited close to the Havant to Rowlands Castle road, hence Staunton's remark about the 'bad approach'.[69] Kent's elegant Regency design features in two paintings by Gilbert, one of the front façade with its semi-circular Doric porch and the garden elevation (*colour 31*), enhanced by a climber-wreathed loggia and a large conservatory; in this view gardeners tend the island beds in the lawn, which is edged with shrubs and tall specimen trees.

Sale particulars of Garrett's 'Modern Villa' mention the practical aspects of 'Productive Gardens, Green, Pinery and Succession Houses, Melon Grounds, with pleasant and extensive Shrubberies', the whole presenting 'a perfect *ferme ornée*', due to the close proximity of the agricultural buildings,[70] while an 1817 account by William Butler describes the estate in more aesthetic terms:

> The shrubberies are laid out with taste; and from its numerous wood-walks, at different points, are seen many interesting objects of the neighbourhood. The view of Havant Thicket from the hermitage, clad with ivy, upon the mount is of a more sedate kind, highly interesting from its deep shade in summer, its beautiful tints in autumn, and serving as a contrast to the more brilliant views of the sea and its islands. The gardens are planned with great judgement, and furnished with pinery, hot-house, green-houses, and stoves, and surrounded with shrubberies and walks communicating in all directions. The farm buildings, dairy embellished with old china, and pheasantry adjoining, are detached from the mansion, and contribute by their nice arrangement to render this estate one of the most delightful residences in the country.[71]

This is particularly interesting when taken together with Staunton's later reminiscences of his initial visit to Leigh Park, as it suggests that Garrett had achieved a diverse ornamental garden around the house with productive areas within the walled garden and at least one garden building – the Hermitage – out in the fields beyond, probably on the elevated slope to the north where Staunton would later raise his Doric temple.

As we have seen, Gilbert White had set the eremitic fashion in the county with his Hermitage at Selborne, and these thatched cells for contemplation continued to feature in later Regency gardens. In his topographical survey of the area Butler records 'a beautiful garden, embellished with grottos, shady walks and chairs of grotesque workmanship' at nearby **Langstone**.[72] One can almost sense the writer's excitement as he walks the grounds of the 'ingenious owner' – we are never told his name – and comes across 'a Grecian temple, constructed with great simplicity, with thatch and the bark of trees, where slumber, unconscious of their happiness, his pigs'.[73] After threading the walks at Langstone, Butler catches a glimpse of the sea, where 'beneath an umbrageous filbert hedge is the hermit's grotto, from whence the cares of the world are wholly excluded, and every object around invites contemplation'.[74] Butler was so taken with his visit to Langstone that he included an engraving, in an otherwise under-illustrated book, of one of the rustic seats and another of the Hermit's Grotto.

In addition to the pine and melon pits and the stoves alongside the walls of the enclosure, Garrett had built an arbour with a conical thatched roof called the Cone House, and laid out a Dutch Garden with semi-circular flower beds commanded by the 'Swiss House', a mountain chalet that had been popularised by the architectural writer Peter Frederick Robinson.[75] The vogue for things Swiss was to find its ultimate expression in Lord Ongley's 1820s Swiss Garden at Old Warden in Bedfordshire.[76] James King's *Poem on Leigh Park*, although published in 1829 after Staunton had taken possession and begun to extend his grounds, mentions an Indian Temple, which Garrett is thought to have built in 1810 to amuse his nephews:

> What fane is that which sudden meets the sight,
> Half shown, half hidden by the glimmering light?
> Hath then ere now the foot or mortal been
> Amid this wild interminable scene?
> What do I see? A bloody dagger there!
> And here the tomahawks all reeking glare!
> Hath then the blood-stained Indian dared invade,
> With impious foot, this still and peaceful shade?[77]

King's footnote to the verse adds that 'in the midst of this wood is an Indian temple, on the walls and roof of which are painted daggers, tomahawks, and other weapons of Indian warfare', suggesting its close proximity to the Hermitage in High Field to the north. This again links Garrett's layout with Lord Ongley's at Old Warden, which also had an Indian Temple.

Garrett's garden is shown on Charles Lewis's 1842 map of the estate (*colour 32*), by which time the road had been moved eastwards so that the home farm buildings, including the dairy and the pheasantry, could be brought into the pleasure grounds.[78] Lewis's map is proof that Staunton retained Garrett's garden and restricted his improvements to Leigh Water. Sadly the Swiss House, one of the earliest of its kind, has disappeared, but Staunton's octagonal Library still stands in shrubberies close to the Walled Garden, while the original farm buildings function again as they were originally intended.

Only two of the garden buildings around Leigh Water – the Shell House on the circuit walk by what was Temple Lawn, close now to the site of the demolished Victorian Leigh Park, and the Beacon on Beacon Lawn – together with the substructure of the Chinese Bridge survive of what Staunton intended to be an oriental tour. The Shell House (*53*) has lost its coronet, inspired by the Chichester Market Cross and shown in a Gilbert watercolour, while the Beacon is fairly intact if a little careworn. The Chinese buildings must have been made of timber and as such may not have lasted very long. There is a beautiful watercolour by CR Cotton,[79] which shows the trellis-clad Cottage on its island, the Chinese Bridge and the Chinese Boathouse (*colour 33*). Gilbert's views of the East and the West Water (*54*) contrive to include all the buildings, especially the Corinthian Bridge, which was taken directly from Plate 9 of a 'Bridge and Temple' in Papworth's *Ornamental Gardening* (*55*). Papworth's advice to prospective builders of his design is that it 'should be executed in stone, and upon a small scale; for such an edifice, when applied as ornamental chiefly, should be considered rather as a *bijou* than otherwise'.[80] Staunton built the 'Corinthian Portico' in 1835 and published his *Notices of the Leigh Park Estate near Havant*, signalling that his layout was now complete, in the following year.

Not only did Papworth's seminal book become the standard text for owners wishing to create ornamental landscapes and gardens, it also acted as a sales brochure for his own landscape practice. His son's memoir of his father's life and work lists over twenty sites where Papworth was engaged in 'landscape gardening', or where he was designing lodges, estate cottages, dairies, aviaries and, more often than not, conservatories.[81] Papworth's architectural work, other than that on the Lansdown estate in Cheltenham, has remained under-researched in studies on the Regency, while his landscape gardening has never been written about. This is unfortunate, as he seems to provide the horticultural link between Repton and the early Victorians. His last appearance in

53 The Shell House at Leigh Park is one of only two surviving buildings from George Thomas Staunton's exotic layout set around Leigh Water. It has lost its coronet, which was based on the Chichester Market Cross

54 The profusion of eclectic garden buildings around the lake at Leigh Park included both Turkish and Chinoiserie structures. *Hampshire Record Office: 116M88/C53. Photograph by Paul Carter*

55 George Thomas Staunton used John Buonarotti Papworth's design for a templar bridge, from Papworth's *Ornamental Gardening* of 1823, for his own bridge at Leigh Park

Hampshire is at **Cranbury Park**, where he did architectural work inside the house and laid out pleasure grounds for Thomas Chamberlayne, who had inherited the estate on the death of his distant cousin, William Chamberlayne, in 1829.[82]

Wyatt Papworth's entry of 1830-2 for his father's work at Cranbury lists 'library fittings' and minor additions, including 'gates, piers, archway…fountain'. The design of the library bookcases with their incised antae and lotus leaf and anthemion frieze is very close to interior views that Papworth drew for the engravings in Peter Coxe's *The Social Day*, a poem on customs and manners in the Regency published in 1823, particularly his frontispiece for the fourth canto.[83] Intriguingly, William Chamberlayne is listed as one of the subscribers to Coxe's book, so it may have been in the library at Cranbury when Thomas took charge. However Papworth got the commission, he must also have designed the extraordinarily beautiful silk Tent Room, made about 1830, as a copy of Empress Josephine's room at Malmaison, which has affinities with his drawing of the toilet for Coxe's social satire.

Papworth's hand in the grounds is less easy to discern, apart from the great

56 J B Papworth was responsible for the fitting up of the Library and a remarkable silk
Tent Room at Cranbury Park, where he also added ornamental buildings to the
landscape, including this Fountain

circular Fountain on the east front (*56*), which is mentioned by Wyatt
Papworth and marked clearly on an 1859 plan of the estate.[84] Papworth
includes two designs for fountains in his *Ornamental Gardening* in an attempt to
re-instate them in gardens:

> Few architectural embellishments have so interesting an effect as fountains, and
> being capable of an inexhaustible variety of design, situation and magnitude, it
> is rather a matter of surprise that their beauties have been neglected, ever since
> the general abandonment of them nearly a century ago.[85]

There is a circular pool to the north of the house, known as Middle Pond, also
a vaulted chamber housing a spring, on the walls of which there are tablets
inscribed with a verse written by Wordsworth, while close to George Dance's
double colonnaded and bow-fronted Dairy there are two small enclosed
gardens, one of which has a wrought-iron pergola with a domed roof. Here
authorities disagree as to who was responsible. Gordon Nares, who wrote up
the house and grounds in 1956 for *Country Life*, believes that the laying out of
the grounds north of the house was down to Thomas Dummer, 'or possibly his
widow, Lady Dance-Holland', while the EH Register entry implies that most
of these features, including the Middle Pond, were early nineteenth-century in
date and 'possibly by Papworth'. All this sounds like the pleasure-ground

scenery that Loudon sneered at when he visited Somerley in 1835. By then, of course, the stony Italianate had supplanted such elegant, Austen-style 'prettinesses'. The spirited gardens of the Regency, the pictures of an owner's fancy, would soon be forgotten, dismissed as mere fripperies of design, just as their forebears, the Rococo gardens of the 1740s and 1750s, had been swept away by the cold hand of archaeologically driven neo-Classicism.

7

'Their growth has been a floral struggle'
High Victorian Gardens

Heckfield Place, Brockenhurst Park, Minley Manor, Elvetham Hall
Sherfield Manor, Tylney Hall, Dogmersfield Park, Rhinefield House

With the exception of Brockenhurst Park, the Victorian gardens of Hampshire conform to the nineteenth-century taste for brightly coloured flowers and exotic plants. Ubiquitous rhododendrons flourished and avenues of newly imported trees proliferated across the county. The vast numbers of plants used to create ostentatious displays of carpet bedding required considerable labour to grow, plant and maintain, demonstrating the wealth and status of their owners. The railways facilitated travel, and visiting gardens and horticultural shows became easier, popularised by the gardening press. One of the earliest of these layouts was achieved at **Heckfield Place**, near Hook, which had been built between 1780 and 1790 for John Lefevre.[1] Its stable block was extended to residential accommodation in the early 1980s and at the time of writing (2015) the main house at Heckfield was being converted into a hotel. The site was, therefore, inaccessible, and this account relies heavily on published descriptions in the contemporary gardening press.

A landscape park was created at Heckfield for Charles Shaw-Lefevre I around 1818, including two large lakes with islands, which survive in the valley to the northeast of the house.[2] The visitors' car park is beside the large walled garden to the north of the house, occupying the space where the productive greenhouses were; they are now gone. A *Country Life* writer described Heckfield in 1898 commanding 'a great panorama, extending, beyond its lovely gardens, to the distant hills of Oxfordshire and the lordly Woods of Windsor'.[3]

The Victorian gardens at Heckfield were laid out for Charles Shaw-Lefevre II, who was Speaker of the House of Commons from 1839 until his retirement in 1857, when he was created Viscount Eversley.[4] By 1882, at the age of eighty-nine, Eversley still had a zest for life and liked to see his trees increase around him, keeping his gardens in the best order.[5] As a visitor for *The Gardeners' Chronicle* described: 'there is an art which mends Nature, and a wilderness in the precincts of the lawn, with bad weeds, Nettles, Docks, Thistles, would be as intolerable to Lord Eversley as so many recalcitrant Irish MPs'.[6] Eversley's Head Gardener was William Walker Wildsmith, who was the 'presiding genius' over the gardens at Heckfield.[7] He was engaged as a gardener in 1865 and two years later made Head Gardener, a post he held until his death in 1890.[8] Wildsmith was a member of the Fruit Committee of the Royal Horticultural Society and presented several papers to the Society's conferences.[9] Public recognition of the role of head gardener as a respected professional lasted for only a short time, of which Wildsmith's success at Heckfield is a good illustration. His position was reversed by 1898, when *Country Life* gave credit for the gardens to Lord Eversley, rather than to Wildsmith.[10]

The lakes at Heckfield were an important feature of the gardens in the Victorian period, their banks planted with yellow iris and water forget-me-not, the pools filled with water lilies. Beside the lakes was a sub-tropical garden with 'massive banks of pampas grass, the silvery-plumed Arundo conspicua, gorse, rhododendrons and the graceful bamboo'.[11] The island was thickly planted with rhododendrons, described as 'a water-borne bouquet'.[12] Between the upper and lower lakes there is a dam, with a rockery and cascade crossed by a wooden bridge. The gardens extended to 30 acres of 'well-wooded pleasure grounds', populated with large evergreen conifers including *Abies cephalonica*, and the Douglas pine 'in perfect growth and happy contrast' amongst the deciduous trees.[13] Lord Eversley loved trees and approved of planting a few every year: 'A portion of the bracken in the wood beyond this year's boundary is dug under, and in goes a *Cryptomeria japonica* – a favourite tree at Heckfield', while limes and chestnuts grew beside the lawn, reached by winding walks.[14]

A terrace flanks the south and east sides of the house, enclosed by a strapwork balustrade which was in place by 1833.[15] Two-storey canted bay windows were added to the garden front in the mid nineteenth century, overlooking the terrace and the lakes below.[16] The terrace (57), with its 'beautiful outlook over billowy lawns, glorious trees and transcendently beautiful lakes' was Lord Eversley's pride and joy.[17] It is accessed by steps that descend from the path in front of the house to a fountain at its centre. To either side of the central path the terrace is laid to grass, with large artificial stone basket weave planters, which are still in place. In 1882 the planting in the stone baskets included a tangled mass of dahlias relieved with white and golden marguerites and heliotropes,

> with Tropaeolums scrambling among them and falling over the sides here and there, as if escaping from an overladen receptacle. The plants appear to have been inserted, and then as regards their floral outline left to take their chance. Their growth has been a floral struggle as if to represent the survival of the fittest.[18]

57 This archival photograph of the terrace at Heckfield Place shows the stone flower baskets of the Italianate gardens, while Lord Eversley's specimen trees are seen in the parkland beyond. *Country Life Picture Library*

As well as the planted baskets beds were set into the grass. On the north side of the terrace were eight long beds, four on each side of the baskets, while in the centre there were raised round beds and star-shaped beds.[19] 'On the east terrace about 30 various beds and vases are well disposed for effect'.[20] In 1898 the *Country Life* writer was captivated by the blaze of colour:

> Up here on the terrace, too, there is a feast of colour for the eye. The beds are brilliant with glowing hues, but the effect is softened and harmonised by the presence of leafy, sub-tropical plants, which add a peculiar charm to the summer garden.[21]

The main attraction of the terrace planting, to Victorian taste, was 'gorgeous colour' and thus 'every bed and vase is rich with well-contrasted hues'.[22] The dominance of carpet bedding lasted from 1870 until the late 1880s, when Wildsmith was Head Gardener at Heckfield. He became the figurehead of the campaign for colour mixing, emerging by 1880 as the most celebrated gardener of his generation.[23] In 1883 he wrote the chapter on summer bedding for William Robinson's *The English Flower Garden,* thus achieving wide circulation of his views for the remainder of the Victorian period.[24] He used dot plants and patches of herbaceous flowers in his summer beds, creating cluttered bedding patterns, described as 'mosaiculture'.[25]

Honeysuckles, conifers and hollies were also included in the terrace planting to 'create pleasant effects in winter'.[26] The carpet beds included a great variety of succulents that maintained 'a certain amount of freshness all through the dull season'.[27] Wildsmith developed winter bedding into its most complex form at Heckfield, and his beds also included Acubas, Euonymus and Herniaria.[28] In 1875, at the eastern end of the terrace, there were 'two notable examples of the hardy Palm (*Chamaerops Fortunei*, now *Trachycarpus Fortunei*), which were planted ten years earlier and had, by then, reached about 9 feet in height, and would have given a tropical feel.[29]

Impressive Victorian gardens were thrown open to the public on occasion by their proud owners, and in 1874 *The Garden* advertised the opening of Heckfield Place on Mondays throughout September when 'just now the flower beds are at their best, and there is also a piece of decorative bordering in the kitchen garden'.[30] The writer considered that, despite competition from nearby Stratfield Saye, Elvetham and Dogmersfield Park, and 'although not so palatial in character as either of these residences, [Heckfield Place] is yet the most beautiful in all that relates to gardenesque effects'.[31]

Heckfield was also famous for its production of grapes, and there were eight large glasshouses to the west of the walled garden which were devoted to their cultivation.[32] The grapes in the earliest house were ready at the end of April and late grapes, including a whole house devoted to Lady Downes, were fully ripe in October.[33] There was a Grape Room capable of storing 2,000 bunches over winter, ensuring that grapes were available for the table all year round. In the Kitchen Garden itself, peaches were particularly successful, their blossoms protected by a hemp covering attached to rollers, while early potatoes and asparagus were forced in brick pits.[34] Pears were trained on a trellis arched over a border of hardy plants, 'a curious and interesting form of gardening'[35], and there was also a flower border, providing blooms for picking without damaging the ornate parterres. Cactus and dahlias were trained up a hedge of *Cupressus Lawsoniana*, providing 'an original effect and a particularly happy one'.[36] Through the walled gardens ran a long rose walk, the roses trained over a pergola arched over the paths between the gates.[37]

While much remains of the Victorian gardens at Heckfield, those at **Brockenhurst Park** have not fared so well. When John Morant III succeeded to Brockenhurst in 1857 he began a series of alterations and improvements designed by Thomas Wyatt, remodelling the house in the style of a French château.[38] Wyatt also designed the North Lodge, an ornate carriage arch in the same

Renaissance style over the main entrance drive into the park. This leads from the house to Brockenhurst, and also to a halt on the main London and South Western Railway. Wyatt's house was demolished in 1958 and, as we have seen, was replaced by a 1960s building designed by Harry Graham.

Morant also carried out considerable work in the park, creating a degree of formality by planting three avenues. The north entrance drive was lined with an avenue of chestnuts between 1840 and 1860; this was replanted in the 1990s. A broad lime avenue was planted across the park from east to west, on high ground to the south of the house. This was badly damaged by a storm in 1990, but most of the trees were pollarded and successfully re-erected. The third avenue ran west from the house towards the church, and Morant moved the portico of the former Georgian house on the site to the end of this avenue to act as an eye-catcher. The portico was demolished in 1958, at the same time as the house. Morant also remodelled the late eighteenth-century walled garden to the south of the house, replacing the kitchen garden with extensive Italianate gardens, while a new complex of kitchen gardens was laid out further from the house, to the west of Church Road.

A long, stone-edged Canal, described on the 1890s map as a fish pond, with a fountain at the end nearest to the house, extends along the south side. A *Country Life* photograph shows this to have had a large shell-shaped bowl raised on a rock-like base and topped with an ornate urn.[39] This has disappeared, but the Canal survives, with the new house set at its head (*colour plate 34*). Beyond the Canal is a double set of rising steps that lead to hedged garden compartments with fountains, pools and seats.[40] More urns were set on the steps, and small statues of *putti* decorated the corners of the Canal, while standard topiary trees in octagonal pots lined the sides.[41] The 1890s map shows three fountains, and there was another in the centre of the front entrance court. The gardens were decorated with statues, which have since been dispersed, themed on Ancient Rome.[42] The first garden at the top of the steps was called the Emperors' Court, and another photograph reveals that the statues were herms, recessed into a series of arched topiary niches cut into the yew hedge.[43] The *Country Life* writer, clearly impressed by the place, described 'the truly imperial aspect of the great court, dignified by its busts of the Caesars, the noble descent to the long water be-gemmed with lilies – all these possess an individuality quite their own'.[44] The yew hedges were topped with topiary obelisks and balls and formed a series of compartments, while more statues on plinths, set against the dark yew, created a refined ambience, unusually for this period, devoid of flowers.[45]

This was not the case at **Minley Manor**, near Yateley, which was conceived as a grand house of a piece with its correspondingly magnificent, flower-filled gardens. Built between 1858 and 1862 by Henry Clutton for the banker Raikes Currie of Glyn & Co., it was one of the earliest English houses inspired by the design of French Renaissance châteaux.[46] It was extended in 1885-6 by George Devey, matching Clutton's style, for Currie's son, Bertram.[47] Devey added a stable block to the northwest of the house, also the main lodge and gateway, and in 1887 the neo-Elizabethan Arch Cottage, as well as the Orangery and Loggia.[48] On the crest of the hill, the square brick water tower with its octagonal cupola, designed by Arthur Castings, Devey's chief draughtsman, was added in 1896.[49] This has a Gothic summerhouse incorporated in its base, and was built for Bertram's son Laurence, who inherited on his father's death in 1896.[50] Devey also created the formal gardens around the skirts of the house.[51]

The main entrance is through the red brick lodge and gates on Minley Road, which are on an axis with the arched entrance of Arch Cottage and the gates north of the Orangery. A second entrance from the southwest of the estate is through Fleet Lodge, designed by Devey but built by Castings for Laurence Currie in 1899.[52] From here, the drive leads on a serpentine route through Minley Wood to the west side of the forecourt. This drive branches to Home Farm, southeast of the house, which was a model farm, built by Castings in 1900.[53] The entrance to the house is through a courtyard enclosed by a low brick wall. The *Country Life* writer described how: 'Looking from this into the grounds we see the long grass avenue, with its Wellingtonias, Limes, and Douglas firs, the Wellingtonias and Limes being, in alternate sequence, all down the line'.[54] James Veitch Junior planted this avenue.[55] It must have been planted as soon as the house was built, as a visitor in 1864 recalled how he 'could see the outlines of what would some day be a splendid avenue'.[56] The Veitch nurseries were specialists in exotic trees and in the 1840s grew trees from the first monkey-puzzle seed and *Cryptomeria japonica*.[57] The redwoods and Wellingtonias of California were discovered in the 1850s, and thus the avenue at Minley Manor was at the forefront of the latest garden fashions. The avenue was originally 600 metres long, and the 'two stately Douglas Firs [were planted] as *avant courriers*'.[58] The visual climax of the avenue, as it approached the house, was an ornate Renaissance-style fountain in the entrance courtyard, which has since gone.[59] At the entrance to the courtyard, opposite the front door, were 'a splendid pair of gates, once, we were told, the property of the great Napoleon'.[60]

Through an archway from the entrance court is a cloister, at the centre of which was another Renaissance-style fountain, topped with a statue of Venus wringing out her hair, which has also disappeared.[61] To the southwest of the house is a large rectangular garden, divided into two sections. The upper part is enclosed on two sides, and is commanded by an Orangery in Dutch seventeenth-century style (*58*), while along the eastern side runs a pent-roofed Loggia with carved wood columns. The steps up to this garden were flanked with statues, and more statues occupied the niches on either side of the entrance to the Orangery.[62] A terrace runs in front of the Orangery, which has

58 The Dutch Garden at Minley Manor is overlooked by the seventeenth-century style Orangery; statues flank its entrance, while those that originally lined the steps have gone

59 The sunken Winter Garden at Minley Manor was laid out in the form of a family crest using miniature conifers, an early instance of bonsai

a stone seat at either end, backed by yew hedging; one seat is dated 1861, the other 1909. The lower part or Winter Garden is a sunken area, bordered in stone with circular steps descending at each corner (59). The 1899 photographs show that stone urns flanked the steps and there was a fountain with a classical statue, possibly of Diana, on a plinth at the centre of the garden.[63] The circular basin of the fountain survives, but the statues and urns are gone. Robert T Veitch, with his landscaper FW Meyer, was responsible for the planting of these gardens.[64] The 1891 *Gardeners' Chronicle* describes how, in the Winter Garden,

> the groundwork is formed of dark Yews, edged with white Euonymus radicans. No fewer than eighty thousand seedling yews were employed, and their dark foliage serves to set off to advantage the scrolls and devices, which are worked out in gold and silver Retinosporas [juvenile cypresses]...Other portions of the design represent the family coats-of-arms and the monograms of Mr. and Mrs. Currie. Mound-like beds, arranged in panels of Golden Queen Holly, alternating with Hodgen's Holly, lend brightness, without glare, to the scene, even in the dullest winter day.[65]

This innovative geometric garden used dwarf trees as bedding plants and was contemporary with the first interest in bonsai.[66] All the formal gardens around the house were ornamented with wooden Versailles-style tubs, painted white, and each was planted with standard bays, 'specimens worthy of Belgium or Italy, but which are rarely seen so fine in this country'.[67] In winter they were housed in the Orangery.[68]

Commentators on the design of the Minley Manor layout highlighted the juxtaposition of formal geometric gardens and more naturalistic areas moving out into the countryside. Beyond the Winter Garden, linking it to the wild woodland in the distance, the Veitchs were in 1891 'contriving a garden which will be full of interest at all seasons'.[69] Known as The Plain, this is bordered by a ha-ha to the south, dividing it from the woodland beyond. It consisted of 'a series of bold beds, separated by grass, and devoted each to one description of herbaceous plant, or flowering shrub'.[70] These included clumps of herbaceous plants, beds of roses and brambles, broom, weigela, rhododendrons and azaleas, 'of any and everything that is choice, beautiful and fitting'. There would be 'no fear of monotony in such a garden, no meaningless wiggle-waggles and purposeless meanderings'.[71] In 1893, Bertram Currie employed the Veitchs to design pleasure grounds for the opposite side of the Minley Road.[72] This included Hawley Lake, planted with water lilies, which had several islands. On the largest island was a thatched summerhouse, and there was a boathouse, now Boathouse Cottage.[73] To the northeast of the house, adjacent to the stables, is a large square walled Kitchen Garden. This was quartered with paths in the traditional way and glasshouses were built against the furthest, south-facing wall. The quarters were separated by 'Ilex crenata, Osmanthus Retinosporas' and other low hedges.[74] An unusual feature was the growth of pyramidal apples and pears on broad grass verges, with credit for keeping the whole establishment in order given to gardeners Mr Profit and Mr Tubb.[75] East of the house is a rustic circular Summerhouse with a tall thatched roof, which was probably built in the 1890s.[76]

Elvetham Hall, the spikily Gothic mansion designed by Samuel Sanders Teulon between 1859 and 1862 for Frederick Gough, 4th Baron Calthorpe, now functions as a hotel. Characteristic of Victorian Gothic architecture in its asymmetry and polychromy, the house is highly coloured in bright red brick, garishly striped and spotted with black detail. The original house burnt down in 1840, and in replacing it Teulon embellished his interior with decorative elements reflecting his interest in its Tudor and Elizabethan past. To the rear of the house Teulon built a terrace with a pierced brick parapet overlooking a formal garden. He also built stables, now The Court, and a gardener's cottage. In the gardens to the east of the house he planned a parterre in a crescent shape, reflecting the crescent lake created by the Earl of Hertford for Queen Elizabeth's 1591 visit.[77] This large lake, sited to the northeast of the house, remained full throughout the Victorian period, although it has now disappeared. Below the house a balustraded bridge crosses the river and beyond it an avenue of Wellingtonias, planted in 1860, extends across New Park.[78] William Wildsmith's pupil, Mr Jones, was the gardener at Elvetham and he followed Wildsmith's practice of mixing and shading the beds with a wide variety of plants, abolishing formality and geometry in favour of deliberately cluttered bedding to give a sense of profusion rather than control.[79] Writing in *The Garden* in 1889, Wildsmith praised the success of the scheme:

> The whole terrace is a perfect plateau raised to the level of the ground-floor rooms of the mansion, the whole being supported on the south and west by a retaining wall that is so completely covered with rare climbers in variety as to make it one of the finest features of the garden. Escallonia macrantha, Magnolias, Clematises, Wistarias, Roses, Pyrus, &c, commingle together in such natural and wild profusion, that one is compelled to stop and admire.[80]

The front of the house itself was dressed from top to bottom in typical Victorian style: 'covered with creepers that are allowed to ramble in the same natural way' including fragrant 'Chimonanthus, Wistarias and sweet-scented Clematises'.[81] The flowerbeds, described as 'of immense size', were 'planted in such a loose, natural manner as to completely destroy all formality' in a riot of heliotropes, lobelia, alyssum, pelargoniums, salvia and geraniums.[82] One of the large beds contained abutilons and eucalyptus as standard plants; clearly this

60 This pool is a lone survivor of the busy Victorian layout at Sherfield Manor, where
the extensive pleasure grounds were strewn with beds of flowering shrubs and trees

was a departure from conventional planting, as Wildsmith concluded that 'the
general effect is, I consider, unique'. However, not all Wildsmith's comments
were complimentary and he judged that 'an avenue of Irish Yews and variegated
Maples (*Acer Negundo variegata*) has a terribly funereal appearance'.[83] Lord
Calthorpe was particularly partial to sweet-smelling plants, and Jones obliged.
Wildsmith records how, 'every nook and corner under the windows are filled
with Heliotropes, scented Geraniums, the scented Verbena (*Aloysia*), Roses,
Violets and Wallflowers'.[84] Sadly, all this planting has disappeared.

The walled Kitchen and Fruit Garden was well stocked with various fruit
trees, but one of the quarters was also given over to scented plants: 'Mr. Jones,
the gardener here, having visions of the requirements in the scented plant line
for the furnishing of the rooms of the mansion in winter'.[85] There was also a
good collection of orchids in one of the plant houses, while fruit houses
contained peach, fig, cherry and apricot, as well as vines.[86] In 1912 William
Goldring designed an oval enclosure planted with azaleas.[87] Goldring's remodelling also included a ha-ha and a sunken Rose Garden with a pond below the
terrace, which is overlooked by a 1901 Summerhouse.[88]

Much of the horticulture of the Victorian layout has also disappeared at
Sherfield Manor (*60*), now Sherfield School, northeast of Basingstoke, which
was built in the 1860s for John B Stane.[89] He demolished an existing house on

the site called Archer Lodge and named his new house Buckfield, as it was built in the middle of Buckfield Wood.[90] In 1880 it was sold to Charles Lethridge, who changed the name to Sherfield Manor.[91] It was then purchased in 1898 by James B Taylor, a South African mining financier, who largely re-built the house in 1898-9 to designs by Wade and Frankiss.[92] There is a wide terrace along its southern side, and climbing plants were used to cover the house, including a *Magnolia grandiflora* 40 feet high, and an equally large *Rosa Rêve d'Or*. Part of the terrace wall was planted with the fragrant, white-flowered *Clematis flammula*, 'which when in flower pervades the whole atmosphere with its delicious scent'.[93]

The estate extended to approximately 200 acres, of which the pleasure grounds covered around 30 acres.[94] They were planted with beds of flowering shrubs and trees, with emphasis on rhododendrons, planted a hundred to a bed, surrounded by large quantities of *Lilium auratum* 'to prevent these Rhododendron beds appearing dull in summer'.[95] These were under-planted with daisies, forget-me-nots and foxgloves 'to hide the soil'.[96] Deciduous flowering shrubs were also used, including magnolias, weigela, forsythia and spiraea.[97] There was a profusion of roses, and standard roses were planted singly on the lawns, while the Rose Garden, which survives, was enclosed by a yew hedge. An archway at each entrance to the Rose Garden was covered with *Rosa wichuraiana*.[98]

In the walled garden there was a Palm House, which was constructed by Messenger & Co. in 1898-9, but it is now in the grounds of a private house.[99] In 1904 the visitor writing for the *Gardeners' Chronicle* described it as 'a lofty structure well furnished with *Hibiscus rosa sinesis*, a glowing crimson-coloured variety with blooms fully 8 inches in diameter'.[100] It also contained '*Passiflora edulis*, Bougainvilleas and *Ipomoea Horsefieldii*', which were covering the roof.[101] Leading from the Kitchen Garden towards the house was a large Pergola built of larch, 200 yards long, nine feet high and equally wide.[102] It was covered with assorted climbing plants, while at its base was a margin of stones planted with alpine plants.[103] The Kitchen Garden had an archway 50 yards long, on which were grown blackberries, loganberries and wineberries: 'the growth is so free that they meet in the middle, the fruit hanging down in huge clusters'.[104] Fruit trees included apples, pears and figs, while plum trees were grown in pots; exotics, including *Gloriosa Superba* and *Ixora Westii*, were grown in the plant stove.[105]

In the Reading Horticultural Show, held on 24 August 1904, Taylor was judged to have the best four specimen stove and greenhouse plants. He was ranked first in the Open Division with 'four exotic Ferns having fine examples of *Davallias fijiensis* [*Davallia fejeensis*] and polyantha, *Adiantum cardiochlaena* and *Woodwardia radicans*'.[106] In the Palm House 600 Chrysanthemums were cultivated for exhibition.[107] In the Winchester Chrysanthemum exhibition, held in the Guildhall on 15 and 16 November 1904, in the Cut Bloom category, first prize went to Mr G Hall, gardener to Lady Ashburton at Melchet Court, but Mr J Wasley, Taylor's gardener at Sherfield, was a close second.[108]

The lake was an important feature of the gardens. It had rocks around its margins, and in 1901 Wasley created a rockery connected to it with waterfalls made of Derbyshire stone. It was planted with evergreens, bamboos and ferns, as well as cistus and campanulas.[109] Planting around the lake included tritomas, which produced flowers 6 feet high, and *Arundo Conspicua*.[110]

Tylney Hall, near Rotherwick, has also been converted into a hotel. The original house was built in 1878 for Charles E Harris to designs by Edward Birchall. Harris had purchased land to create the estate from the 1870s, which was acquired in 1899 by Sir Lionel Phillips, the South African gold and diamond millionaire.[111] The house was then almost entirely rebuilt for him by RS Wornum between 1899 and 1902.[112] It is Jacobethan in style, of red brick with Bath stone dressings, and has projecting wings enclosing the forecourt. The porch, interiors and garden works were carried out by Robert Weir Schultz in 1901-5.[113]

The 1905 *Gardeners' Chronicle* states that Harris had planted most of the trees which were then in the grounds, but because many had been cut down a century before, 'there is now a scarcity of desirable trees in the park and elsewhere'.[114] By 1905 the long straight carriage drives had been 'altered to suit the more modern styles of arrangement'.[115] One led to the village of Rotherwick, about a mile to the north, and was flanked by an avenue of limes, planted by Harris. The other drive led to Hook station and in 1905 was 'recently' planted with chestnuts by Phillips.[116] There are lodges designed by Wornum on each of these drives where they enter the park.[117] The writer continues:

> On the western side there is a delightful grass glade some 40 yards wide, well furnished with *Sequoia gigantea* [Wellingtonia] and *Pseudotsuga Douglasi* [Douglas Fir], 40 feet high; *Abies grandis*, 60 feet; *Cedrus atlantica*, *Cupressus nootkatensis*, &c. These are growing grandly, and will soon require more space.[118]

This avenue is aligned on the west front of the house and frames a view across the park from the small terrace beneath the loggia.

Roses were an important feature of the gardens and a hedge 200 yards long on either side of the carriage drive was composed entirely of climbing varieties such as euphrosyne and crimson rambler.[119] To the west of the house was a large circular garden enclosed by a yew hedge, which survives. This was a rose garden containing 'hybrid perpetuals with Crimson Rambler trailing over the central arches'.[120] Most Victorian rosaries, like this one, were planted well away from the main house, so as not to interfere with the views.[121]

The spectacular formal gardens laid out behind the house descend in a series of terraces. On the upper balustraded terrace (*61*) is a delicate Ionic loggia with a polygonal stone stair tower, latticework and flower carving, 'a

61 The garden terrace at Tylney Hall has an Ionic loggia, derived from Loire châteaux, which was added to the existing Jacobethan-style house by Robert Weir Schultz; climbing plants that still flourish on the walls of the house were introduced by Gertrude Jekyll

miniature piece of Blois or Chambord', added by Schultz to give access to the internal gallery.[122] The planting on the upper terrace was by Gertrude Jekyll and included a yellow Banksian Rose 'luxuriating on the walls of the house'.[123] Bay trees clipped into pyramids and grand specimen plants of *Hydrangea Hortensia* were 'employed with good effect in suitable positions outside the dwelling-house'.[124] Below the terrace is the Italian Garden (*colour 35*), designed by Wornum. It is enclosed with a balustraded wall bristling with obelisks, and which has a pair of attractive ogee-roofed Summerhouses at its outer corners, based on the Jacobean banqueting houses at Montacute in Somerset. From these there are steps to the lawn below, which slopes steeply down to a pair of lakes. There was a boathouse on the northern side of the upper lake, of which only the base survives.[125] The lower lawn was bordered with trees beneath which rhododendrons and bamboo were planted, while bulbs, including narcissus, sternbergias, colchicums and anemones, were naturalised under the trees and in the grass.[126] A winding woodland path was made beneath the trees, planted with iris, cotoneaster, bamboos, kniphofias and *Anemone japonica*. Wornum also designed a sunken Dutch Garden, between the house and the Kitchen Garden, which is entered through a beautiful pair of floral-designed wrought iron gates by Schultz.[127] This garden now has a swimming pool, inserted by Lord Rotherwick in 1935.[128]

In the walled Kitchen Garden to the southwest of the house, designed by Wornum as an integral part of the garden scheme, is an Orangery, which is a modern reconstruction of the original designed by Schultz.[129] Some of the associated garden buildings including the gardener's house, bothy, potting shed, apple store, grape store and mushroom house survive.[130] Vine houses against the walls contained varieties such as Muscat of Alexandria, Black Hamburgh and Gros Colman, with one house devoted to each variety.[131] Peach Houses on the south and west walls contained trees which were 'remarkably healthy and carry full crops of promising fruits'.[132] Melons were successfully cultivated in houses, while apple and pear trees in pots were a feature, and the plant houses also grew flowers for decorating the house, such as begonias, carnations and 1,500 chrysanthemums.[133] In a further walled garden is a large Water Tower with a polygonal stair turret on the side, designed by Schultz.[134] To the south of the Kitchen Garden is the Water Garden, which has two ponds linked by a series of pools running through rock-work (colour 36). This garden was created from the canal that formed part of the eighteenth-century formal layout.[135] It was made by Schultz around 1906, with planting by Jekyll, and partly re-worked by William Wood of Taplow in 1935-6.[136] It is overlooked at the southern end by an attractive octagonal covered seat with a bell-shaped roof and rustic wooden columns.

Although the fire in 1981 destroyed the larger part of the house at **Dogmersfield Park**, yet another Hampshire hotel, an account in the *Gardeners' Chronicle* of 1883 sheds light on the gardens in the Victorian period, which

> for sixteen years past...have been thrown open to the public on three successive Mondays in August and September, and this act of kindness on the part of Sir Henry St. John Mildmay, Bart., is greatly appreciated by the residents of Odiham, Winchfield and district, who go there in large numbers, and who annually find something fresh and attractive to admire.[137]

Mildmay, who liked fashionable carpet bedding, had entirely remodelled the formal gardens.[138] In 1883 the gardens were managed by Mr W Fowle, and were famous for his apples and pears, which were grown both on the walls and as pyramid trees, and for which he won many prizes in London shows.[139] Although brief mention is made of the wider landscape, where there were 'fine specimens of trees and shrubs in the pinetum',[140] the focus was on the planting in the areas close to the house:

> In the conservatory there are some beautiful specimens of various-coloured

Begonias, Palms, Tree Ferns, Liliums, &c. The fernery, adjoining the conservatory, is a new feature, having been extended and remodelled; the Ferns are planted out in bark-covered borders, one above the other, to the top of the house, and the plants appear to be so much at home as to form one dense luxuriant bank.[141]

Ivy-leaved pelargoniums were also grown in the Conservatory, and were 'much used in hanging baskets'.[142] The Conservatory was in the principal walled garden, entered through the 'Golden Gates', which were ornate wrought iron gates edged with trailing leaves. This garden was not immediately next to the house, but was reached by a walk through the Orange Court, in which large orange trees and palms were set out during the summer.[143] The Flower Garden, which still survives as a walled garden to the east of the house, had a central path, known as the Broad Walk, with beds of various designs cut in the grass on either side. There were four raised beds, planted with fuchsias surrounded with ivy-leaved pelargoniums, while eight circular beds were filled with 'large clumps of the scarlet *Lobelia fulgens*'.[144] Rectangular carpet beds were edged with *Herniaria glabra* and planted with *Alternanthera* and *Mesembryanthemum cordifolium variegatum*.[145] The walls of the garden were covered with tea roses and 'masses of *Magnolia grandiflora*'. The plants chosen for the summer beds in the Flower Garden were 'only those which make a bright and striking display of colour', while the less showy plants were relegated to the Kitchen Garden.[146] Intersecting the central path was the Long Walk, running across the garden and terminating in the Garden House (*62*), a small building with a double-arched loggia and broken pediment recessed into the garden wall. This path was flanked with wide, double herbaceous borders planted with *Herniaria glabra* as ground cover, dotted with brightly coloured fuchsias, begonias and zinnias, backed by a yew hedge.[147]

The Kitchen Garden, less showy than the Flower Garden, was considered somewhat more dated, with 'its borders fringed with the deep lines of the old-fashioned herbaceous plants', and, as in the Fruit Garden, 'the walks are run under the purple masses of clematis on arches'.[148] Here there was 'an old-fashioned corner' with a rustic seat on an old apple tree, described in 1901 as overlooking 'nothing but the sweet-smelling herbs and Elizabethan flowers of the Tudor days'.[149] This Kitchen Garden was closed off from the Flower Garden by a high holly hedge, which was 'a special feature of the Dogmersfield gardens'.[150]

C H Holloway, the Head Gardener at Dogmersfield, kept a gardening diary of his time there between 1884 and 1885.[151] In November and December, he records getting strawberries into frames, putting in chrysanthemum cuttings and getting the hyacinths into the stove for the winter, as well as composting peach trees and getting some tea roses into the Early Vinery. Holloway also

62 The Garden House at Dogmersfield Park, where an arched loggia set in the wall of the Flower Garden, offered views out across formal gardens, its central path flanked by double herbaceous borders

had responsibility for the house plants, and mentions bringing plants into the house for a shooting party, and 'Doing the Dinner Table', 'doing a vase with flowers for the Breakfast Table' and 'taking plants to the Dining Room for the Ball'.[152] In April he was busy potting lobelia, fuchsia and coleus cuttings, putting strawberries in the Vinery to ripen, and shifting geraniums from the Vinery into frames.[153] Although he recorded a Feast on Christmas Day 1884, on Boxing Day he was back at work putting stakes into the Vinery.[154] Holloway was clearly a good gardener, as his chrysanthemums won first prize in the Winchester Horticultural Society Exhibition in 1893, and his flowers won first prize at the Portsmouth Floricultural Society in the same year.[155]

Rhinefield House, close to Brockenhurst in the heart of the New Forest, is also a hotel. The entrance is from Rhinefield Road, past a small brick lodge, the drive flanked by an avenue of trees that was planted in the 1890s. The house was built in Elizabethan style with Gothic features between 1888 and 1890 for Lionel Walker Munro.[156] It was designed by William Henry Romaine-Walker and Augustus William Tanner to reflect the status of Miss Mabel Walker, who had married Munro. She was heiress to a considerable coal-mining fortune, and was reputed to be one of the wealthiest women in England.[157] Romaine-Walker and Tanner also laid out formal gardens to the

63　This pool at Rhinefield is a survivor of the elaborate Victorian gardens, which were laid out around the house in the 1890s

south of the house. However, there had already been much development of the wider landscape at Rhinefield. In 1856, 10,000 acres of the New Forest were enclosed, and a nursery was formed under the charge of the Forest nurseryman, JE Nelson. By 1859 it was his home, and he set out an arboretum and Ornamental Drive in the late 1850s.[158] Rhinefield Ornamental Drive is now separate and managed by the Forestry Commission. The Drive, which is a narrow road running north from the Lodge, is flanked by tall Douglas fir trees, as well as common silver fir, Lawson cypress and Sitka spruce. It also has some of England's tallest Wellingtonias, one measuring 50 metres in 2003,[159] and is lined with a mixture of rhododendrons and azaleas. Within the grounds of the hotel there is a Douglas fir avenue that has many huge conifers. In the lower avenue is a western red cedar, which measured 42 metres in 2006.[160]

The Walker-Munro family sold the house in 1951, and the gardens subsequently declined to a point in the 1980s where only earthworks, pools (63) and some planting remained.[161] The house was converted into a hotel after 1982 and the gardens were restored between 1986 and 1990, using historic photographs, together with aerial and archaeological surveys.[162] Kim Wilkie introduced a modern design into the gardens, using a chequer-pattern of stone blocks and lavender.[163] A sculpture made from a Douglas fir by Simon Thomas commemorates the centenary of the gardens and their restoration. To the west of the gardens is a grass amphitheatre, also added in the late 1980s.[164] The centrepiece of the gardens is a long Canal (*colour 37*), part of the original 1890s design, which has a fountain at its centre. The Canal runs from the house southwards, terminating in a pair of wrought iron gates which were moved here from the Kitchen Garden and offer views out over the New Forest. On either side of the Canal are yew-hedged enclosures, which were restored to their original designs in the late 1980s.[165]

8

'Life has many shadows but the sunshine makes them all' – The Edwardians

Avon Tyrrell, High Coxlease, Berrydown Court, New Place, Marsh Court
Amport House, Townhill Park, Weir's Barn, Macartneys, Compton End
Little Boarhunt, Hailie, Ashford Chace, Hinton Admiral
Walhampton House, Moundsmere Manor, Melchet Court
Winchester College War Cloister

While the record of Victorian gardens in Hampshire is poor, with many of the layouts having disappeared or represented only by stony fragments, the county is particularly rich in surviving Edwardian gardens, many of which were designed by the real heavyweights of the age. Due to its geographical proximity to her home county, Surrey, there are several planting schemes by Gertrude Jekyll, two combined with hard landscaping by Edwin Lutyens, at Marsh Court and Amport Park; a rare layout at Avon Tyrrell by the writer on architectural aesthetics and symbolism, William Lethaby; designs by the architect and prolific garden writer, Harry Inigo Triggs; a matchless remodelling at Hinton Admiral House by Harold Ainsworth Peto; Leonard Rome Guthrie's loggia-flanked enclosure at Townhill Park, which has undergone a brilliant restoration; modest houses and gardens designed especially for themselves by Mervyn Macartney, George Herbert Kitchin, Robert Weir Schultz and Triggs; and a stony sunken enclosure by Sir Reginald Blomfield, promoter of the architectural garden, at Moundsmere Manor. This vibrant flourishing of the Arts and Crafts style in all its architectural guises climaxes with the coming of peace after the First World War in a classical memorial cloister at Winchester College designed by Sir Herbert Baker, which is perhaps the most numinous and heart-wrenching garden space in the entire county.

If anyone came close in the period to defining the essential character of the Art and Crafts garden it is probably Lawrence Weaver, architectural editor of *Country Life*, who, together with Gertrude Jekyll, published a seminal study on the subject just before the outbreak of war in 1913. The opening sentences can be taken for an Arts and Crafts garden manifesto:

It is upon the right relation of the garden to the house that its value and the enjoyment that is to be derived from it will largely depend. The connection must be intimate, and the access not only convenient but inviting.[1]

Interestingly, there is no mention of architectural style, merely a fitness of the hard landscaping and the planting regimes for the terrain and the parent house. Weaver advocates that the house be built on a slight platform, that there should be 'one wide easy terrace on the sunny side', and for structure 'our noble English yew is nearly always beneficial in the garden landscape...no tree is more satisfactory for emphasising important points'.[2] Add to these a spacious lawn punctuated with a sundial, herbaceous borders, a pergola, perhaps a small loggia 'notched into the house itself', or a summerhouse, a pool or water tank, a rose garden and tennis lawn, and, for productivity, a kitchen garden and an orchard, and all the necessary ingredients of a small country house garden would be included.[3]

The real value of the book for prospective owners and designers is the wealth of plans and illustrations of architectural details (*64*). As the writers of *Gardens for Small Country Houses* freely admit: 'we have been glad to avail ourselves of several sketches for pools, walls and the like, which Mr. Inigo Triggs has kindly placed at our disposal'.[4] It may be that this favour was returned by their detailed focus on a Hampshire garden designed by Triggs: Little Boarhunt at Liphook. Little Boarhunt will be retained for a later digression on architects' own houses and gardens, while this overview must begin chronologically with a rare house and garden by an architect of mystic pretensions, who designed very little, but who was, nevertheless, an important influence on the development of the Arts and Crafts aesthetic.

William Richard Lethaby was brought up by Bible Christian parents in Barnstaple and began his architectural career articled to a local practice in 1871. For the next eight years he was successively articled to architects in Devon, Derbyshire and Leicester, before winning the Soane Medallion and Travelling Scholarship in 1879. With the prize money he went to France to sketch thirty cathedrals, the drawings for which appeared in *Building News* and were spotted by Richard Norman Shaw, who engaged him in the same year as chief assistant in his London office.[5] At this time, Shaw's assistants would meet regularly to discuss art and architecture, calling themselves the St George's Art Society, out of which grew the Art Workers' Guild. Lethaby became immersed in this intellectual community and was a founder Guild member and Master in 1911. After ten years with Shaw, he set up practice on his own, joining Reginald Blomfield, Mervyn Macartney, Ernest Gimson and Sidney Barnsley in the founding of Kenton & Company, with the intention of making furniture. He supplemented his architectural work by designing pottery, woodwork, leadwork and embroidery for manufacturers. In this he was a true Arts and Crafts

64 A design for a summerhouse and pergola by Harry Inigo Triggs, intended to direct prospective garden owners, from Jekyll and Weaver's 1913 *Gardens for Small Country Houses*

practitioner, designing holistically from first principles with great simplicity in the manner of his hero Philip Webb, and in an attempt to further the aims and ideals of John Ruskin and William Morris. Of Webb he wrote:

> The happy chance of close intimacy with Philip Webb at last satisfied my mind about that   mysterious thing we call 'Architecture'. From him I learnt that what I was going to mean by 'Architecture' was not mere designs, forms and grandeurs, but buildings, honest and human, with hearts in them'.[6]

To this overarching precept of simplicity and honesty to materials, Lethaby added symbolism, but not symbols of the arcane and opaque variety. Quoting César-Denis Daly, the French architectural editor and journalist, he asserted: 'if we would have architecture excite an interest, real and general, we must have a symbolism, immediately comprehensible by the great majority of spectators'.[7] Lethaby developed these ideas in a seminal book, *Architecture, Mysticism and Myth*, which looked for a new architecture to express the spirit of the age: 'What then, will this art of the future be? The message will still be of nature and man, of order and beauty, but all will be sweetness, simplicity, freedom, confidence, and light'.[8] These abiding tenets suffuse his work and make it instantly recognisable.

They are nowhere more apparent than in the entrance forecourt to **Avon Tyrrell**, the house he designed for Lord Manners in 1891, the same year in which his book was published.9 The walled enclosure is punctuated by a gateway which displays the Manners coat of arms, but whose gable apex is topped by a bouquet of flowers (*65*). The garden theme is continued on the roofline of the entrance front, where two stone peacocks, ubiquitous exotics in the gardens of the Edwardian period, face each other on either side of the central chimneystacks. On the garden front there is a wide terrace, as Weaver advocated, with a Garden House at one end and a Sunken Garden at the other. The Garden House (*66*) has a round-arched arcade with celestial images, suggesting prosaically its versatility for all times of day and night, but perhaps more symbolically for Lethaby of the earth within the universe, 'a chamber lighted by the sun, moon, and stars'.10 The terrace is bordered by a robust balustrade set with circular stone planters decorated with rope moulding (*colour 38*), while the Sunken Garden has bulbous scrolls to the steps and more stone planters filled with bay trees. In 1910 there were 'well-grown orange trees' in 'good square tubs', on the terrace and 'on the lower levels' a rose garden and tennis lawn and rock garden'.11 The Sunken Garden was originally laid out with a chequerboard of square beds mirroring the flint flushwork on one of the chimneybreasts of the house, each bed centred by standard roses.12 It is simple landscape architecture, but combines effectively with the assured free vernacular style of the main house.

Much less of Lethaby's layout survives at **High Coxlease**, near Lyndhurst in the New Forest, designed for Thomas Eustace Smith, heir to a Tyneside shipping empire, yet the 1901 house betrays a similar obsession with symbols. The garden front is patterned with brickwork crenellations and zig-zags, and the two gabled wings carry carvings of the sun and a five-pointed star. The terrace is now mostly laid to lawn, though there are patches of incised brickwork under the walls of the house, while the rock and water garden beyond the terrace wall, photographed for Jekyll and Weaver's book, has disappeared.13

With the work of Edwin Lutyens, particularly when he was designing in concert with Gertrude Jekyll, there is more documentation and there are many more contemporary images. This is due, in part, to Edward Hudson's influence on the architect's career – many of Lutyens's early Surrey vernacular style houses and gardens were featured in *Country Life* – and Lawrence Weaver's *Houses and Gardens by E. L. Lutyens*, which came out in 1913. Oddly, however, his earliest house in Hampshire is not well documented and there are no surviving garden plans, so it is a matter of conjecture as to what was intended in the grounds. What is beyond doubt is that **Berrydown Court** is one of Lutyens's most assured vernacular houses, with a stunning range of white-harled subsidiary buildings and a vast walled garden close to the house. A succession

65 William Lethaby's garden symbolism at Avon Tyrrell is expressed on the entrance gateway by a be-ribboned bouquet of flowers

66 Lethaby's 1891 Garden House at Avon Tyrrell has symbols of the sun, moon and stars expressing its practical function for all times of day and night

of owners, beginning with the financier Archibald Grove, who commissioned the house in 1897, have made alterations to both the house and the gardens. The house was extended in 1926, and from 1976 until 2001 the Tholstrup family owned Berrydown; they changed the garden layout to accommodate a swimming pool. In 2008 the house was sold to the present owner, who has undertaken a most sensitive and scholarly restoration, while adding a series of important artworks to the grounds.

The approach to the house from the gatehouse to the entrance forecourt emphasises the rectilinearity of the area and mirrors the series of terraces and yew-enclosed garden rooms to the rear. Double avenues of blockish pleached limes set in square planting beds march towards harled and tile-topped containing walls, which guard a building that looks more like a semi-fortified French *manoir* of the Perche rather than a Hampshire country house. Figs climb the retaining walls, while simple planting along the skirts of the façade gives a welcome softening to the slightly forbidding exterior. This is a Janus house, for the architectural register changes completely on the garden front to cosy Surrey vernacular. Here huge tile-hung gables sweep down to a lattice of mullioned windows, which overlook an expansive lawn and the descending terraces (67). These are yew-bordered and create a series of green rooms set parallel to the mature planting of the wider woodland. The trees, rhododendrons and azaleas in this area may be due to William Robinson, who in August 1899 was called in to rescue the planning of the garden, 'which seems to have gone awry'.[14] Grove sold the house in 1900, so it is likely that 'the 19th solution' for the grounds was tried and failed.[15] Thereafter, as well as the introduction of the swimming pool in place of a sunken enclosure, a Norah Lindsay-style garden, designed by Mary Keen and Pip Morrison, has been planted along the south terrace. The drifts of soft blues and greys make a perfect counterpoint to Lutyens's green angularity.

The creative partnership between Lutyens and Jekyll is easier to grasp at **New Place**, Shedfield, Lutyens's stripped-down, angular Jacobean-style house, which was built after 1906 expressly to take the rescued interiors from John Langton's 1623 mansion that had commanded the quayside on Welsh Back in Bristol.[16] Weaver included it in his 1913 book on the architect, just after the house was complete, but when the gardens were still bare, apart from brick retaining walls, stone steps and narrow stone paths.[17] The borders were all cut and waiting for planting, their edges defined by young sprigs of yew. Correspondence between Lutyens and Jekyll, who by this time was directing her designs via letter rather than on-site visits, survives to record the proposals.[18] However, as at Berrydown, much of what was planned was never executed and the gardens around the house have been altered, so the correspondence between the two is a vital resource in retrieving the initial proposal. Essentially, Lutyens proposed a broad terrace on the garden front, terminated

47 The south front of Reginald Blomfield's greatest country house, Moundsmere Manor, is based on Wren's façade at Hampton Court. Blomfield's formal gardens accord perfectly with the 'Wrenaissance' character of the house

48 Blomfield designed all the ancillary buildings for Moundsmere, including this combined Gardener's House and Glasshouse, which commands the Walled Garden

49 Thomas Darcy Braddell's 1914 Pavilion in the Dutch Garden at Melchet Court was
   once flanked by stone columns with obelisk finials, long since gone. At the other
   end of the Canal is a Lutyens-style arched bridge with a waterspout

50 Sir Herbert Baker's War Cloister at Winchester College, dedicated in 1924, commemorates in
   one united shrine 500 Old Wykehamists who fell in the Great War

51 A cascading wisteria over the Pergola in the renamed Sundial Garden at Exbury

52 The Long Walk at Hinton Ampner House is another original Victorian feature adapted and given a neo-Georgian feel by the eighteenth-century enthusiast Ralph Dutton

53 The Nymphaeum at West Green House was designed by Quinlan Terry in the 1970s for Lord MacAlpine, as part of their Philosophical Garden

54 The Wallingers' Rose Garden at the Manor House in Upton Grey is a faithful recreation of a Gertrude Jekyll design

55 Kim Wilkie's arcing green amphitheatre glimpsed from the forecourt of the late-seventeenth-century house at The Holt; green angularity in perfect harmony with the ordered classical façade

56 Wilkie's retrieval of a mediaeval landscape in a criss-cross of water channels at Shawford, seen from the air. *By kind permission of Kim Wilkie*

57 Curving beds of mixed perennial planting, cambered paths and sharp-edged lawns make Piet Oudolf's design at Bury Court one of the great contemporary gardens of Hampshire

58 From working farmyard to a sylvan setting for weddings and opera at Piet Oudolf and John Coke's Bury Court

59 Robert Adam's Millennium Pavilion at Preston Candover
combines eighteenth-century garden traditions with modern
technology to produce a structure of great presence and beauty
for the Hampshire landscape. ©*ADAM Architecture*

67 Edwin Lutyens's sequence of yew-enclosed terraces creates intimate garden rooms at
Berrydown Court

at either end by summerhouses, with steps down to a *patte d'oie* of avenues
flanked by formal gardens giving on to 'big herbaceous borders – grass paths
right and left – fruit trees – gooseberries – [a] sort of fruit garden gradually into
wild and away'.[19] It is not clear how all this would have worked, and there is
little surviving on site today, apart from the terrace walls and two stone-flagged
areas in the lower sector of the grounds, to show their joint intentions.

This is not the case at **Marsh Court**, set on a spectacular site overlooking
the Test Valley on the edge of Stockbridge. This white clunch and black flint
flushwork house with its sweeping clay tile roofs, soaring brick chimneys and
battery of mullioned windows shows, as Weaver wrote in 1913, 'the art of Mr.
Lutyens in its gayest mood'.[20] It is one of Lutyens's greatest designs, the 'last
and most important of the houses...[he] deliberately built in the Tudor
manner',[21] wrapped around with gardens of brilliant invention, which are
undergoing a most informed and sensitive repair and restoration.

Marsh Court was built between 1901 and 1904 for Herbert Johnson. The
grounds are the epitome of the architectural garden, signalled as the visitor
approaches along a deep-delved entrance drive to arrive at a balustraded
entrance court accessed via a bridge across a dry, green moat. The service court
wall to the left has Portland stone gate piers with obelisk finials and walls with
deep-set circular niches, while to the right are more piers and semicircular
steps that cascade down to a long southwest terrace – the Long Walk –

68 Lutyens in joyful mood as his stone steps, a symmetry of semicircles and circles, curve down to the Long Walk, which skirts the chalk-walled west elevation of Marsh Court, its pavement patterned with herringbone tiles

running parallel to the west wing (*68*). The edges of its borders were originally planted with the large-leaved saxifrage, *Megasea cordifolia*, and the beds with 'rectangular and equidistant clumps of peony', which formed 'buttress-like divisions of the border'.[22] The Long Walk leads, at the southwest corner of the house, to the Pool Garden, 'sunk in a setting of steps, and surrounded by a balustraded wall...a rich retreat in architectural fancy'.[23] Local materials proliferate here – principally herringbone-laid brick tiles and flint chequer work – while the space is enlivened by lead cisterns, from which water is fed down to the central pool, and spouting seahorse finials rising out of cubes of clipped box (*69*). In the early twentieth century it was planted up with China roses and lavender-cotton, while against the walls climbed figs, vines and clematis.[24] Steps up from the Pool Garden give onto a Pergola of tiled piers supporting massive oak beams, which extends across the south retaining wall of the garden lawn. This is an ingenious feature which doubles as a rose arbour and another water garden decorated with robust architectural niches and more flushwork (*colour 39*), while the Piazza Lawn above has an obligatory sundial, its stone pedestal inlaid with lead to reflect the chequer theme. A further pergola, vine-clad and decorated with circular niches, strides along the south wall of the ballroom, which was added in 1926.

There are no planting plans for Marsh Court, but Gertrude Jekyll's planting schemes for the Manor House at Upton Grey, a 1908-09 commission for

69 Lutyens's water-filled Pool Garden at Marsh Court, where lead cisterns conduct water down to the central tank, which is sprayed by seahorse finials rising out of box cubes. *Neil Simpson*

Charles Holme the editor of *The Studio*, survive in the Reef Point Collection in California and have driven a remarkable restoration by Rosamund and John Wallinger. As such, their achievement will be reserved for the last chapter of this book in a section on twentieth-century historic recreations in the county. Jekyll was also responsible for the 1925 plan for the walled kitchen garden at Hursley Park, with its blue and mauve borders, but it is unclear if this was ever carried out.[25] She may also have provided planting schemes for the Sunken Garden, which survives at Hursley, though altered. It is certain, however, that she produced designs for another of Lutyens's layouts at Amport House, near Andover, for her planting plans for the two water terraces survive. These have been reproduced and discussed in some detail by Jane Brown.[26]

Amport House was built in a bleak Jacobethan style in 1857 to designs by William Burn, and bought in 1922 by Colonel Sofer-Whitburn, who commissioned Lutyens to remodel the gardens and Jekyll to supply the planting. Prior to their arrival the top terrace to the northwest of the house was given a box parterre garden, which was laid out between 1896 and 1909, when it was photographed for a *Country Life* article, to represent the Winchester coats of arms around a central pool.[27] This enclosure has survived with its crowns, spirals and domes of topiary. The extraordinary U-shaped avenue of limes in the field beyond was planted after Lutyens and Jekyll had left, as it does not appear on Ordnance Survey maps until the mid twentieth century.

The partnership's work was centred on the two terraces below the south front of the house where Lutyens laid out water gardens, which accord well with Burn's house in that they appear more Victorian in feel than twentieth-century (*colour 40*). Indeed, they bear little resemblance to any of Lutyens's other water gardens, like that at Hestercombe, which are far more inventive. Perhaps the twin garden houses, planned for the ha-ha but never built, would have given the layout the architectural containment it lacks. However, water is fed ingeniously through each pool via iris rills and thence to the lower terrace before it is collected for recirculation. The pool on the top terrace has a double rim to accommodate another iris rill, while the whole layout is punc-tuated by geometrically clipped yews and rectangular beds planted originally by Jekyll with roses from the famous rose breeders, Dickson's of Newtow-nards, County Down. The roses came from their 1927 catalogue and reflect the blush and salmon shades of hybrid teas they were developing at the time.[28] Jekyll also designed a raised-bed rock garden at the east end of the lower terrace, containing lavender, hyssop, santolina, iberis, nepetas, rock pinks, ferns, sedums and yuccas. This has been replaced by a part-sunken square of drystone walls planted with shrubs and herbaceous plants.

Jekyll's most significant Hampshire design was surely that for **Townhill Park** on the outskirts of Southampton. After a period of severe neglect the gardens have been restored by the Friends of Townhill Park House Gardens with the co-operation and support of the Gregg School, which owns the site. The Hampshire Gardens Trust, which initiated the formation of the Friends Group, has given generous grants and valued advice towards the ongoing restoration.[29]

In 1910 the then owner, Lord Swaythling, commissioned Leonard Rome Guthrie to remodel the existing house on the site; the work was completed after the hiatus of war in 1922.[30] *Country Life* visited in 1923 and photographed the house and its gardens, particularly those on the west commanded by a colonnade along the length of the façade. These are a series of formal terraces leading to a Sunken Garden, which is bordered on three sides by pergolas and centred by a circular pool. Beyond this, on a lower level, there is a Herb Garden, the planting for which was also drawn up by Jekyll. By the 1980s much of the layout was in decay and the Pergola was in ruins, but after its listing in 1989 and the formation of the Friends, restoration began (*70*). Wide Jekyll-inspired herbaceous borders backed by crisply cut yew hedges lead the eye down to the Sunken Garden (*colour 41*), its Pergola and Summerhouse restored, the brick paving re-laid and its beds planted up busily with ornamental grasses in and amongst coreopsis, penstemon, santolina and lavenders. Lady Swaythling's Seat has been repaired and is ready again for a contemplative visitor

70 One arm of the great Pergola at Leonard Rome Guthrie's Townhill Park, completed in 1922 as a frame for planting by Gertrude Jekyll in the sunken area it encloses

(*colour 42*). Steps lead down from the Summerhouse into the Herb Garden, where the mood changes to one of tranquility, with more open paving and less dense planting. Perhaps a new benefactor might commission a new Italian wellhead for the circular lawn here, like that shown in 1923 photographs. Unlike the Wallingers' intensely scholarly recreation of Jekyll's original planting schemes at Upton Grey, the informed volunteers at Townhill, especially Rosaleen Wilkinson and Janet and David Harley, have re-planted using Jekyll's plans but adapting them when they saw fit to do so. The restoration is nothing short of a triumph and should be much better known.

As David Ottewill has remarked, 'for those who believed in the Arts and Crafts Movement it was almost a religious duty to design the whole environment in which they lived'.[31] At the same time that Lutyens was laying out the stony enclosures at Marsh Court, Robert Weir Schultz was devising his own grounds and house around existing barns at Phoenix Green, Hartley Wintney. His friend Ernest Newton had already built a cottage for himself at Hazeley Heath, though Shultz probably got to know this part of north Hampshire through Dr WS Playfair, for whom he laid out a small formal garden at West Green House.[32] At **Weir's Barn** Schultz converted one of the existing sixteenth-century barns into a house and laid out a sunken flower garden to the rear. Two dramatic topiary peacocks frame the entrance gateway (71), which gives on to a densely planted front garden with a pergola. Over the door there is

71 Sentinel peacocks, a ubiquitous feature of most Art and Crafts topiary, guard the front gate of Robert Weir Schultz's Barn at Hartley Wintney

a leadwork plaque with the motto: '*Parva Domus Magna Quies*' (Small House Great Peace), Schultz's initials and the date, 1901. The garden is now busy with clipped box shapes and centred by an urn (*colour 43*), but Schultz's diamond-patterned brick planters for alpines are still in place on the raised borders. These were backed by the topiary and standard roses, while beyond there were climbers – flowering quince, roses and honeysuckle – trained against diagonal trellises.[33] At the heart of the lawn was a sundial of 1906 supported by a lead 'putto', which was inscribed: 'Life has many shadows but the sunshine makes them all', reflecting the theme of Schultz's bookplate, 'Shadows Pass', designed by his friend Lethaby.[34] Beyond the Sunken Garden is a bowling alley underneath one of the outbuildings, which gives on to a vast lawn, originally used for croquet.

In 1895 Mervyn Macartney, another ex-pupil of Richard Norman Shaw, founder member of the Art Workers' Guild and a leading authority of the English Renaissance revival, bought a pair of fire-damaged cottages on a plot of land at Silchester Common, demolished them and built a country cottage for himself and his family. The house, **Macartneys**, which was originally called Rosebank, 'a home for the week-ends and the holiday month', is a simple vernacular brick building with black weatherboarding and mullioned, leaded lights.[35] To the front there is a sunken lawn, originally a bowling green, and a small circular pool. A long, yew-bordered path runs axially from the front gate

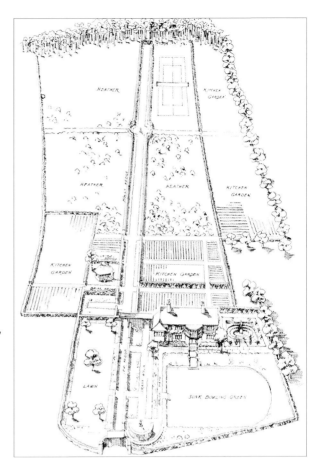

72 Mervyn Macartney's
gardens at his weekend
holiday cottage, Rosebank,
feature productive areas
and enclosures for leisure

to the woodland at the back, out of which Macartney carved a series of garden
compartments (72). The last sector of the grounds, where there was a tennis
court and an extension to the kitchen garden, has now been sold off, but there
is enough of Macartney's layout surviving to appreciate his design. His reten-
tion of a small bothy in the plan reflects the charmingly homespun nature of
the place, which cost a mere £760.[36]

George Herbert Kitchin effected much the same at **Compton End**, near
Shawford, with what his close friend Henry Avray Tipping would later
describe as 'A Quarter-Acre Example' in his 1933 book, *The Garden of To-Day*.
Kitchin bought the run-down farm cottage, originally surrounded by barns, in
1894 and set about transforming the garden. He worked up to the outbreak of
war in 1914 and continued to live in the house until his death in 1951. Tipping
captures perfectly the extent and rustic charm of the place:

The lawn and border should not be the final features of the layout, for even in
a small garden it is a restriction not to be able to pass from formal to wild, not

to have a suggestion of woodland, and how the latter can be included even where the Garden of Pleasure is to occupy no more than a quarter of an acre is well exemplified in the garden laid out for his own enjoyment around an old thatched cottage near Winchester by Mr. G.H. Kitchin, F. R. I. B. A...From a garden room added to the south end of the cottage we step out along a path formally edged with borders but ending with rough segmental steps taking you down into a slight hollow, shady and tree set, its banks and broken ground spangled with many a modest flower, growing as it were wild in this miniature natural valley which succeeds in giving you some feeling of reclusiveness despite its measuring only about 10 yards in width and 30 in length.[37]

As we have seen in the Introduction to this book, Tipping included a plan of the layout in his 1933 book (2), which he had originally reproduced in his 1925 *English Gardens* accompanying an article on the house and grounds. This conveys precisely the busyness of Kitchin's garden, its separate rooms (73) and the way in which the cottage connects with the spaces, especially via the Garden Room on the southwest which links with the formal parterre. From here much of the gardens can be viewed, except the Wild Garden which is in a declivity below the retaining wall, the vista reaching as far as the Garden House, a later addition to the grounds of 1926. Writing in 1919, Kitchin explained the accretive nature of the garden spaces he had created and described how the surrounding beds of the square lily pond were planted 'chiefly with bush roses and scarlet phlox, with tall tulips for the earlier show', while the formal garden by the Garden Room was originally a brick-paved, bedding-out garden, with box and saxifrage-edged beds.[38] Much of the layout that Tipping and Kitchin described survives and is being thoughtfully restored by the present owner.

The same attention to scholarly detail has underpinned the restoration of another owner-architect house and grounds, where an existing house was again refurbished and extended and then given an appropriate garden. In 1910 Harry Inigo Triggs, illustrator of Jekyll and Weaver's *Gardens for Small Country Houses*, bought an eighteenth-century farmhouse on the outskirts of Liphook, built a timber-framed gatehouse from cottages on the approach, excavated the farmyard to the rear of the house to produce a sunken garden and renamed the house **Little Boarhunt**. The retaining walls of the enclosure were studded with saxifrages, pinks and veronica, while in the centre of the geometrically-planned rose beds, set into lawn, a canal-like rill was dramatised by a brick column topped by a *putto*, a copy of one at the Baptistery in Florence. Overlooking the garden at one corner is an ogee-roofed open Summerhouse from which extend piers and supporting beams intended for climbing roses (74). All of this has been meticulously repaired, even down to the *putto*, which had disappeared. A circular pool was planned for the area beyond the Pergola,

73 George Herbert Kitchin's Lily Pond Garden at Compton End is one of a series of
green rooms in this compact 'Quarter-Acre' example of a garden

known as the Green Court, but was never executed; nearby, at the end of a
brick wall, is a delightful brick dovecote with a tiled roof. The frontispiece to
this book illustrates a Triggs drawing for the gardens at Little Boarhunt, which
is close to what was carried out, but omits the central rill.

Triggs was also asked in 1912 to design a new house, just along from Little
Boarhunt, originally called **Hailie** and latterly Bramshott Rectory. This also
featured a sunken rose garden with a rill and rectangular pool, yew topiary, a
bowling green and a gazebo.[39] Sadly, the gardens fell into disrepair, but new
owners have taken over the house, which has been renamed Hailie, and are
undertaking an informed restoration.[40]

Soon after Triggs bought his Hampshire house he was commissioned,
together with his partner, William F Unsworth, to design a house and grounds
for the explorer and naturalist, Aubyn Trevor-Battye. As well as his *Some architectural works of Inigo Jones* (1901), his *Formal Gardens in England and Scotland* of
1902 and his 1906 *The Art of Garden Design in Italy*, Triggs was just about to
bring out *Garden Craft in Europe*, which included Spanish gardens. It is the
Spanish influence that is most evident at **Ashford Chace**, set on a platform
overlooking a wooded valley threaded by the Ashford Stream below the beautiful wooded hangers at Steep, near Petersfield. Although the house has been
altered, especially around the Sunk Garden and the 'Out-Door Tea House' at
the southeast corner, enough survives to convey the impression of a water-

74 Harry Inigo Triggs's Sunken Garden at Little Boarhunt is overlooked by a
Summerhouse and dramatised by geometric rose beds and a rill; the *putto* on top
of the column is a copy of one in the Baptistery in Florence

filled courtyard reminiscent of the Alhambra.[41] A paved court dramatised with
a Moorish-style Fountain was commanded on the first floor by an arcaded
loggia, now filled in, and the Tea House with its open arcade, now also filled
in. Water from the Fountain was channelled underground through the
retaining wall to issue at a lion's head in a niche and from thence 'through the
maze of a "puzzle-stream", as at the Generalife [*colour 44*], and so down a
tunnel' to the rectangular tank in the lower courtyard.[42] The outer wall of the
lower court, through which the pleasure grounds are reached, supports a
wooden, vine-covered Loggia (75).

It seems that Unsworth had as much to do with this Spanish-style enclosure as Triggs. The 1920 *Country Life* writer was of the opinion that,

> The late Mr. W. F. Unsworth was an architect who remained to the end of a
> long life a student of inextinguishable enthusiasm, ready to gather impressions
> from abroad, but always skilled in grafting them on to native stock. His last holi-
> days were spent in Spain and Algiers, and the fine measured drawings of the
> Generalife at Granada attest to the laborious study he gave to the use of water
> in garden design.[43]

It may be, therefore, that Unsworth was the driving force behind another

75 The Loggia in the Alhambra-inspired garden at Ashford Chace, a joint work by Inigo
Triggs and William Unsworth

formal garden at Ashford Chace, further out to the southwest, at the end of a
long axial walk. The Fig Garden, which has a tile-roofed, arcaded wall facing
the valley is now centred by a pool, but it was originally a paved area with 'a
very old cistern cut out of one solid block of sandstone and lined with lead'.44
The walled retreat also had a rectangular space 'enclosed on three sides by old
fig trees', where there were 'stone seats, four little green plots of grass, iron-
stone paths, and in the middle the four low stone seats of a Persian garden
curling round an octagonal stone table designed for tea'.45

The Ashford Chace Fig Garden is characteristic of the Edwardians' delight
in enjoying the outdoor life, whether spending the warm summer nights
outside in specially constructed sleeping balconies or on roofs, like that above
the Garden Room at Compton End, which connects with Kitchin's bedroom,
taking the air within the shelter of gazebos and garden houses, promenading in
clement conditions under pergolas, or just conversing while relaxing on seats.
Harold Peto provided three of these elements, as well as a rock garden, when
he was brought in at **Hinton Admiral**, near Christchurch, by Sir George
Meyrick in 1905 to remodel the existing grounds.46 In providing a better
access from the house to the gardens, his solution was to construct a wide
terrace along the south front of the house with a balustraded wall and steps to
the lawns below. At the western end of the terrace he introduced one of his

signature seats, curved and conducive to conversation (76), which was originally furnished with a table, and around the corner from Peto's new ballroom on the west front there is a majestic Pergola (*colour 45*) supported on Ionic columns.[47]

While Peto was engaged on the works at Hinton Admiral he often stayed at nearby **Walhampton House**, now a school, which had been bought in 1883 by John Postle Heseltine, who subsequently altered the house.[48] It is thought that Peto was responsible for the Italian Terrace and Sunken Garden and the Roman Arch; these are first recorded on the 1907 Ordnance Survey map.[49] There are clues to Peto's possible authorship on the Italian Terrace. One is the presence of an exedra seat at its termination, while another seat, now beached in greensward, faces the Terrace. Then there are two herms flanking steps down to the lawns; their bodies appear to be antique, but their heads are unmistakably late nineteenth-century in date (*colour 46*). Peto was an inveterate collector of architectural fragments, which he often adapted or modified for display in his gardens, and these may well be his. The somewhat blockish Sunken Garden seems to have been designed as a piece with the Italian Terrace, but the Roman Arch looks too fussy in its detailing to be by Peto or, indeed, by Thomas Mawson, who was brought in by Dorothy Morrison in 1911 to alter the house and gardens; she married Viscount St Cyres in 1912. Mawson was certainly responsible, together with the architect Edmund Fisher, for the robust Loggia to the west of the Music Room, which encloses a garden court. The sunk court had an oval pool and a fountain, and was decorated with statuary; it has been converted into a swimming pool for the school. The Loggia, which had a central closed space for dining, was to have continued all around to produce a cloister, but this was never executed.[50] It is a building of great presence, a symphony of arched brickwork niches, their stone plinths now devoid of statues long gone, sturdy stone Tuscan columns, semi-domes and curved seats set behind Serlian motifs.

Reginald Blomfield gave a similar robust architectural treatment to the environs of his new 'Wrennaisance' house, **Moundsmere Manor** at Preston Candover, when Wilfred Buckley commissioned it in 1908.[51] The house was featured in *Country Life* in 1910, just as it was completed, but before the gardens had been laid out. Blomfield took as his architectural cue the Wren façade at Hampton Court and provided all modern conveniences, including a plethora of bathrooms, for his American lawyer client, who had bought the estate 'to devote himself to the advancement of dairy farming'.[52] As well as the main house, which has been truncated, Blomfield designed many service buildings, all of which survive intact. For the gardens he devised simple rectangular enclosures across the south front of the house, studded with clipped yews, the central section commanded by a raised walk and dramatised by a sunken rectangular pool (*colour 47*). There is a simple Doric Summerhouse, not unlike Mawson's Loggia at Walhampton, to the west, which now fronts a swimming pool, while

76 Harold Peto often introduced curved seats into his designs to encourage conversation, as on his terrace at Hinton Admiral; the table and decorative *putti* have disappeared

at the end of a long west-east axial path there is a vast Walled Garden with a curvilinear Glasshouse backed by the Gardener's House (*colour 48*).

Of more architectural consequence than Blomfield's layout at Moundsmere is Thomas Darcy Braddell's Sunken Garden and Dutch Garden at **Melchet Court**, near Romsey, designed after 1911 for Sir Alfred Mond, who would later become Lord Melchett. Henry Clutton designed the somewhat ponderous main house in Jacobean style for William Bingham Baring, 2nd Lord Ashburton, between 1862 and 1868. The upper terrace with its balustrade and central steps are of this date, so too were elaborate double parterres, centred by star-shaped pools on the lower area, but these have been swept away.[53] However, Braddell's wonderfully intimate Sunken Garden has recently been restored by the staff and boys of the school, and his Dutch Garden survives relatively intact, though divested of its statuary. Great blocks of clipped yew enlivened by rectangular lead cisterns dated 1914, now used as planters, guard the entrance to the Sunken Garden, its curved stone seat beckoning beyond. On the wall of the house above the enclosure is another ubiquitous sundial with the motto '*Sera Nimis Vita Est Crastina Vive Hodie*' (Life is too late tomorrow; live for today). The arcaded Pavilion in the Dutch Garden (*colour 49*) is thought by Arthur Oswald to have been inspired by the loggias at Cranborne Manor in neighbouring Dorset, while the arched bridge at the end of the Canal is reminiscent of many designed by Lutyens, particularly those at

Abbotswood in Gloucestershire and Hestercombe in Somerset.

The yew hedges of the Dutch Garden were originally studded with herms, and two stone seats offered places for contemplation, while the Pavilion was flanked by tall, rose-clad stone columns topped by obelisks and linked by chains; only the plinths for the columns survive. These decorative embellishments, recorded in Oswald's *Country Life* article of 1930, made the garden appear far more Italianate than it does today. Further out on the two terraces in front of the house there were important artworks in bronze and stone by Charles Sergeant Jagger and the Swedish sculptor Carl Milles. These included a pair of bronze wild boar on the upper terrace steps and two fountain groups in the parterre pools below. Milles also sculpted the figure in the middle of the Canal. 'Siren' held a fish in either hand from which spouted little jets of water. Milles's work had first been introduced to England by a Tate Gallery exhibition of 1927 and these artworks at Melchet Court had only recently been acquired when Oswald saw them.

A fitting postscript to this chapter of these gay, in the Edwardian sense of the word, gardens, full of people active in sports, conversing at leisure or just walking contemplatively, accompanied by peacocks, 'with their great fans extended and blazing with purples and greens',54 is a numinous memorial garden raised to 500 Wykehamists killed during the war that ended this golden afternoon. The **War Cloister** at Winchester College was the vision of Headmaster Montague Rendall, who conceived the idea of a cloister to commemorate a lost generation of young men who gave their lives in the Great War. Rendall commissioned Sir Herbert Baker who, together with contributions from the Art Master, RMY Gleadowe, devised the great roofed quadrangle. In his proposals to the War Memorial Committee in 1918, Baker wrote that 'the essential need…is to enclose and surround in one united shrine, with all the reverence which architecture can give, the spirit and the long roll of names of those who have fallen in this Great War'.55 Work began in 1922 and the memorial was dedicated by the Duke of Connaught on 31 May 1924.

Unlike William of Wykeham's mediaeval cloister at the College, which is completely dominated by the two-storey Fromond Chantry Chapel, Baker's quadrangle is spacious and open, centred only by a stone cross, emblazoned with two crusader knights, set on an octagonal plinth (*colour 50*). The bright white Portland stone arcades and russet-tiled roofs lend it a Lombardic feel, while the knapped flint walls and sturdy oak beams of the cloister walks define its English, and specifically Hampshire, character, an entirely appropriate register for the last stirrings of the Arts and Crafts Movement. But the building reaches out beyond the shire and the country, to the four quarters of what was then a worldwide Empire, commemorated at each corner, while the 120 regiments in which Old Wykehamists served are recorded in the badges on the roof corbels and beams.

The planting scheme for the Memorial was drawn up by Jekyll from Baker's plans and used her favourite pastel colours, drifting from pinks through mauves to blues, with China roses throughout. This soft and gentle look was in stark contrast to Baker and Rendall's intention to have simple and austere forms. The dying back of the herbaceous foliage in the autumn and the consequent bare soil made any recreation of the Jekyll planting, which had disappeared long ago, problematic. The current gardeners have decided, therefore, to plant a new scheme of eighteen blocks of yew for the main structure, mirroring the columns of the Tuscan colonnade, and providing twenty-eight planting beds. For the shady side of the cloister they have chosen hostas, ferns and brunerras, while the sunny side has astrantias, trifoliums and ceratostigmas. 'The four corners will remain "forever England" with pure white roses bringing in light, reminiscent of the war cemeteries of Flanders'. Snowdrops have been scattered everywhere to signal the return of life after the winter and 'hidden among all this symmetry and organization is a single Gertrude Jekyll Rose in memory of the original garden designer'.

Walking the shadowed pavements of the cloister, one could be forgiven for thinking that it was a garden loggia, like that at Hinton Admiral, Townhill, or Walhampton, and that in a recess around one of the corners was a typical Edwardian touch: a welcoming seat and a table laid for tea. But when the garth is entered, and the names of those who fell, inscribed on the outer walls, come into sight, the full enormity of that great loss of humanity hits home. Paradoxically, in its quiet, understated way, this is powerful architecture that speaks for the entire country, not just for Hampshire.

9

'This subliminal connection with nature' Twentieth-Century Gardens and beyond

▼

Exbury House, Mottisfont Abbey, Lake House Northington
Hinton Ampner, Longstock Park, Sir Harold Hillier Gardens
West Green House, Mountbatten House
The Beeches, The Manor House Upton Grey, Tudor House
Queen Eleanor's Garden, King John's House Romsey
Dean Garnier Garden, Hyde Abbey, Rotherfield Park, The Holt
Shawford Park, Bury Court, Preston House

It is approaching a century since the end of the First World War, years that have seen huge social, economic and cultural change. The gardens in this chapter cover this entire period and present a wide range and diversity of both design and planting, perhaps unprecedented in any previous century. They range from specialist plantsmen's gardens, concerned little with design, as at Exbury and the Hillier Gardens, to carefully researched re-creations of historic gardens as at Tudor House and Upton Grey. There are those that deploy garden buildings and architectural features to provide meaning, like the layout at West Green House, and then there are others which are intensely design-led and concerned with landscape, such as the amphitheatre at The Holt. Finally, there are gardens which, within a small space, as achieved at Bury Court, succeed in combining design and planting to create an intensely tranquil place in the frenetic modern world.

Lionel Rothschild became a managing partner of NM Rothschild & Sons bank after the death of his father Leopold in 1917. In 1919 he acquired **Exbury House**, sited on the east bank of the Beaulieu River in the New Forest, where he remodelled and enlarged the eighteenth-century house to designs of WH Romaine-Walker and GH Jenkins.[1] The house has views over its parkland to the Isle of Wight, and Rothschild extended Exbury village to provide housing for his staff.[2] Lionel created the gardens over a twenty-year period from 1919 until the outbreak of the Second World War.[3] After his death in 1942, the Royal Navy requisitioned the house as an HQ for the D-Day landings, but after the war Lionel's son Edmund continued the development of the gardens and they were opened to the public from the 1950s.[4]

To the south of the house Lionel retained the eighteenth-century layout with an open lawn, bounded by a ha-ha, beyond which is parkland with small clumps of trees. The new gardens were laid out to the southwest on a sloping site extending to some 200 acres between the house and the river, in an area of New Forest oak woodland, and are mainly planted with species of hybrid rhododendrons, camellias, azaleas and rare trees.[5] The size of the site allowed Lionel to indulge his passion for plants, gradually adding to his collection, and by 1942 the gardens had 20 miles of paths and walks, interspersed with woodland glades, lily pools and a rock garden.

Lionel sponsored plant collectors. Home Wood, a native oak, beech and pine wood close to the house, was planted with rhododendron species grown from seed, sent back by Frank Kingdon-Ward, George Forrest and Joseph Rock.[6] Trees include magnolias, Japanese cherries, maple, liquidambar and parrotia.[7] There is a fine *Davidia involucrata* (pocket handkerchief tree) as well as a monkey puzzle tree and a rare *Quercus glauca* (evergreen blue-leaved oak).[8] The water gardens and streams are planted with candelabra primulas, irises and day lilies, while the bog garden displays Japanese irises and *Primula florindae*, the giant cowslip.[9] The gardens continue to be developed: a new Camellia Walk was planted in 1999-2000 and the Rose Garden (*colour 51*) was replanted with exotic plants in 2004 and renamed the Sundial Garden.[10] Although the colours in spring appear bright and gaudy to the modern eye, appearing perhaps as if a child has daubed paint indiscriminately, the overall result is a testament to Lionel's quest for botanical exploration, bringing together a vast collection of trees and shrubs from across the world.

While Exbury is essentially a twentieth-century garden, **Mottisfont Abbey**, sited on the bank of the River Test, has a much longer history. It was founded as a priory of Austin Canons in 1201, and after its dissolution in 1536 Lord Sandys, as he had done at The Vyne, converted the buildings into a large new house, set around two courtyards, completing his second home by his death in 1540.[11] Although elements of the monastic and Tudor buildings remain, the present red brick house is by Richard Mill, who succeeded in 1706, while the wings were enlarged in the Victorian period.[12] Gilbert Russell, a great-grandson of the 6th Duke of Bedford, purchased the house in 1934, and he and his wife Maud, a great patron of the arts, again renovated it and added a wing.[13] In 1957 Mrs Russell conveyed Mottisfont to the National Trust, who continue to own and manage it.[14]

The Russells made alterations to the gardens close to the house, for which they commissioned Norah Lindsay and Geoffrey Jellicoe. On the south side is a sloping lawn extending down to the river. In the area immediately in front of the house, enclosed by its wings, is a box parterre devised by Lindsay in 1935.

The square symmetrical design reflects the glazed pattern above the doorway in front of the parterre.[15] Lindsay was an inveterate socialite, beautiful, well travelled and well connected.[16] But in 1924, at the age of 51, her marriage fell apart and, facing financial ruin, she began a career in garden design, taking some of her closest friends as clients.[17] Having visited many of the great gardens of the Continent, she used topiary and geometric-shaped hedges and trees to contrast with herbaceous plants.[18] In England she visited Hidcote, Cothay Manor and Lionel Rothschild's gardens at Exbury, and remained influenced by Gertrude Jekyll.[19] She arrived at Mottisfont at the same time as Rex Whistler was painting the interior and shared a walk with him to admire the completion of her planting.[20] Norah wrote to her sister Madeleine of her work:

> Arrived at the Gilbert Russell's. Mottisfont is magnificent and romantic too. It is all stone, rushing rivers, vast old yew trees, cedars and lawns and a charming atmosphere of the past...We gardened in pelting rain two days running – and in mud up to one's knees.[21]

The formal layout on the north side of the house is by Geoffrey Jellicoe. The area is a level lawn enclosed by ashlar walls and a curved ha-ha that forms the northern boundary with the park. The gardens were embellished with statues bought by Maud Russell in 1936, including a marble statue of St George, four herms and an urn on a plinth.[22] Jellicoe's plan included a paved octagon at the northwest corner of the house, enclosed with clipped yew hedges, with a stone plinth supporting a lead urn at the centre. The Octagon connects the path along the rear of the house to a raised walk of pleached limes extending across one side of the garden (77), reached by steps from the Octagon. Jellicoe also designed herbaceous planting beside the house at the request of the owners, to provide colour close to the main rooms.[23]

In 1975 Jellicoe accepted another commission in Hampshire, for Sir John Baring at **Lake House, Northington**.[24] The new house, by architect Francis Pollen, was sited on the opposite side of the lake to The Grange, the former house of the Baring family, and Jellicoe created an island vantage point, with a view of The Grange. Beside the lake there was a typical Jellicoe mound with a cascade, christened Monte Jellicoe by his client.[25]

The lands around **Hinton Ampner**, a few miles south of Alresford, belonged to St Swithun's Priory in Winchester until the Dissolution, being appropriated to the Almoner, of which 'Ampner' is a corruption.[26] A Tudor house was then built on the site, demolished in 1793, and replaced by a small Georgian mansion. This, in turn, was enlarged to form a mock-Tudor house in 1867, though the Georgian house survived as the core.[27] The Victorian house had an extensive garden of formal parterres.[28] However, the present day gardens are largely the creation of Ralph Dutton, 8th Lord Sherborne, who

77 Geoffrey Jellicoe's 1930s
Octagon and raised walk
with its pleached limes at
Mottisfont Abbey

inherited the estate in 1935. He considered the Victorian house 'a monstrosity',
and commissioned the architects Lord Gerald Wellesley and Trenwith Wells
to rebuild it, revealing the Georgian core and giving it an eighteenth-century
appearance.[29] Though he considered the garden an 'attractive example of mid-
Victorian design' he swept away much of it to create a new garden more in
keeping with his neo-Georgian house.[30]

This first phase of rebuilding and garden layout took place between 1935
and 1939, and the gardens continued to be developed up to Dutton's death in
1985. He was a knowledgeable horticulturalist, author of the 1937 *English
Garden*, who planted in an English landscape style on the existing Victorian
framework using plants unavailable in the eighteenth century to create a twentieth-century garden in a Georgian setting.[31] Thus there is a lime avenue dating
from between 1740 and 1794,[32] but now clumped, running from the Temple at
the northern end to an Obelisk at the southern end, very much to classical
Georgian tastes, but actually only incorporated into the garden by Dutton
during the war.[33] The terraces around the house were intended to provide 'a

leafy and mellow coloured podium from which the house rises',[34] and are planted accordingly, while a Long Walk (*colour 52*), 180 metres in length, links the garden from east to west, with a vista to a statue of Diana.[35] Again, the Walk combines earlier yew planting from the Victorian garden with shrub rose borders laid out only in 1954. At the mid-point it opens onto the Sunken Garden, planted with formal raised beds in 1935, and with yew topiary in the shape of staddle stones – a modern take on Georgian formality. There are yet more yews in the Yew Garden, which replaced an earlier rose garden.[36] The Lily Pond, on the site of the Victorian croquet lawn, uses the idea of a water feature from earlier centuries but has no less than nine varieties of water lily, as well as a bed of roses underplanted with *Diascia barberae* and *Verbena rigida*.[37]

Described in *Country Life* as no less than 'Britain's finest garden featuring waterside perennials and aquatics',[38] the water gardens at **Longstock Park**, near Stockbridge, have their origins in 1870. In that year gravel was extracted from the banks of the River Test, Hampshire's most famous trout river, to make a new driveway in the park, creating a lake. A map shows this lake in the 1890s surrounded by what was described as a Water Copse. However, it was only after 1946, when John Spedan Lewis, founder of the John Lewis Partnership, purchased the 200-acre estate, that a relatively modest water feature underwent its remarkable transformation.[39] Acting with the advice of the botanist Terry Jones, Lewis trebled the size of the existing water garden to almost 5 acres, adding islands, bridges and promontories to the lake, fed from the Test. Because of the marshy nature of the site almost all the work had to be done by hand and it took ten years to complete the project. The planting mixes native species with exotics, which prosper in the damp soil, while further away a woodland garden has been laid out which suits a range of woody plants and acid-loving perennials preferring less waterlogged conditions.[40] As well as many waterside and bog perennials, there are ferns in profusion and, in summer, a spectacular display of water lilies.

Harold Hillier first began laying out his gardens and arboretum in 1953, on a 42-hectare site around the eighteenth-century Jermyns House, near Romsey, now called the **Sir Harold Hillier Gardens**. This was two years after he and his family had acquired the property. He chose Jermyns, at least in part, because its acidic soil suited the planting he had in mind.[41] The family firm, Hillier Nurseries, had been established since 1864 and had built a formidable reputation in the cultivation of temperate woody trees and shrubs, many of them rare. Indeed, the *Hillier Manual of Trees and Shrubs,* first published in 1964, is still in print and a standard reference work. Hillier could draw on this resource for his planting scheme, which he amplified through travels to gather seeds and plants and through his extensive contacts amongst fellow-collectors. But as *Country Life* observed, writing about the gardens over twenty years later:

From the first the arboretum was envisaged as a collection rather than a land-
scaped garden. Thus, with space at a premium, grand vistas, vast lawns and mass
displays of a few selected cultivars had to be forsaken in order to accommodate
the large and ever increasing collections of woody plants.[42]

Moreover, 'it became the unwritten policy of Mr Hillier that only two specimens of each tree or shrub should be planted in the arboretum',[43] so as to
maximise the breadth of the collection and ensure that many rare and endan-
gered species could be represented. By 1977, when the site was given in trust
to Hampshire County Council, there were over 10,000 different plants in the
gardens and arboretum. Twenty years later the site had expanded to 70
hectares and contained over 42,000 plants of 12,000 different taxa.[44] It is an
astonishing collection. Many of the original trees are still present in the
arboretum areas, such as the Pinetum, known in its early days as Little Switzer-
land. Also planted in the early days of the gardens is the area now called
Himalayan Valley, with a profusion of rhododendrons, hydrangeas, azaleas and
pieris, as well as many other species. There are other gardens such as the Bog
Garden, the Heather Garden and the Pond Garden, remaining true to Hillier's
concept, but requiring more regular renewal.

West Green House in Hartley Wintney was built around 1714, and
enlarged between 1730 and 1740 with a two-storey polygonal bay for General
Henry 'Hangman' Hawley of Culloden.[45] The house has a walled forecourt and
on the first floor are roundels with busts of Bacchus and Roman emperors in
place of windows.[46] The house was remodelled in 1898-1909 by Robert Weir
Schultz and again, between 1974 and 1980, by Quinlan Terry for Lord
McAlpine.[47] The National Trust took over the management in 1971, and the
first tenant was Lord McAlpine, who lived at West Green until 1990. As well
as his work on the house, Terry transformed the gardens for McAlpine, adding
a collection of garden buildings and ornaments to the earlier layout.[48]
Australian-born Marylyn Abbott acquired the lease in 1993, and she has
continued a programme of restoring and developing the gardens.

The lake was remade by Abbott in 1999, and the Terry buildings around the
lakeside were restored. These include a Laugier-inspired primitive Doric
Temple with tree trunk columns, a flint Grotto with a fountain inside and, on
the island in the centre of the lake reached by a Chinese Bridge, a large ornate
birdcage topped with a pineapple finial.[49] Beside the lake is an Obelisk with a
statue of Thomas Mann, the gardener at West Green from 1946 to 1986,
leaning against it (78). At the end of a lime avenue a quarter of a mile to the
north of the house is a tall column with rusticated bands and a Latin inscription: 'This monument was built with a large sum of money, which would
otherwise have fallen, sooner or later, into the hands of the tax-gatherers'.[50]
Beyond is a Triumphal Arch, topped with flint obelisks, which bears a plaque

78 The Obelisk, raised in memory of Thomas Mann, gardener at West Green
House, is one of a series of classically-inspired garden buildings around the
lake designed in the 1970s by Quinlan Terry for Lord MacAlpine

dedicating it to the 'first lady Prime Minister of Great Britain'. Terry and
McAlpine also made a 'Moon Gate' in the west wall of the eighteenth-century
walled garden, through which is the Philosophical Garden. This is a flight of
brick steps flanked by rills, leading to a Nymphaeum (*colour 53*), modelled on
the fountain of Santa Maria della Scala in the Via Garibaldi, Rome.[51] It is
inscribed with a quotation from Pope: 'A little learning is a dangerous thing,
drink deep or taste not the Pierian Spring'. In the Walled Garden Oliver Ford
designed two large ornate fruit cages for McAlpine. Marylyn Abbott added to
this garden in 1999 by planting a double *allée* of yew trees and creating water
steps.[52] One of her most impressive additions, made in 2004, is the Paradise
Courtyard (79), a water garden with rills and fountains inspired by traditional
Islamic gardens. Apple trees appear to be growing directly out of the water,
their white blossom mirroring the white trunks of *Betula Utilis,* which are
planted around the edge.[53]

While classical symbolism was being deployed at West Green, the multi-
level gardens of **Mountbatten House**, known locally as the 'Hanging
Gardens of Basingstoke', were being designed in parallel with the building
itself and are highly innovative in the way in which they integrate the garden
into the built form. When paper manufacturers Wiggins Teape commissioned
architects Arup Associates to design their new headquarters offices (then

79   Marylyn Abbot's 2004 Islamic Paradise Courtyard at West Green House, where
apple trees appear to flourish from water

called Gateway House) in 1973, Arup in turn commissioned the landscape
gardener James Russell to design an extensive planting scheme for the planned
roof gardens and the perimeter landscaping. At the time Russell was resident
horticultural consultant at Castle Howard, but continued to work as a free-
lance consultant, with Arup Associates as one of his main clients.[54] The
elevated site was designed so that most staff could look out on to open country
with a sunny aspect to the south and east, as well as providing pleasant recreation spaces.[55] There had to be ample opportunities to go outside, so that staff
could avoid any feeling of 'being cooped up'.[56] This meant that the roof
gardens were laid out over five different levels (*80*), accessible from the office
space, which Russell planted both to give a different atmosphere at each level,
and to reflect environmental conditions. As a result, it has been described as a
large and elaborate chest of drawers; the drawers all open to different extents
and each is filled with overflowing shrubs, trees and trailing creepers.[57]

Arup's brief to Russell was also for the planting to be 'romantic rather than
formal'.[58] So at level two, which is sheltered, there is a pond, planted around
with mature azaleas, hydrangeas and ferns. At level three there is primarily a
lawn, surrounded by trees and low-growing shrubs, including lavender, poten-
tillas, viburnum, heathers and eucalyptus. Level four is given over to a Wisteria
Terrace and a Vine Terrace with a central platform planted with ceanothus.

80 James Russell's Hanging Gardens of Basingstoke enliven a series of levels at
Mountbatten House, built in 1973 as the headquarters of paper manufacturers
Wiggins Teape

Level five, more exposed, contains both a golden-brown themed area, with
maple, *Lonicera*, *Berberis* and *Philadelphus*; and a silver-grey themed area with
silver wild pear, buddleia and willow. Level six has three small gardens: a Herb
Garden, a Winter Garden of mainly *Mahonia* and *Garrya* species, and a
Japanese Garden with dwarf pines and azaleas. Finally, at ground floor level,
there is perimeter planting of beech, sycamore, maple, lime, willow and poplar
trees, with underplanting. Although a few gaps have opened up and there has
been replacement planting, much of Russell's original design survives.

One of the most unusual and intriguing private gardens in Hampshire is at
The Beeches in the village of Weyhill, near Andover. It was the creation of
Stanley Norbury who, after the Second World War, bought the site and corru-
gated iron hut, which his family had previously rented, and over the next
twelve years replaced the hut with a self-designed bungalow, living there with
his mother. At the same time he began experimenting with cement structures,
formed using wooden moulds, which he then carved over a ten-day period
before the cement had set too hard. Norbury also began excavating a small
swimming pool in the centre of the garden. After his mother's death in 1966,
the pool was abandoned and planted as a rockery, but in 1974 Norbury was
inspired to convert the pool excavation into a sunken garden of carved cement
and Purbeck stone, which grew ever more ornate.[59] As Norbury put it in 1985:

81 Is it Granada or Seville? Neither. This is Stanley Norbury's The Beeches in Weyhill, a riotous cement fantasy land worthy of Tolkien

> In a way it grew by its own momentum. At no stage even as each fresh feature appeared, did the outcome result from a preconceived idea. The various features, one with another, came into being by the suggestion of what was already complete.[60]

The principal elements are a domed pavilion, two tall towers, a trefoil-shaped fountain and a semi-circular fretwork entrance archway supported on four columns (*81*). These are all contained within a balustraded wall decorated with niches containing vases and figures. Steps lead down from the garden into this wonderfully claustrophobic enclosure, a fantasy capriccio of the Alhambra and Seville. Everything is ornately carved with plants, animals, birds and fish; there are pots brimming with plants, climbing roses and variegated ivies every-where.[61] Unfortunately, following Norbury's death in 1996, the whole garden became overgrown, but has now been restored by the present owner.

One of the themes of modern gardens developed in Hampshire in recent years is the recreation of historic gardens, and several have been made covering a wide range of historic periods. When Rosamund Wallinger and her husband John acquired the **The Manor House at Upton Grey** in 1983, the building was 'shrouded in dripping climbers and weeds' and on the brink of becoming derelict.[62] The oldest part of the house is an early fifteenth-century hall, to which a cross wing was added in the early seventeenth century.[63] In 1907 Ernest Newton added a central timber-framed gabled porch and a tall timber-framed gabled bay on the garden side for Charles Holme, editor of *The Studio*.[64] Holme commissioned Gertrude Jekyll to design the gardens between 1908 and 1909, and her plans were used by the Wallingers to inform the restoration.[65]

The forecourt has brick gate piers topped by cherubs seated on stone balls, between which is a nineteenth-century wrought iron gateway. The land rises to the front of the house and Jekyll's plan for this area shows it to be the Wild Garden.[66] It begins with a formal area closest to the house where the grass beyond is laid out in a series of wide semi-circular steps, forming an amphitheatre. Surrounding this, spring bulbs are followed by rambling roses on supports, which give colour as well as height and structure. Beyond, the garden is increasingly informal, with curving paths leading around a pond at the top, and a small orchard of walnut trees. When the Wallingers arrived it was overgrown with brambles, ground elder and nettles, but clearing these revealed an area of natural wild flowers including wood anemones, pyramidal orchids and *Fritillaria meleagris*.[67] The line of a Roman road cuts diagonally across this garden and at the top, where the road crosses the drive, is an ancient yew tree, estimated to be between 1,800 and 2,000 years old.[68]

To the south of the house the land falls away and the gardens are terraced to four levels with dry stone walls, each terrace reached by descending central stone steps. The upper terrace is paved and a pergola leads from the house to the top steps. In 1983 the walls had collapsed and required rebuilding. The lowest, small wall between the bowling green and the tennis court had been included in Jekyll's plans, but marked 'thrown out' and was not implemented. The Wallingers elected to build it, as Jekyll originally intended, and to plant it with dianthus to her plan.[69] The pergola on the upper terrace was built and planted by the Wallingers according to Jekyll's designs and its oak posts support roses, Virginia creeper and *Aristolochia macrophylla*, focusing on the rose arbour at the bottom of the formal gardens.[70] Descending the steps, the Rose Garden occupies the second terrace (*colour 54*). This is laid out with four square stone beds each surrounded by four trapezoidal beds forming a larger square in a rigid geometric pattern. Soft planting is used in contrast to the structure, with a combination of roses and peonies in pale pink, edged with soft grey *Stachys lanata*.[71]

The herbaceous borders were also cleared and replanted according to Jekyll's plans, and the attention to detail means that the overall effect today is probably just as it was a century ago. The colours run in Jekyll style from white and pale pink and blue at the ends to hot red and orange in the centre. Wallinger admits that her approach of recreating and maintaining the gardens as closely as possible to the original design leaves them in an unnatural time warp.[72] But having discovered the Jekyll plans, she has succeeded in her aim 'to recreate a horticultural work of art almost precisely to those plans, following colour, shape, texture, structure and proportion to the letter'.[73] The Wallingers' extraordinary achievement has been recorded in a beautiful bird's-eye view of the whole site by Jonathan Myles-Lea, which is reproduced on the back cover of this book.

There is another recreated garden at **Tudor House** in Southampton, a rare late mediaeval town house, built by Sir John Dawtrey between 1491 and 1518, which faces onto Bugle Street within the mediaeval town walls.[74] The house was restored in the early twentieth century, and presented to the town council as a museum in 1911.[75] In the square walled courtyard behind the house there is a garden, which was designed by Dr Sylvia Landsberg using plants and design features typical of the Tudor period. There is an interlaced knot at its centre, surrounded by open knots, so called because it is possible to walk between the beds. Landsberg has used cotton lavender, winter savory, wall germander and box with corners of thrift and pinks.[76] The Knot Garden is also planted with other plants appropriate to the period including columbine, peonies, marigolds, iris, and a wide range of herbs. Knot pattern plants were described by Thomas Hill in his 1568 *The Proffitable Arte of Gardening*, which included a design for the first 'proper knot' that he stated 'may be set either with Tyme or Isop, at the discretion of the Gardener'.[77] In an earlier book Hill included two designs for mazes, which he recommended 'mai be set ether with Isope and time, or winter Savory and time, for these will indure grene all the yeare thorow'.[78] For the more adventurous gardener, he noted that 'there be some which set their Mazes with Lavender Cotten, Spike, Marjoram and such like'.[79] The use of scented herbs was a part of the pleasure of walking through a maze. Box was not used until later; its smell was described by John Gerard in his *Herball*, published in 1597, as 'evil and lothsome', and it was never recommended for making knots before 1600.[80]

A path runs along two sides of the Knot Garden where features typical of the Tudor period have been placed. A bee skep has been inserted into a bole in the back wall of the café, and a fountain within a small square area enclosed with low green and white painted rails has been set to one side of the path, although in practice fountains would have probably occupied a more central focal position. Beyond the fountain is a stone seat in a small vine-covered arbour, in front of which are two tall painted columns supporting heraldic beasts (*82*). One is a unicorn, for Sir John Dawtrey, and the other a stag for Sir Richard Lyster, Lord Chief Justice of the King's Bench, who married Dawtrey's widow, Jane, whose portrait by Holbein is in the Royal Collection.[81] Beyond the arbour an orchard is represented by a medlar and a turf bench. A covered walk runs along the far side of the Knot Garden, planted with vines for shade, as well as honeysuckle and jasmine, providing a scented walk with views onto the garden.[82] The path passes through an arch that came from St Denys

82 The Arbour at Sylvia Landsberg's recreation of a Tudor garden at Tudor House, Southampton. The colourful columns with their heraldic beasts – a unicorn and a stag – are typical features of Tudor garden design

Priory.[83] It extends to the ramparts of the adjoining twelfth-century King John's House, which survives as a shell and can be viewed from above.

Behind the Great Hall in Winchester is a modern mediaeval garden, also designed by Sylvia Landsberg, which was opened by the Queen Mother in 1986 as part of the Domesday 900 celebrations. **Queen Eleanor's Garden** is named after the queens of Henry III and Edward I, who would have used such a garden at the Castle as their private retreat. The size and positions of the three herbers, as such gardens were then called, made by Henry III are unknown, since they were sited between buildings that no longer exist, but there was certainly a turf area on the south side of the Great Hall, the site of Queen Eleanor's Garden.[84] Landsberg took her inspiration for the garden from contemporary illustrations as well as authentic plant lists of the period. Although the new garden is an awkward triangular shape, constrained by the base of Christopher Wren's seventeenth-century King's Palace on one side and the new Law Courts on the other, it provides a quiet city centre oasis. The stonework of the walls and paving is Purbeck limestone, matching that of the Great Hall. So too is the Fountain column, whose design is copied from the 1292 tomb of Peter de Sancto Mario in St Cross.[85] It is topped with a bronze falcon based on a carving in the choir stalls of the Cathedral (83), while water flows from four leopard-head masks, which reflect those in a description of a

83 At Queen Eleanor's
Garden in Winchester
Sylvia Landsberg
designed a mediaeval-
style Fountain crowned
by a bronze falcon,
which was inspired by a
carving on the choir
stalls in the Cathedral.
Helen Lawrence-Beaton

fountain dating from 1275 at Charing Cross Mews, Westminster.[86] The garden
also has a tunnel arbour built from curved chestnut poles, and a pentice roofed
with oak shingles, which houses white doves.[87]

This intimate garden was designed as one in which a queen might sit, with
turf benches in a rose-trellised herber. The centre of the garden is grass,
providing a peaceful green space, planted with daisies to represent a flowery
mead.[88] Taking fidelity as a central theme, Landsberg uses evergreen plants to
symbolise permanence.[89] In the mediaeval period, plants were associated
symbolically with religious and personal virtues, and the holly, ivy and bay
represent faithfulness.[90] Specimen plants include golden broom, once named
Planta genista, the emblem of the Plantagenet Kings, including Henry III and
Edward I.[91] Iris, peony, rose and Madonna lily (*Lilium candidum*), dedicated to
the Virgin, provide authentic seasonal colour, which can be appreciated from
turf seats. Red *Rosa Gallica* and white *Rosa x Alba* combine with honeysuckle
on the trellises, while a vine, symbolising everlasting life, which was often
grown over a church entrance, colours the doorway of the Hall.[92] The holly-
hock or Spanish Rose may well have been imported to England from the Holy
Land by Eleanor of Castile, who is known to have brought gardeners to
England from Spain.[93] Other Mediterranean plants such as lavender, wallflowers and pot marigolds are likely to have been introduced by her.[94]

To the east of the Market Place in the centre of Romsey, opposite the Abbey, is **King John's House**, another surviving mediaeval town house, with another recreated garden. It is a thirteenth-century hall house, with the hall on the upper floor, and is linked to the sixteenth-century Tudor Cottage that houses the tourist office.[95] The house was first given its name in 1927 when the owner, Miss Mabel Moody, asked a local historian to investigate the roof space where mediaeval heraldic graffiti were revealed, and the link with King John, who is recorded as having a hunting lodge in Romsey, was suggested.[96] In fact, dendrochronology carried out on the central tie beam in 1995 dated it to a tree felled in spring 1256, forty years after the death of King John.[97] Miss Moody presented the house to the townspeople of Romsey in 1969.[98] Tudor Cottage was acquired in 1979 and a Trust was established to care for both buildings.[99] Further land was later acquired to the rear of the houses, which was used to create gardens by a team of designers and volunteers from 1990, and the gardens were officially opened in 1995.[100] The small enclosures are attractive, but are not designed with historical features, although they do use planting confined to pre-seventeenth-century introductions to complement the houses, which they surround on three sides.[101] A shelter was added later, near the bridge, funded by the Hampshire Gardens Trust. A pentice was added in 2000, and in 2002 a small courtyard was created at the entrance with a fountain and restored iron gates.[102]

Within the precincts of Winchester Cathedral, the **Dean Garnier Garden** was opened in 1995. It is a walled garden in the shadow of the Cathedral, accessed by a flight of steps leading off the Inner Close through a thirteenth-century doorway, and is built on the site of the monks' dormitory of the mediaeval Priory of St Swithun.[103] When the monastery was dissolved in 1538 the monks' dormitory was demolished and the site became part of the Dean's garden.[104] The Deanery is on the south side, with the remains of the Deanery bakehouse.[105] In 1992 part of the Dean's garden was donated to create a public garden to be run by a Friends group under the auspices of the Hampshire Gardens Trust.[106] It was dedicated to the memory of Thomas Garnier, Dean of Winchester from 1840 to 1872, who was a founder member of the Hampshire Horticultural Society and planted many of the trees that now surround the Cathedral.[107] The Garden is maintained by volunteers and is open to the public in the summer months. It is divided into three areas, beginning with the Dorter Garden, which has a lawn with a medlar tree, surrounded with stone paths and bordered by the Monks' Herb Garden. Across the garden is a triple-arched arbour which echoes the arcade of Norman arches on the Cathedral below.[108] Beyond is the Presbytery Lawn, backed by yew buttresses, where a little stone fox lies curled under a bench sheltered by a large beech tree. At the far end, behind a yew hedge, is the Lady Chapel Garden, planted with flowering and foliage plants.

The forces of William the Conqueror arrived in Winchester in November 1066 and began building a new castle the following year.[109] Under William the centre of Winchester changed dramatically. Around 1070 the King decided to expand his royal palace close to the existing Cathedral on land confiscated from the New Minster, while in 1079 work began on a new cathedral.[110] Under Henry I the monks of the New Minster moved outside the city walls, to a new monastery at Hyde Mead known as **Hyde Abbey**, which was founded in 1110 and built specifically to accommodate them.[111] The coffins containing the skeletons of King Alfred and his son King Edward the Elder were taken with them and were reinterred, immediately in front of the high altar.[112] Hyde Abbey was dissolved in 1539; the buildings were demolished and much of the stone was used in other parts of the city.[113] Only the lower storey of the Abbey's gatehouse, which stood between the forecourt and the outer court, survives, as does a bridge that led from the outer to the inner court.[114] The royal graves were forgotten and in 1788, when Bridewell Jail was built, the workmen found what was potentially King Alfred's coffin, stripped it of its lead and treasures, picked up the bones and scattered them around.[115] The footings of the nave of the Abbey Church lie beneath King Alfred Place where, between 1995 and 1999, a community archaeological excavation of the Abbey Church, led by Winchester Museums Service, revealed the foundations of the church and some human bones in the area of the High Altar.[116] A radiocarbon date of the bones suggests that they are of King Alfred himself, or of his son.[117] The modern garden at Hyde Abbey marks the site of the final resting place of King Alfred the Great and King Edward the Elder.

An ingenious glass panel, engraved by Tracey Sheppard, has been set up at the entrance to a new garden at Hyde (*84*), which, when looked through, gives a visual impression of the interior of the Abbey Church.[118] The garden beyond was designed by the landscape architect Kim Wilkie and opened on 2 June 2003 to celebrate the 50th anniversary of the coronation of Queen Elizabeth II. Flint paving marks the site of the church walls, while tall holly columns, bound within stainless steel cages, rise to replicate the church columns.[119] Three large ledger stones, for Alfred, his wife Ealhswith and their son Edward the Elder, indicate the position of the royal graves beneath the altar. Yew hedges have been used to indicate side chapels, and beyond the altar, yew buttresses replace the stone ones of the Lady Chapel, while seats in the Cathedral inspired the oak benches.[120]

It is perhaps no surprise that Kim Wilkie has worked extensively in Hampshire, since it is his home county. He is particularly noted for creating subtle sculptural landforms that respond to the existing terrain on any site. One of his major Hampshire commissions is at **Rotherfield Park**, where the area to the south of the house, which was remodelled in the nineteenth century, looked to him 'as though the builders moved out in the 1870s and left the grass

84 Tracy Sheppard's translucent engraved panel works effectively with Kim Wilkie's
steel-caged holly columns to produce an impression of the interior of the lost
abbey at Hyde

to grow over their heaps of rubble'.[121] A design for the lawn had been proposed
by Russell Page, but was never implemented, and so it remained unresolved
until Wilkie arrived in 2009.[122] He prepared a balsawood model for his clients
that proposed a radical reconfiguration of the land between the south front of
the house and the adjacent stable block into a series of rippling, layered waves
culminating in a tiered mound.[123]

In the event, the owners opted for a less complex design and the result is a
long, partially tiered, sweeping grass curve which enfolds the open lawn on two
sides and rises gently to a large hemispherical mound at the far corner of the
garden. Tapping into landscape craft and archaeology, Wilkie explains that it
was 'made in the local tradition of earth fortifications and tumuli'.[124] It harks
back to ridge and furrow cultivation of the land and the concentric circles
around Neolithic henge monuments like Avebury in Wiltshire. The design is
also in the tradition of Elizabethan and Jacobean gardens with their viewing
mounts – Wilkie cites Sir Thomas Tresham's Lyveden New Bield in Northamptonshire as an influence on his work – and recalls the early eighteenth-
century landforms of Charles Bridgeman; Lyveden and Bridgeman's Claremont
amphitheatre are both illustrated in Wilkie's book.[125] From the top of the
mound there are long views down across the parkland to East Tisted Church
tower in the valley below, and the ridge beyond.

85 Wilkie's encircling green amphitheatre at The Holt has opened up the landscape around the house; it reflects his interest in ancient landforms and recalls Gilbert White's celebrated Zig-Zag path up the Hanger at Selborne

Wilkie's garden at **The Holt**, Upham, which was constructed in 2008, uses far more complex turf architecture spread across a large area that sweeps around two sides of the mellow brick, seventeenth-century house (*colour 55*). The amphitheatre design ascends in six tiers, broken by a central zig-zag path which climbs to an old wrought iron gate (*85*). This is reminiscent of the famous Zig-Zag at Selborne, devised by Gilbert White and his brother in 1753 and which Wilkie has restored for the National Trust. He describes how at The Holt 'the wings mimic a bird in turning flight, with the zig-zag as a spine'.[126] The level grass tiers are shadowed by wild flowers on their rising faces, which provide contrasting detail and help to define the forms. The only planting in the scheme is a single tulip tree half way along the fifth tier. Beyond the gate at the top a path cut into the adjacent field leads to a spiral mound, raised from the chalk spoil. This was sited in a central glade at the heart of a series of radiating tree avenues laid out by Katherine Wake's grandmother. The mound offers vistas along the avenues, as well as being visible as a focus from the ends of the axes where they meet the drive. At the far end of the land-form an existing circular pond was incorporated into the design by building up the level of the surrounding lawn so that it lies within a sunken circle.[127]

Wilkie is passionate about the sustainable management of water meadows to support wildlife, and in Winchester he championed Winchester College's plan to re-introduce cattle grazing and to clear away trees and scrub in order to restore the meadows to their ancient state.[128] Further downstream, at **Shawford Park**, the meadows had been levelled to accommodate a helipad and polo ground, but new owners engaged Wilkie to return the area to wet meadows while protecting the formal, sunken area around the house from floods and deer.[129] Although the 'archaeology and relevance of earlier gardens' on the site had been erased – as we have seen, Shawford once had an elaborate formal layout – Wilkie was intent on responding to the 'language of seventeenth-century design', which he sees as 'strong and architectural'.[130] His solution was to build a large rampart around the garden, hiding a deer fence, and providing a stunning viewing terrace commanding the landscape beyond. A gently curving knot of channels (*colour 56*) was carved out where there had been a 'sprawl of island beds and pampas grass' to provide a pattern of shallow rills, a haven for wildlife, especially the southern damselfly.[131] This atmospheric, elemental landscape is brooded over by Antony Gormley's *Watcher*, which stands sentinel on a corner of the revetment (*86*).

A similar transformation, but of buildings and gardens, has been affected by John Coke, who inherited **Bury Court**, near Hook, in 1994. Until the 1980s the complex was a thriving hop farm and at its heart was a concrete farmyard enclosed on three sides by the house, barn and outbuildings. As Coke describes it: 'There was really no garden to speak of here when we arrived, and the area in front of and to the west of the house was a hideous melange of grossly overgrown Victorian shrubbery, shapeless lawn and even more shapeless tarmac drive'.[132] The farm became the base for a specialist perennial nursery, Green Farm Plants, which Coke ran until 2003 in partnership with Marina Christopher. Now gardens have been created at the farm with the aid of designers Piet Oudolf and Christopher Bradley-Hole, and they provide a beautiful venue for events, weddings and opera.

Bradley-Hole's garden is in front of the farmhouse and was established in 2005. Coke had made a number of visits to wild meadows and grasslands in America, Armenia and Transylvania and 'wanted with this garden to evoke the idea, or spirit, of these wild places, perhaps in a dream-like way'.[133] The garden is laid out in a grid of twenty square beds edged with rusted steel and divided by gravel paths. At its heart is a square, black reflecting pool, next to which a large green oak Tea House, an afterthought, rears up (*87*). Coke was particularly attracted to Bradley-Hole's 'meticulous eye for detail' and minimalist aesthetic. The garden relies on blocks of grasses of different heights, some very tall, 'to add to the dream-like effect'; these are interspersed with colour provided by bright red oriental poppies, red and white sanguisorbas from South Korea, and rare, pure white field scabious.

The garden in the former farmyard, overlooked by the old Threshing Barn which was restored as a wedding venue in 2002, is in a different register

86 Antony Gormley's *Watcher* overlooks the contoured mounds and chalky water channels of Kim Wilkie's restored water meadows at Shawford Park

87 The Tea House soaring above a reflecting pool in the midst of Christopher Bradley-Hole's angular garden at Bury Court

88 Piet Oudolf's brilliant transformation of a working farmyard into a garden of
sweeping curves of perennial planting and hard landscaping at Bury Court

completely. While Bradley-Hole's is darkly angular, all-containing and somewhat oppressive, Piet Oudolf's design is open and curvaceous and wonderfully
bright. It is approached via a series of topiary trees that line the drive. Coke
calls them the Silent Watchers, waiting for the arrival of wedding guests.
Beyond is Oudolf's first garden in England. In 1996 Coke had been planning a
display garden for his nursery by digging beds in the concrete-paved farmyard
when, by happy coincidence, Oudolf came to visit just as the machinery was
moving in. He asked Coke what he was intending and suggested instead that
he should do a drawing for the site. Coke had recently visited Hummelo in
Holland, where he acknowledged that the grasses created a mysterious beauty,
but Oudolf's initial sketch for Bury Court did not accommodate Coke's practical notion for the space. Nevertheless, he acknowledged that a speedy
decision had to be made: 'Piet has never been one for compromising, the
design and planting were not up for negotiation, it was a take it or leave it
moment'. Oudolf's style of planting, originally called the 'Dutch Wave' and
later the 'New Perennial Movement', would earn him worldwide fame, and this
garden at Bury Court is typical of his naturalistic style. It deploys ornamental
grasses and hardy perennials to give shape and form to every inch of the courtyard (*88*). A gently curving, cambered path of setts divides the area into grassy
meadow and perennial borders (*colour 57*). It all seems so effortless and
unplanned, so natural and, above all, so tranquil. Coke describes the effect of

Oudolf's planting succinctly:

> He believes strongly in our subconscious desire to connect with nature, and uses
> natural-looking perennials – plants which we might expect to see in meadows
> and woodland fringes...in particular members of the Umbellifer family, so remi-
> niscent of the ubiquitous hedgerow 'cow parsley'...And then, of course, there
> are grasses, in much greater variety and number than were hitherto used in
> gardens. Grasses are the most basic constituents of any open natural landscape,
> and bringing them into a garden situation enhances this subliminal connection
> with nature.[134]

The Coke-Oudolf garden – for John Coke has adapted and modified the original design, particularly in front of the Barn where a paved terrace had to be
introduced to cater for guests – is both inward and outward-looking. The
restored farm buildings enclose and embrace the horticulture (*colour 58*), while
the Summerhouse in the far corner extends the prospect across the countryside beyond, creating a connection with the natural world. It is a place of rare
beauty and one of the county's greatest modern gardens.

It seems fitting to end this chapter of Hampshire's latest historic gardens
and landscapes with another garden building by Robert Adam, whose Doric
pavilion at his own house in Crawley featured in the Introduction. It is never
easy to predict which gardens will be considered in the future as worthy of the
distinction of historic, whether Oudolf's perennials will endure, or Wilkie's
earthworks survive to be seen as this century's polite equivalents of Stone Age
landforms. What is not at issue, however, is the durability of most built structures, especially those associated with gardens, which are often the only
reminders of layouts long since gone. Adam has spent his entire career working
in the classical language of architecture, modifying and adapting it dextrously
to contemporary needs.[135] He has, naturally, been in great demand as a country
house architect and, as such, has often, together with his co-directors at Adam
Architecture, been commissioned to introduce garden structures into the
landscape.[136] Perhaps the most impressive of these is the Pavilion at **Preston
House**, Preston Candover.

The owner wanted a pavilion in the landscape to commemorate the turn of
the Millennium, reflecting the new age as well as the classicism of the parent
house.[137] It was to be a landmark on rising ground seen from the front of the
house (*colour 59*). The design is a traditional classical rotunda as a destination
on a walk from the house, with views out to the surrounding countryside. The
Pavilion is located on the line from the house where the sun would finally set
at the end of the second Millennium. It develops a well-established classical
idea of the dome suspended in or representing the sky, and uses the most up-
to-date structure, designed by engineer Tony Hunt, to give the impression of

a dome floating over Corinthian columns. The column capitals have no abacus on the top, but instead specially-cast bronze leaves open out to reveal a stainless steel ball from which, like a stamen, a narrow tapering pin emerges to support the copper dome. Thin steel wires brace the structure where the entablature would have been, while the dome is based on a spiral grid with a spiral copper covering. The circular rotunda sits on an elliptical paved base, which is cut into the hill at the rear, and the flint retaining wall becomes the back to a seat. In the floor in the centre of the pavilion is a circular plaque cut by stone carver Gary Breeze, with the names of prominent Britons from the last 2,000 years. The Millennium Pavilion is a perfect tribute to the enduring appeal and influence of the classical idiom and the ceaseless desire of mankind to make its mark upon the landscape.

Introduction

1 Timothy Mowl & Laura Mayer, *Cambridgeshire and the Isle of Ely* (Bristol, 2013), p. 8.

2 The survey is preserved at Rotherfield. We are grateful to Sir James and Lady Scott for their warm hospitality and for making the archives accessible for study.

3 H Avray Tipping, *English Gardens*, 1925, p. 111. We are grateful to Laura Westbury for alerting us to the endpapers in Tipping's book.

4 Edward Wedlake Brayley & John Britton, *The Beauties of England and Wales: Hampshire*, vol. 6, 1804, p. 237. The portraits arc listed in a 1795 catalogue of pictures at Highclere (Highclere Castle Archives: Box 51A, no.1), and again in a manuscript catalogue of 1853; they are further listed in a printed 1880 catalogue of the principal pictures at Highclere, hanging on the Stone Staircase: Hampshire Record Office (hereafter HRO), 15M84/23/46. Sir Richard Kingsmill owned Highclere at his death in 1600. Crux Easton Manor House was purchased by the 3rd Earl in 1836, but has since been demolished. We owe much of this information to the Highclere Archivist, David Rymill.

5 Brayley & Britton, *Hampshire*, 6, p. 237.

6 John Butt (gen. ed.), *The Twickenham Edition of the Poems of Alexander Pope*, 6 vols, 1961-4, 6, Minor Poems, p. 353.

7 British Library, Add. MSS 15,776: 'An Account of a Tour in Hampshire & Sussex' (1743).

8 Brayley & Britton, *Hampshire*, p. 236.

9 Henry Howard Molyneux, 4th Earl of Carnarvon, *The Herberts of Highclere* (printed for private circulation, 1908), p. 94; HRO, 75M91/Z4.

10 Butt, *Poems of Alexander Pope*, 6, p. 354.

11 Ibid., p. 353.

chapter 1

1 Minta Collins, *Medieval Herbals: The Illustrative Traditions*, 2000, p. 25.

2 Maria Amalia d'Aronco, 'Gardens on Vellum: Plants and Herbs in Anglo Saxon Manuscripts', Peter Dendle and Alan Touwaide (eds.), *Health and Healing from the Medieval Garden* (Woodbridge, 2008), p.122.

3 Richard Marsden, *The Cambridge Old English Reader* (Cambridge, 2004), p. 17.

4 Thomas Oswald Cockayne (ed.), *Leechdoms, Wortcunning, and Starcraft of Early England, Being a Collection of Documents Illustrating the History of Science in this Country before the Norman Conquest*, 2 vols (Cambridge, 1865; reprint 2012), 2, p. 33.

5 Ibid., p. 67.

6 Ibid., p. 353.

7 Michael Bullen, John Crook, Rodney Hubbuck & Nikolaus Pevsner, *The Buildings of England: Hampshire: Winchester and the North*, 2010, pp. 33-34.

8 Ibid., p. 34.

9 http://www.winchester-cathedral.org.uk/our-heritage/our-history.

10 *Victoria County History of Hampshire and the Isle of Wight*, 5 vols, 1903, 2, pp. 108-115.

11 http://www.winchester-cathedral.org.uk/our-heritage/our-history.

12 http://www.kemble.asnc.cam.ac.uk/node/162 (accessed 30 November 2014).

13 FL Cross and EA Livingstone (eds.), *The Oxford Dictionary of the Christian Church* (Oxford, 2005), p. 1765.

14 http://www.winchester-cathedral.org.uk/our-heritage/our-history.

15 Cockayne, *Leechdoms*, 2, p. 397.

16 GW Kitchin (ed.), *Compotus Rolls of the Obedientiaries of St Swithun's Priory*, Winchester, 1892, p. 12.

17 Ibid., p. 249.

18 *VCH*, 2, pp. 108-115.

19 Kitchin, *Compotus Rolls*, pp. 400-402.

20 John Harvey, *Mediaeval Gardens*, 1981, p. 92.

21 Ibid.

22 Ibid.

23 Ibid., p. 422.

24 Ibid.

25 Ibid., pp. 422-3.

26 Ibid., p. 423

27 Ibid., p. 111.

28 Ibid., p. 292.

29 Kitchen, *Compotus Rolls*, p. 281.

30 Ibid.

31 Harvey, *Medieaval Gardens*, p. 211.

32 Ibid., pp. 220, 503.

33 Ibid., p. 110.

34 Martin Biddle, 'Excavations at Winchester, 1970: Ninth Interim Report', *The Antiquaries Journal*, vol. 52 (Oxford, 1972), pp. 93-131; p. 124.

35 Bullen *et al*, *Hampshire*, p. 641.

36 Ibid.

37 Ibid., p. 642.

38 Martin Biddle & Beatrice Clayre, *Winchester Castle and the Great Hall* (Winchester, 1983), p. 4.

39 Ibid., pp. 4-5.

40 Ibid., p. 5.

41 Ibid., p. 8.

42 Ibid., p. 4.

43 Ibid., p. 8.

44 Harvey, *Mediaeval Gardens*, p. 11.

45 R Allen Brown, H M Colvin & A J Taylor, *The History of the King's Works, Volume 2: The Middle Ages*, 1963, p. 1006.

46 Bullen *et al*, *Hampshire*, p. 640.

47 Biddle & Clayre, *Winchester Castle*, p. 12.

48 Sylvia Landsberg, *The Mediaeval Garden*, 1998, p. 120.

49 Harvey, *Mediaeval Gardens*, p. 6.

50 Ibid.

51 Ibid.

52 Ibid.

53 Ibid.

54 Ibid., p. 11.

55 Ibid., pp. 79-80.

56 Howard M Colvin, 'Royal Gardens in Medieval England', in Elizabeth B MacDougal (ed.), *Mediaeval Gardens* (Washington D C, 1986), p. 9.

57 Harvey, *Mediaeval Gardens*, p. 106.

58 Ibid., p. 78.

59 Anne Jennings, *Mediaeval Gardens*, 2004, p. 21.

60 Colvin, *King's Works*, 2, p. 862.

61 John Wareham, *Three Palaces of the Bishops of Winchester: Wolvesey, Bishop's Waltham Palace, Farnham Castle Keep*, 2000, p. 25.

62 Ibid., pp. 17, 25.

63 Ibid., p. 9.

64 Lucy Toulmin Smith (ed.), John Leland, *The Itinerary of John Leland in or about the years 1535-1543*, 5 vols., 1907, 1, p. 270.

65 Colvin, *King's Works*, 2, pp. 862-3.

66 Wareham, *Three Palaces*, pp. 17-19.

67 Biddle & Clayre, *Winchester Castle*, p. 13.

68 John McIlwain, *The Hospital of St Cross and St Cross Church* (Andover, 1999), n.p.

69 Ibid.

70 Ibid.

71 Christopher K Currie, 'Earthworks in St Cross Park, near Winchester, Hampshire', *Proceedings of the Hampshire Field Club and Archaeological Society*, vol. 53 (1998), pp. 169-182; p. 171.

72 Ibid.

73 Ibid.

74 TF Kirby (ed.), *Wykeham's Register*, 2 vols (1896), 2, pp. 532-4.

75 Currie, 'Earthworks in St Cross Park', pp. 169-182.

76 Ibid., p. 173; pp. 176-7.

77 Ibid., p. 176.

78 Ibid.

79 Landsberg, *Mediaeval Garden*, pp. 71-72.

80 Sarah Richards, 'An Assessment of Hampshire Dovecotes', *Hampshire Field Club and Archaeological Society Newsletter* 32 (Autumn, 1999), pp. 26-29; p. 26.

81 Giles Jacob & TE Tomlins, *The Law Dictionary: Explaining the Rise, Progress and Present State of the English*

Law, 6 vols (New York, 1811), 5, p. 150.

82 Lise Hull, *Understanding the Castle Ruins of England and Wales: How to Interpret the History and Meaning of Masonry and Earthworks* (Jefferson, NC, 2009), p. 156.

83 Wareham, *Three Palaces*, p. 35.

84 Elizabeth Lewis, 'Excavations in Bishops Waltham; 1967-78', *Proceedings of the Hampshire Field Club and Archaeological Society,* vol. 41 (December, 1985), pp. 81-125; p. 81.

85 Edward Roberts, 'The Bishop of Winchester's Deer Parks in Hampshire, 1200-1400', *Proceedings of the Hampshire Field Club and Archaeological Society,* vol. 44 (August, 1988), pp. 67-86, p. 67.

86 Anthony Emery, *Greater Mediaeval Houses of England and Wales; 1300-1500,* 3 vols (Cambridge, 2006), 3, p. 312.

87 Lewis, 'Excavations in Bishops Waltham', p. 81.

88 Emery, *Greater Mediaeval Houses,* p. 312.

89 Ibid., pp. 312-13.

90 Ibid., pp. 315-16.

91 Ibid., p.317.

92 Wareham, *Three Palaces*, p. 35.

93 Emery, *Greater Mediaeval Houses,* p. 317.

94 Toulmin Smith, *Itinerary of John Leland,* 1, p. 285.

95 Hubert Hall (ed.), *The Pipe Rolls of the Bishopric of Winchester for the Fourth Year of the Pontificate of Peter des Roches, 1208-1209* (1903), p. 2.

96 Ibid. p. 3.

97 NR Holt (ed.), *The Pipe Roll of the Bishopric of Winchester, 1210-1211* (Manchester, 1964), p. 115.

98 Hall, *The Pipe Rolls of the Bishopric of Winchester, 1208-1209,* p. 2.

99 Ibid., p. xxvi.

100 Ibid., p. 5.

101 Holt, *The Pipe Roll of the Bishopric of Winchester, 1210-1211,* p. 120.

102 Joan Greatrex (ed.), *The Register of the Common Seal of the Priory of St. Swithun, Winchester, 1345-1497* (Winchester, 1978), p. 186.

103 Hall, *The Pipe Rolls of the Bishopric of Winchester, 1208-1209,* p. 1.

104 Ibid.

105 Holt, *The Pipe Roll of the Bishopric of Winchester, 1210-1211,* p. 115.

106 Ibid., p. 114.

107 Hall, *The Pipe Rolls of the Bishopric of Winchester, 1208-1209,* p. 3.

108 Ibid.

109 Ibid., p. 5.

110 Holt, *The Pipe Roll of the Bishopric of Winchester, 1210-1211,* p. 118.

111 Ibid., p. 114.

112 Ibid., p. 117.

113 David A Hinton, 'Excavation at Beaulieu Abbey, 1977' in *Proceedings of the Hampshire Field Club and Archaeological Society,* vol. 34 for 1977 (July 1978), pp. 49-52; p. 50.

114 *Country Life,* 17 November 1906.

115 Ibid., p. 21.

116 Ibid., p.8.

117 Ibid., p. 2.

118 Paul Meyvaert, 'The Mediaeval Monastic Garden', in Elisabeth B Macdougall (ed.), *Mediaeval Gardens* (Washington, DC, 1986), p. 45.

119 Ibid., p.3.

120 *Country Life,* 17 November 1906.

121 S F Hockey (ed.), *The Account-Book of Beaulieu Abbey,* 1975, p.10.

122 Lord Montagu of Beaulieu, *Beaulieu,* no date, p. 22.

123 Quoted in Meyvaert, 'The Mediaeval Monastic Garden', p. 28.

124 Montagu, *Beaulieu,* pp. 18-19.

125 Ibid., p. 19.

126 Hockey, *The Account-Book of Beaulieu Abbey,* X., p. 3.

127 Ibid., pp. 44-45.

128 Ibid., p. 123.

129 Ibid., p. 199.

130 Ibid., pp. 163, 199.

131 Ibid., pp. 39-40.

132 Ibid., p. 192.

133 Ibid.

134 Ibid., p. 193.

135 Ibid., p. 238.

136 John Goodall, *The English Castle: 1066-1650*, 2011, p. 158; R Allen Brown, 'Royal castle-building in England 1154-1216', in Robert Liddiard (ed.), *Anglo Norman Castles* (Woodbridge, 2003), pp. 133-178; p. 135.

137 Ibid., p. 158.

138 Colvin, *King's Works*, 2, p. 766.

139 David Allen and Nick Stoodley, 'Odiham Castle, Hampshire: Excavations 1981-85' in *Hampshire Studies 2010: Proceedings of the Hampshire Field Club & Archaeological Society*, vol. 65 (Winchester, 2010), pp. 23-101; pp. 30-31.

140 Allen & Stoodley, 'Odiham Castle', p. 27.

141 Ibid., p. 31.

142 Ibid.

143 Ibid.

144 Colvin, *King's Works*, 2, p. 767.

145 Ibid., pp. 766-7.

146 Allen & Stoodley, 'Odiham Castle', p. 23.

147 English Heritage Register entry.

148 Edward Roberts & D H Miles,'Edward III's lodge at Odiham, Hampshire', *Medieval Archaeology*, vol. 39 (1995), pp. 91-106; p. 100.

149 Colvin, 'Royal Gardens', pp. 18-19.

150 Johanna Bauman, 'Tradition and transformation: the pleasure garden in Piero de'Crescenzi's *Liber Ruralium Commodorum*', *Studies in the History of Gardens and Designed Landscapes*, vol. 22, issue 2 (2002), pp. 99-111; p. 102.

151 Colvin, *King's Works*, 2, p. 767.

152 Harvey, *Mediaeval Gardens*, p. 87.

153 Ibid.

154 Colvin, *King's Works*, 2, pp. 767-8.

155 Colvin, 'Royal Gardens', p. 11.

156 Ibid., p. 9.

157 Maggie Campbell-Culver, *The Origin of Plants: The People and Plants that have shaped Britain's Garden History since the Year 1000*, 2001, p. 71.

158 Harvey, *Mediaeval Gardens*, p. 126.

159 Ibid.

160 Ibid., pp. 126-7.

161 Teresa McLean, *Mediaeval English Gardens*, 1981, p. 194.

162 *The Riverside Chaucer*, (Oxford, 2008), p. xiv.

163 Gillian Rudd, *Geoffrey Chaucer*, 2001, p. 9, p. 14 & p. 15.

164 *The Riverside Chaucer*, 'The Parliament of Fowls', pp. 183-191.

165 www.winchestercollege.org.

166 Bullen *et al*, *Hampshire*, p. 644.

167 Ibid.

168 Arthur F Leach, *A History of Winchester College*, 1899, p. 110.

169 Ibid., pp. 645-6.

170 Emery, *Greater Mediaeval Houses*, 3, p. 424.

171 McLean, *Mediaeval English Gardens*, p. 117.

172 Harvey, *Mediaeval Gardens*, pp. 109-110.

173 McLean, *Mediaeval English Gardens*, p. 117.

174 Ibid., pp. 117-118.

175 Ibid., p. 118.

176 Ibid., p. 110.

177 Leach, *A History of Winchester College*, p. 111.

chapter 2

1 Nikolaus Pevsner & David Lloyd, *The Buildings of England: Hampshire and the Isle of Wight* (Harmondsworth, 1967), p. 641.

2 English Heritage Monument number 242155 (consulted 4 February 2015).

3 National Archives, E101/490/12.

4 RR and S Morgan, 'Warblington Castle', *Hampshire Field Club and Archaeological Society: Section Newsletters,* New series, no. 15 (Spring, 1991), p. 1.

5 EH Monument number 242155 (consulted 4 February 2015).

6 'Warblington', in *A History of the County of Hampshire: Volume 3*, ed. William Page (London, 1908), pp. 134-139; http://www.british-history.ac.uk/vch/hants/vol3/pp134-139 (accessed 30 January 2015).

7 RR and S Morgan, 'Warblington Castle', p. 2.

8 Pevsner & Lloyd, *Hampshire*, p. 28.

9 EH Monument number 242155 (consulted 4 February 2015).

10 Ibid.

11 Ibid.

12 RR and S. Morgan, 'Warblington Castle', p. 2.

13 EH Register entry.

14 John Leland, *The Itinerary of John Leland the Antiquary*, vol. 4, part 1 (Oxford, 1769), p. 9.

15 Maurice Howard, *The Vyne* (Swindon, 2010) p. 45.

16 Bullen *et al*, *Hampshire*, p.531.

17 Howard, *The Vyne*, pp. 42-43.

18 Howard, *The Vyne*, p. 39.

19 William Moss, *A Correct Survey of The Vine belonging to Thomas Chute*, 1776 (HRO, 31M57/1210).

20 Bullen *et al*, p. 539.

21 Howard, *The Vyne*, p. 39.

22 Bullen *et al*, *Hampshire*, p. 539.

23 Howard, *The Vyne*, p. 39.

24 Bullen *et al*, *Hampshire*, p. 539.

25 Howard, *The Vyne*, p. 40.

26 Timothy Mowl & Brian Earnshaw, *Architecture Without Kings* (Manchester, 1995), p. 221.

27 John Harris, 'A Far Cry From Ancient Rome: Summer Houses at The Vyne', *Apollo,* April 2002, pp. 32-35.

28 Mary Hill Cole, *The Portable Queen: Elizabeth I and the Politics of Ceremony* (Amherst, MA, 1999), pp. 183, 196, 201.

29 Mavis Batey, 'Basing House Tudor Garden', *Garden History,* Vol. 15, No. 2 (Autumn, 1987), pp. 94-109, pp. 96-97.

30 David Allen & Alan Turton, *Basing House: A Tudor mansion destroyed in the English Civil War* (Andover, 2010), p. 4: 'Parishes: Basing or Old Basing', in *A History of the County of Hampshire*: vol. 4, ed., William Page, 1911, pp. 115-127; http://www.british-history.ac.uk/vch/hants/vol4/, pp. 115-127 (accessed 6 February 2015).

31 'Parishes: Basing or Old Basing', in *A History of the County of Hampshire*: vol. 4, ed., William Page, 1911, pp. 115-127; http://www.british-history.ac.uk/vch/hants/vol4/, pp. 115-127 (accessed 6 February 2015).

32 Ibid.

33 Batey, 'Basing House Tudor Garden', p. 95.

34 Allen & Turton, *Basing House*, p. 12.

35 Ibid., p. 5.

36 Bullen *et al, Hampshire*, pp. 432-433.

37 Allen & Turton, *Basing House*, p. 5.

38 Hill Cole, *The Portable Queen*, p.224.

39 John Nichols, *The Progresses and Public Processions of Queen Elizabeth,* 3 vols (1823), 1, p. 87.

40 Ibid., 3, p. 566.

41 Ibid., 1, p. 150.

42 Ibid., 3, p. 566.

43 William Brown, Survey of Basing, 1798; HRO 11M49/E/B1/22.

44 Bullen *et al*, *Hampshire*, p. 433.

45 Batey, 'Basing House Tudor Garden', p. 96.

46 Allen & Turton, *Basing House*, p. 10.

47 Batey, 'Basing House Tudor Garden', p. 107.

48 Ibid., p. 100.

49 John Hare, 'Netley Abbey: Monastery, Mansion and Ruin', *Proceedings of the Hampshire Field Club and Archaeological Society*, vol. 49 (February 1993), pp. 207-227; pp. 207-8.

50 H Arthur Doubleday &William Page, (eds.), 'Houses of Cistercian monks: Abbey of Netley', *A History of the County of Hampshire: Volume 2*, 1903, pp. 146-149; http://www.british-history.ac.uk/vch/hants/vol2/, pp. 146-149 (accessed 17 April 2015).

51 Hare, 'Netley Abbey', p. 212.

52 William Page (ed.), 'Parishes: Hound with Netley', *A History of the County of Hampshire: Volume 3*, 1908, pp. 472-478; http://www.british-history.ac.uk/vch/hants/vol3/, pp. 472-478 (accessed 17 April 2015).

53 Doubleday & Page, 'Abbey of Netley', pp. 146-149.

54 Ibid., pp. 472-478.

55 Ibid., pp. 472-478.

56 Hare, 'Netley Abbey', p. 218.

57 Page, 'Hound with Netley', pp. 472-478.

58 Hare, 'Netley Abbey', p. 218.

59 Cole, *The Portable Queen*, p. 180.

60 Hare, 'Netley Abbey', p. 211.

61 Pevsner & Lloyd, *Hampshire and the Isle of Wight*, p. 349.

62 WS Lewis (ed.), *The Yale Edition of Horace Walpole's Correspondence*, 48 vols (1973-83), 35, p. 251.

63 Pevsner & Lloyd, *Hampshire*, p. 629.

64 'Houses of Premonstratensian canons: Abbey of Titchfield', in *A History of the County of Hampshire: Volume 2*, H Arthur Doubleday & William Page (eds.), 1903, pp. 181-186; http://www.british-history.ac.uk/vch/hants/vol2/, pp. 181-186 (accessed 23 January 2015).

65 WH St John Hope, 'The Making of Place House at Titchfield, Near Southampton, in 1538', *Archaeological Journal*, vol. 63 (December 1906), pp. 231-243; p. 232.

66 Ibid., p. 240.

67 'Parishes: Titchfield', *A History of the County of Hampshire: Volume 3*, William Page (ed.), 1908, pp. 220-233; http://www.british-history.ac.uk/vch/hants/vol3/, pp. 220-233 (accessed 23 January 2015).

68 'Houses of Premonstratensian canons: Abbey of Titchfield', in *A History of the County of Hampshire: Volume 2*, H Arthur Doubleday & William Page (eds.), 1903, pp. 181-186; http://www.british-history.ac.uk/vch/hants/vol2/, pp. 181-186 (accessed 23 January 2015).

69 Leland, *Itinerary*, p. 281.

70 'Parishes: Titchfield', *A History of the County of Hampshire: Volume 3*, William Page (ed.), 1908, pp. 220-233; http://www.british-history.ac.uk/vch/hants/vol3/, pp. 220-233 (accessed 23 January 2015).

71 John Goodall, *The English Castle*, 2011, p. 426.

72 Ibid., pp. 426-427.

73 'Parishes: Titchfield', *A History of the County of Hampshire: Volume 3*, William Page (ed.), 1908, pp. 220-233; http://www.british-history.ac.uk/vch/hants/vol3/, pp. 220-233 (accessed 23 January 2015).

74 http://m.english-heritage.org.uk/daysout/properties/titchfield-abbey/history-and-research/.

75 St John Hope, 'The Making of Place House at Titchfield', pp. 231-243.

76 Ibid., p. 233.

77 Ibid., p. 240.

78 William Shakespeare, *Venus and Adonis*, lines 249-254.

79 William Shakespeare, *Rape of Lucrece*, lines 1200-01.

80 'Parishes: Titchfield', *A History of the County of Hampshire: Volume 3*, William Page (ed.), 1908, pp. 220-233; http://www.british-history.ac.uk/vch/hants/vol3/, pp. 220-233 (accessed 23 January 2015).

81 St John Hope, 'The Making of Place House at Titchfield', p. 233.

82 Ibid.

83 Susan M Youngs, John Clark & Terry Barry, 'Medieval Britain and Ireland in 1985', *Medieval Archaeology*, vol. 30 (1986), pp. 114-198; p. 147.

84 John Clark & Terry Barry, 'Medieval Britain and Ireland in 1984', *Medieval Archaeology*, vol. 29 (1985), pp. 158-230, p. 182.

85 'Parishes: Hursley', *A History of the County of Hampshire: Volume 3*, William Page (ed.), 1908, pp. 417-422; http://www.british-history.ac.uk/vch/hants/vol3/, pp. 417-422 (accessed 14 July 2015).

86 Ibid.

87 Ibid.

88 Ibid.

89 Ibid.

90 HRO, COPY/390. The original is preserved at Hursley. Our thanks go to David Key for an informed tour of the grounds.

91 Walter Thornbury & Edward Walford (eds.), *Old and New London*, 6 vols, 1878, 4, p. 377.

92 Samuel Johnson & George Steevens (eds.), William Shakespeare, *The Plays of William Shakespeare, Volume the Sixth*, 1778, p. 489.

93 Shakespeare, *King Henry VI, Part III*, III. I.

94 'Parishes: Elvetham', *A History of the County of Hampshire: Volume 4*, William Page (ed.), 1911, pp. 74-76; http://www.british-history.ac.uk/vch/hants/vol4/, pp. 74-76 (accessed 22 January 2015).

95 'The Honourable Entertainment gieven to the Quene's Majesie in Progresse, at Elvetham in Hampshire, by the Right Honble the Earl of Hertford, 1591', John Nichols, *The Progresses and Public Processions of Queen Elizabeth*, 3 vols., 1823, 3, p. 114.

96 Cole, *The Portable Queen*, p. 42.

97 Ibid., p. 46.

98 Ibid., p. 46.

99 Zillah Dovey, *An Elizabethan Progress* (Stroud, 1996), p. 3.

100 Nichols, *Progresses*, 3, p. 101.

101 Ibid., p. 102.

102 Ibid., p. 101.

103 Ibid., p. 110.

104 Ibid., p. 101.

105 Ibid., p. 102.

106 Ibid., p. 103.

107 Ibid., p. 108.

108 Ibid., p. 114.

109 Ibid., pp. 110-111.

110 Ibid., p. 110.

111 Denis Brailsford, *Sport and Society: Elizabeth to Anne* (Abingdon, 2007), p. 59.

112 Nichols, *Progresses*, 3, p. 117.

113 Ibid., p. 118.

114 Ibid.

115 Ibid.

116 Ibid.

117 Ibid., p. 119.

118 Ibid.

119 'Bramshill Park, Hampshire – II', *Country Life*, 15 April 1899.

120 Christopher Hussey, 'Bramshill, Hampshire – I', *Country Life*, 2 June 1923.

121 Helen Hills, 'Bramshill House, Hampshire – I', *Country Life*, 10 October 1985.

122 Ibid.

123 Louis A Knafla, 'Zouche, Edward la, eleventh Baron Zouche (1556-1625), *Oxford Dictionary of National Biography* (Oxford, 2004), online edition, January 2008 (*DNB*); http://www.oxforddnb.com/view/article/30301 (accessed 5 April 2015).

124 Ibid.

125 Deborah Harkness, *The Jewel House: Elizabethan London and the Scientific Revolution*, 2007, p. 25.

126 Anna Parkinson, *Nature's Alchemist: John Parkinson, Herbalist to Charles I*, 2007, pp. 112-113.

127 John Gerard, *The herball or Generall historie of plantes*, 1597, p. 347.

128 Patrick Taylor (ed.), *The Oxford Companion to the Garden* (Oxford, 2008), p. 69.

129 Helen Hills, 'Bramshill House, Hampshire-II', *Country Life*, 17 October 1985.

130 *DNB*.

131 Charles Kingsley, 'My Winter Garden', *Fraser's Magazine*, vol. 57 (1858), pp. 408-25, reproduced in Kingsley, *Sir Walter Raleigh and his Time, with Other Papers* (Boston, 1859), p. 415.

chapter 3

1 Quoted in Christopher Hussey, 'Stratfield Saye House, Hampshire – II', *Country Life*, 26 November 1948. By 1792, when a survey of the park had been made, the gardens had disappeared, although two of the long formal avenues had been retained, while the 'numberless little meanderings' of the Loddon had been reshaped to give it the serpentine 'scope and dimensions of a fine river which now flows for nearly two miles almost as wide as the Thames'. The estate survey, preserved in the Estate Office, is illustrated in the current guidebook.

2 Christopher Morris (ed.), *The Illustrated Journeys of Celia Fiennes c.1682-c.1712*, 1982, p. 74.

3 Ibid., p. 66. The gardens were also seen by Defoe; see Daniel Defoe, *A Tour Thro' the Whole Island of Great Britain*, 4 vols (3rd ed., 1742; facsimile edition, Garland Publishing, New York, 1975), 1, p. 245

4 HRO, 11M49/418; see I Sanderson, 'Duke of Bolton's Gardens at Abbotstone, Near Alresford, Hampshire', *Hampshire Archaeology and Local History Newsletter*, vol. 2, no. 3 (Spring, 1972), pp. 1-4.

5 British Library, Add. MS. 14296, f.62; quoted in *Victoria County History: Hampshire*, vol. 4, p. 192. There was

also at least one banqueting house in the formal gardens at Somerley Park, Ringwood. The old, Flemish-gabled house, which was pulled down in 1803-11, had a walled court with a banqueting house at one corner. Steps from this led down to the gardens beyond. An eighteenth-century engraving of this view is given in Christopher Hussey, 'Somerley, Hampshire – I', *Country Life*, 16 January 1958, plate 3.

6 Quoted in Hampshire Gardens Trust Research Register entry.

7 Wilkie's work at Shawford is discussed in Chapter 9.

8 HRO, 46M72/E2: Hampshire Disbursements book of Henry Mildmay, 1660-1708.

9 HRO, 46M72/E2, f.135 and following pages.

10 HRO, 46M72/E38: 'Plan of that part of the Shawford Estate proposed to be sold to Lady Mildmay'.

11 Morris, *Celia Fiennes*, p. 75.

12 George London & Henry Wise, *The Retir'd Gardner,* 1706, Chapter III: 'Of the different sorts of Parterres, and single Knots, with their Rise, and the Manner of Bordering and Planting them with Box'; p. 129.

13 For the development of the wilderness we are indebted to the research done by James Bartos, particularly his MA Garden History dissertation: 'The Artinatural Wilderness – 1700-1740' (Bristol, 2009), and his PhD thesis: 'Wilderness and Grove – Gardening with Trees in England, 1688-1750' (Bristol, 2013).

14 Timothy Nourse, *Campania Foelix*, 1700.

15 See John Harris, 'The Artinatural Style', Charles Hind (ed.), *The Rococo in England*, 1986, pp. 8-20.

16 Philip Miller, *The Gardener's Dictionary*, 1731.

17 For the genesis of the house, its variant designs and the attribution to James see Sally Jeffery, 'John James and George London at Herriard: Architectural drawings in the Jervoise of Herriard Collection', *Architectural History*, vol. 28 (1985), pp. 40-70; see also Christopher Hussey, 'Herriard Park, Hampshire', *Country Life*, 1 July 1965, written when the house was being demolished. Repton and Armstrong's work is discussed in Chapter 6. George Frederick Prosser, *Select Illustrations of Hampshire*, 1833, p. 70, under Herriard House, states: 'The old mansion having been burnt down, Thomas Jervoise, Esq., grandson of the above-mentioned Sir Thomas Jervoise, built the edifice which is here represented in the reign of Queen Anne, under the directions of Mr James, the architect of Stanstead House in Sussex, and Hursley Park in the county, the seat of Sir William Heathcote, Bart'.

18 HRO, 44M69/P1/61.

19 HRO, 44M69/P1/65.

20 HRO, 44M69/P1/39.

21 Jeffery, 'John James and George London at Herriard', p. 53.

22 HRO, 44M69/P1/65.

23 HRO, 44M69/P1/39.

24 JC Loudon, *The Landscape Gardening and Landscape Architecture of the Late Humphry Repton*, 1840 (Thoemmes Press, Bristol, 2001), within which is a facsimile of Repton's *Sketches and Hints on Landscape Gardening*, 1795, p. 66, footnote.

25 Ibid.

26 Morris, *Celia Fiennes*, p. 73.

27 Defoe, *Tour*, 1, p. 201.

28 Ibid.

29 Ibid., p. 202.

30 Ibid.

31 Badeslade's engraving is included in volume 4 (1739) of *Vitruvius Britannicus*.

32 EH Register entry.

33 The wilderness, which survives in part, is shown on an nineteenth-century map: HRO, 10M57/P12.

34 Christopher Hussey, 'Rotherfield Park, Hampshire – I', *Country Life*, 23 April 1948.

35 The information on Chawton given here is taken from Kate Felus, 'Chawton House, Hampshire: Parkland Plan', March 2010.

36 This, together with the Mellichamp painting, is preserved at Chawton House Library.

37 Robert Williams, 'Fortified Gardens', Christopher Ridgway & Roberts Williams (eds.), *Sir John Vanbrugh and Landscape Architecture in Baroque England* (Stroud, 2004), pp. 49-70.

38 *The Family Memoirs of the Rev William Stukeley, MD and the Antiquarian and other Correspondence of William Stukeley, Roger & Samuel Gale*, Surtees Society, vol.73 (1882), p. 115.

39 John Cornforth, 'Castles for a Georgian Duke', *Country Life*, 8 October 1992.

40 *The Family Memoirs*, Surtees Society, vol.73 (1882), pp. 114-115.

41 We are grateful to the archivist, Susan Tomkins, for her help with the images and to Lord Montagu for allowing their use in this book.

42 The paintings are at Audley End House, Essex.

43 For an analysis of the houses on the site see Alison M Deveson, 'The Lost Mansions of Hurstbourne Park', *Hampshire Field Club and Archaeological Society*, Newsletter 43 (Spring 2005), pp. 31-6.

44 HRO, TOP 173/2/5.

45 A 1792 directory and the 1842 tithe map describe the figures as Hercules and Antaeus, while an estate history notes that 'a statue of George III dressed as Julius Caesar' was placed on the top of the building in 1851. Information from Helen Lawrence-Beaton, 'A Forgotten Baroque Master: Thomas Archer (1668-1743)', PhD thesis, Bristol, 2015, vol.1, p. 225. The figure looks as if it might be Mercury in the Griffier painting.

46 Cited in David Jacques, 'The Formal Garden', Christopher Ridgway & Robert Williams (eds.), *Sir John Vanbrugh and Landscape Architecture in Baroque England* (Stroud, 2000), p. 42, from Switzer's *Hydrostaticks and Hydraulicks*, 1729, II, p. 411.

47 For Vanbrugh's Claremont Belvedere and his obsession with mediaevalism, see Timothy Mowl, 'Antiquaries, Theatre and Early Mediaevalism', Christopher Ridgway & Robert Williams (eds.), *Sir John Vanbrugh and Landscape Architecture in Baroque England* (Stroud, 2000), pp. 71-92; plate 47.

48 Timothy Mowl, 'Thomas Archer and the Hurstbourne Park Bee House', *Architectural History*, vol. 30 (1987), pp. 467-75.

49 British Library, Add. MSS 15,776: 'An Account of a Tour in Hampshire & Sussex' (1743).

50 Ibid.

51 Lawrence-Beaton, 'Thomas Archer', vol.1, chapter 13.

52 The plan is preserved at the house. We are grateful to Helen Lawrence-Beaton for supplying us with images of the plan.

53 Stephen Switzer, *The Nobleman, Gentleman, and Gardener's Recreation*, 1715, revised and enlarged as *Ichnographia Rustica*, 1718, Preface, p. xvii.

54 For the *ferme ornée* see Timothy Mowl, *Gentlemen & Players: Gardeners of the English Landscape* (Stroud, 2000), chapter 10, pp. 124-135.

55 Batty Langley, *New Principles of Gardening, Or, The Laying out and Planting Parterres, Groves, Wildernesses, Labyrinths, Avenues, Parks, &c., After a more Grand and Rural Manner* 1728, p. 198.

56 Ibid., p. 199.

57 Ibid., p. 197.

58 For Heythrop and its stylistic relationship to Wary Wood see Timothy Mowl, *Historic Gardens of Oxfordshire* (Stroud, 2007), pp. 54-62.

59 Lawrence-Beaton, 'Thomas Archer', vol.1, p. 270.

60 HRO, 116M88/B2: 'A Topographicall Discription of the Lands of ye Right Honourable ye Lord Marquesse of Winton known by the name of Hackwood Parke'.

61 The damaged plan is illustrated in *Country Life*, 10 December 1987; the design that was followed is in the Bodleian Library, Oxford, MS. Gough Drawings, a. 4 f. 34; it is illustrated in Peter Willis, *Charles Bridgeman and the English Landscape Garden* (Newcastle-upon-Tyne, 2002), plate 200.

62 HRO, COPY 392/3.

63 Lord Curzon employed John Veitch to plant out the canal basin as a 'Wild Garden'; HRO, 54M98/E/B1/35.

64 Frances Collins & John Hurst, *West Meon, Hampshire: Some Chapters of its History* (Petersfield, 1972), pp. 56-7; East Sussex Record Office, SAS/G/56/42.

65 GH Kitchin, 'Lainston House, Nr Winchester', *Country Life*, 8 March 1919.

66 Quoted in the EH Register entry, which gives the date for Evelyn's visit and his *Diary* entry as 5 July 1714. This cannot be accurate because Evelyn died in 1706. In his *Country Life* article on the house of 8 March 1919, GH Kitchin states that Merrill 'must have built the great octagonal dovecot...and the hexagonal walled garden and planted the long avenue'. Kitchin gives a good general plan of the garden layout at Lainston.

67 HRO, 10M48.

68 HRO, 36M66/94.

69 HRO, 58M71/E/T31 (sale for £35,000, 6 Nov 1718) and HRO, 58M71/E/T33 (final concord of sale in 1719).

70 HRO, 63M84/93, 94, 109.

71 Howard M Colvin, *A Biographical Dictionary of British Architects 1600-1840*, 2008, p. 517.

72 See Mowl, *Gentlemen & Players*, p. 84-86.

73 HRO, 63M84/190.

74 We are indebted to Hursley's archivist, David Key, for bringing this letter to our attention and for an informed tour of the site.

75 See Gordon Nares, 'Cranbury Park, Hampshire – I', *Country Life*, 25 October 1956, plate 6.

76 HRO, 76M83/1.

77 John Evelyn visited Rueil in 1644 and marvelled at the 'Arco of Constantine painted in Oyle on a Wall, as big as is the real one at Rome, so don to the life, that a man very well skilld in Painting may mistake it for stone'. Quoted in Mowl, *Gentlemen & Players*, p. 5.
78 Surveyed by Charles Ley for Sir Harry Burrard. The School holds a scholarly report on the grounds by Sybil Wade: 'Walhampton House Historic Landscape Restoration & Management Report on the Grounds of Hordle Walhampton School', 1999. We are indebted to David Hill for making this known to us and for giving us an expert tour of the estate.
79 Stephen Switzer, *Ichnographia Rustica, or, The Nobleman, Gentleman, and Gardener's Recreation*, 3 vols., 1718, 2, p.135.
80 Switzer's plan for Nostell Priory is illustrated in Gervase Jackson-Stops, *An English Arcadia 1600-1990*, plate 22; pp. 46-8.
81 It is not known if this had been an existing moat, like that at nearby Yateley Hall, east of Eversley Cross, which was converted into a canal in about 1704, the date of a walled garden on the site.
82 For the enlargements to the house and alterations to the landscape made at this period see Christopher Hussey, 'Warbrook House I & II, Hampshire', *Country Life*, 11 & 18 March 1939.
83 John James, *The Theory and Practice of Gardening*, 1728, p. 41.
84 Maynard Mack, *Alexander Pope: A Life*, 1985, p. 649.
85 George Sherburn (ed.), *The Correspondence of Alexander Pope*, 5 vols., 1956, 3, p. 306.
86 Ibid., p. 424.
87 Ibid., 3, p. 427.
88 Mack, *Alexander Pope*, p. 620.
89 Sherburn, *Correspondence*, 3, p. 430.
90 Ibid., p. 487.
91 Defoe, *Tour*, 1, pp. 204-5.
92 British Library, Add. MSS 15,776: 'An Account of a Tour in Hampshire & Sussex' (1743).
93 Ibid.

chapter 4
1 This should not be confused with Farleigh House at Farleigh Wallop, near Basingstoke. It is now Farley Mount Country Park, at the centre of which is an obelisk-like monument on a mount to a famous horse, 'Beware Chalk Pit', owned by Paulet St John. Taylor's map depicts a summerhouse, which probably pre-dated the erection of the monument.
2 The Blandy map is in HRO, 52M88/1; the Bull map is preserved at the house. We are most grateful to the Highclere archivist, David Rymill, for his generous help with the archives, and to the Countess of Carnarvon for allowing publication of images from the collection, as well as photographs of the landscape and its buildings.
3 Mark Girouard, 'Highclere Castle, Hampshire – I', *Country Life*, 18 June 1959.
4 Molyneux, *The Herberts of Highclere*, p. 5.
5 Ibid.
6 British Library, Add. MSS 15,776; quoted in Girouard, 'Highclere Castle, Hampshire – I'.
7 HRO, 52M88/2.
8 HRO, 75M91/Z4.
9 Richard Pococke, *The Travels Through England of Dr Richard Pococke*, ed. by James Joel Cartwright, 2 vols (Camden Society, 1888-9), 2, p. 49.
10 See Introduction to this study.
11 British Library, Add MSS 15,776: 'An Account of a Tour in Hampshire & Sussex' (1743).
12 Ibid.
13 Ibid.
14 John Bold & John Reeves, *Wilton House and English Palladianism: Some Wiltshire Houses*, 1988, pp. 89-91. Plate 126 illustrates William Stukeley's 1723 view of the garden, showing the arch on a hill to the south of the great Caroline garden.
15 British Library, Add MSS 15,776.
16 Charles Lyttelton in a letter to Sanderson Miller of 1756, quoted in Girouard, 'Highclere Castle, Hampshire – I'.
17 Copies of Brown's general plan for Highclere are in HRO, 116M88/B15 & 116M88/C15.
18 HRO, COPY/573/22 and COPY/573/23.
19 HRO, 15M52/437.
20 Tim Mowl & Brian Earnshaw, ' Milford Lake House, Hampshire', *Country Life*, 30 October 1986.

21 Both Bull's map and the vignette are illustrated in Mowl & Earnshaw, *Country Life*, 30 October 1986, plates 5 & 8. A copy of Bull's map is in HRO, COPY/570/1-44.

22 For these see Roger White, 'John Vardy, 1718-65', Roderick Brown (ed.), *The Architectural Outsiders*, 1985, pp. 75-6. Robert Adam was also active at Hackwood in the 1760s and produced a drawing for a rustic lodge; see Roger White, 'Robert Adam's Rustic Designs', *The Georgian Group Journal*, vol. 23 (2015), pp. 167-178; figure 9. The drawing is in the Soane Musuem (Adam drawings, vol. 46/148).

23 Lord Mahon (ed.), *The Letters of Philip Dormer Stanhope, Earl of Chesterfield*, 4 vols., 1845, 3, pp. 105-112.

24 Mahon, *Letters*, 3, p. 106.

25 Mowl & Earnshaw, *Country Life*, 30 October 1986.

26 Mahon, *Letters*, 3, p. 108.

27 Ibid., p. 111.

28 Mark Girouard, 'Echoes of a Georgian Romantic: Follies at Dogmersfield Park, Hampshire', *Country Life*, 2 January 1964, plates 1, 2 & 3.

29 Pococke, 2, pp. 161-2.

30 See Timothy Mowl, *Historic Gardens of Wiltshire* (Stroud, 2004), pp. 85-7; also Bold, *Wilton House*, pp. 80-93.

31 William Stukeley, *Abury, a Temple of the British Druids*, 1743, Preface; quoted in Mowl, *Wiltshire*, p. 87. For Stukeley's antiquarian interests see Stuart Piggott, *William Stukeley: An Eighteenth-Century Antiquary*, 1985.

32 Girouard, 'Echoes of a Georgian Romantic'.

33 Girouard, 'Echoes of a Georgian Romantic'. Girouard cites a nineteenth-century extract from the original accounts that was in the possession of Colonel Wallington in 1964.

34 Timothy Mowl & Marion Mako, *Historic Gardens of Somerset* (Bristol, 2010), pp. 63-78.

35 Nigel Temple, 'A Hermit for Cadland?', *The Follies Journal*, no. 3 (Winter 2003), pp. 3-16; pp. 7-10.

36 Its positioning, though appropriate, has been questioned by David Standing, 'Some Observations on the Layout of Gilbert White's Garden, Selborne: (1) The Location of the Hercules Statue', *Hampshire Field Club and Archaeological Society*, Newsletter 41 (Spring, 2004), pp. 11-13.

37 We are grateful to Christopher Francis for the translations.

38 Standing, 'Some Observations', p. 12.

39 Richard Mabey, *Gilbert White: A Biography of the Author of The Natural History of Selborne*, 1999, p. 88.

40 Ibid., p. 89.

41 Gilbert White, *The Natural History and Antiquities of Selborne*, 1788 (1832 edition), p. 403.

42 Mabey, *Gilbert White*, p. 90.

43 Ibid., p. 91.

44 Ibid.

45 Ibid., p. 92.

46 Ibid.

47 Ibid., pp. 92-3.

48 Ibid., p. 93.

49 HRO, 31M57/1210.

50 This is illustrated in Michael McCarthy, *The Origins of the Gothic Revival*, 1987, plate 129. There is a variant Chinoiserie bridge design by Chute in HRO, 31M57/639/27.

51 John Martin Robinson, 'Alresford House, Hampshire', *Country Life*, 5 January 1978.

52 The property had just been sold when research was in progress for this book, so access to the house and grounds was not possible. This account is, therefore, taken from published sources including the E H Register entry and from Fiona Cowell, *Richard Woods (1715-1793) Master of the Pleasure Garden* (Woodbridge, 2009), pp. 223-224.

53 From the key, quoted in Cowell, *Woods*, p. 224.

54 Illustrated in John Redmill, 'A House Ahead of its Time, The Grange, Hampshire-I', *Country Life*, 8 May 1975, fig. 2.

55 Redmill, *Country Life*, 8 & 15 May 1975; C K Currie, 'Recent work at The Grange, Northington', *Hampshire Field Club and Archaeological Society*, Newsletter 40 (Autumn, 2003), pp. 5-8; Alison M Deveson, 'The Early History of The Grange, Northington', *Proceedings of the Hampshire Field Club & Archaeological Society*, vol. 60 (2005), pp. 198-208.

56 The five drawings for The Grange are in the Soane Museum (Adam drawings, vol. 51/25).

57 Quoted in Jane Geddes, 'The Grange, Northington', *Architectural History*, vol. 26 (1983), pp. 35-48; p. 42; also EH Register entry.

chapter 5

1 As Brown's tercentenary in 2016 approaches, new research is constantly revising this figure; see John Phibbs, 'A List of Landscapes that have been attributed to Lancelot 'Capability' Brown', *Garden History*, vol. 41:2 (Winter, 2013), pp. 244-77, and John Phibbs, 'A List of Landscapes that have been attributed to Lancelot 'Capability' Brown – Revisions', *Garden History*, vol.42:2 (Winter, 2014), pp. 281-86. The current (2015) figure of firm commissions and attributions has exceeded 300.

2 For Brown's employees and followers see David Brown, 'Lancelot Brown and his Associates', *Garden History*, vol. 29:1 (Summer, 2001), pp. 2-11.

3 William Gilpin, *An Essay upon Prints; containing Remarks upon the Principles of picturesque Beauty*, 1768, Explanation of Terms, p. 2.

4 William Gilpin, *Remarks on Forest Scenery*, 2 vols., 1791, 1, p. 189.

5 Ibid., pp. 189-91.

6 Ibid., pp. 191.

7 Ibid.

8 Ibid., p. 192.

9 Ibid., p. 193.

10 Ibid., p. 193.

11 Ibid., p. 193.

12 Richard Payne Knight, *The Landscape, A Didactic Poem*, 1794.

13 Joseph Craddock, *Village Memoirs: In a Series of Letters between A Clergyman and his family in the Country, and his son in Town* (2nd ed., 1775), p. 69. The wagon refers to Brown's machine for transplanting trees that were often as much as thirty feet in height.

14 Ibid., p. 70.

15 Ibid., pp. 70-71.

16 Gilpin, *Forest Scenery*, 1791, 1, p. 194.

17 Ibid., p. 195.

18 Ibid.

19 Ibid., pp. 189-90. For Brown's work at Blenheim see Jeri Bapasola, *The Finest View in England: The Landscape and Gardens at Blenheim Palace* (Woodstock, 2009), pp. 61-73.

20 Dorothy Stroud, *Capability Brown*, 1975, p. 137.

21 Humphry Repton, *The Theory and Practice of Landscape Gardening*, 1803, quoted in JC Loudon, *The Landscape Gardening and Landscape Architecture of the late Humphry Repton*, 1840, p. 266.

22 Humphry Repton, *Sketches and Hints on Landscape Gardening*, 1794, quoted in Loudon, *Landscape Gardening*, p. 53.

23 Dorothy Stroud, *Capability Brown*, p. 137.

24 The drawing is illustrated in Stroud, *Capability Brown*, plate 25b.

25 A photograph of Brown's design for remodelling the Orangery is in HRO, 116M88/B14. It is illustrated in Gervase Jackson-Stops, 'Broadlands, Hampshire – II', *Country Life*, 11 December 1980, plates 8 & 10.

26 Stroud, *Capability Brown*, p. 138.

27 Tim Mowl & Brian Earnshaw, 'Milford Lake House, Hampshire', *Country Life*, 30 October 1986.

28 Stroud, *Capability Brown*, p. 160.

29 Ibid.

30 Ibid.

31 Molyneaux, *The Herberts of Highclere*, HRO, 75M91/Z4.

32 David Rymill informs us that there are updates on this work in letters written to Lord Porchester, the future 3rd Earl, while he was travelling on the Continent, from his father: HRO, 75M91/E4; the extensive works were being supervised by a Mr Strong.

33 Mark Girouard, *The Victorian Country House*, 1979, plate 105.

34 Ibid., pp. 130-31.

35 Copies of the general plan are in HRO, 116M88/B15 & 116M88/C15.

36 Illustrated in Mowl & Earnshaw, 'Milford Lake House', plate 5.

37 David Rymill informs us that the rhododendrons were the work of J R Gowen, sometime Royal Horticultural Society secretary, and confidential secretary to the early earls of Carnarvon. He is credited with *Rhododendron altaclerense*, the specific name being a Latinisation of Highclere.

38 Molyneaux, *The Herberts of Highclere*, p. 81; HRO, 75M91/Z4.

39 Ibid.

40 Ibid.

41 Ibid., p. 82.

42 Ibid.

43 Ibid., p. 83.

44 Ibid., p. 84.

45 Ibid.

46 Ibid.

47 HRO, 573/22.

48 HRO, 75M91/Z4, p. 88. It is David Rymill's view that this may be an exaggeration, especially as the Blandy map shows little evidence of a 'village' as such near the house. He believes that there was a policy over a long time of consolidating the estate by taking property in hand as it became available or leases came to an end; a rather different situation than the wholesale moving of villages that occurred on other eighteenth-century estates.

49 HRO, 75M91/Z4, p. 105.

50 Stroud, *Capability Brown*, p. 236; see also *Country Life*, 17 September 1938.

51 William Gilpin, *Remarks on Forest Scenery*, 2 vols., 1808, 2, p. 228.

52 Gilpin, *Forest Scenery*, 1808, 2, p. 228-30.

53 Ibid., p. 186.

54 Ibid., pp. 187-88.

55 Ibid., p. 186.

56 Ibid.

57 Ibid.

58 Stroud, *Capability Brown*, plate 36b.

59 Richard Payne Knight, *The Landscape: A Didactic Poem*, 1794, lines 286 & 298 respectively.

60 George Frederick Prosser, *Select Illustrations of Hampshire*, 1833, p. xlv.

61 Ibid.

62 Stroud, *Capability Brown*, p. 217.

63 The EH Register entry gives 1958 for demolition, whereas Roy Strong, Marcus Binney & John Harris (eds.), *The Destruction of the Country House*, 1974, p. 189, give 1956.

64 Stroud, *Capability Brown*, plate 33b.

65 Ibid., plates 16c and 31.

66 Ibid., plate 32a.

67 EH Register entry.

68 Thomas Lee Dummer's re-erection of part of the mediaeval ruins of Netley Abbey, which he set up alongside a Gothic tower as an eye-catcher to be viewed from Cranbury Park, is in a similar spirit of Picturesque appropriation; see Gordon Nares, 'Cranbury Park, Hampshire – I', *Country Life*, 25 October 1956, plates 1 & 2. A classical dairy, designed by George Dance when he was altering the house for Dummer also survives in the park; see Dorothy Stroud, *George Dance, Architect 1741-1825*, 1971, plate 26b.

69 Howard M Colvin, *A Biographical Dictionary of British Architects 1600-1840* (4th edition, 2008), p. 499.

70 Stroud, *Capability Brown*, p. 241.

71 Ibid.

72 Christopher Currie has argued that the Park Pond was not made by Brown, but was created after 1818: 'Recent Discoveries at North Stoneham Park', *Hampshire Field Club and Archaeological Society*, Section Newsletters, New Series, No. 15 (Spring, 1991), pp. 11-12. Currie quotes George Prosser's 1833 account, which mentions 'an ornamental piece of water, formed about ten years ago' below the terraced Italianate gardens. We interpret this body of water to be the Shrubbery Pond, rather than the Park Pond.

73 *The Gardener's Magazine*, vol. 1, new series (1835), p. 162.

74 Charles Tomkins, *A Tour of the Isle of Wight*, 2 vols (1796), 1, p. 27.

75 British Library, Add MSS 15,776: 'An Account of a Tour in Hampshire & Sussex' (1743); the building is marked as the 'Banqueting House' on Isaac Taylor's 1759 map of Hampshire.

76 Prosser, *Select Illustrations*, p. 196.

77 A survey of 1818, showing the layout of the park and gardens with the projected new house, is in Southampton Archives D/Z 639; a map of the same is in HRO, 84M94/58/8.

78 *The Gardener's Magazine*, vol. 1, new series (1835), p. 162.

79 Ibid.

80 Ibid.

81 Prosser, *Select Illustrations*, writes of 'an ornamental piece of water, formed about ten years ago, and supplied by springs in the park' (p. 198).

82 Stroud, *Capability Brown,* pp. 177-8.

83 See Timothy Mowl, *Historic Gardens of Dorset* (Stroud, 2003), pp. 89-91.

84 Gilpin, *Forest Scenery*, 1808, 2, p. 202.

85 Stroud, *Capability Brown*, p. 177.

86 Ibid., p. 178.

87 We are most grateful to Mrs Gilly Drummond for allowing us access to the Cadland drawings and for an informative tour of the landscape.

88 Gilpin, *Forest Scenery*, 1808, 2, p. 203.

89 Clive Aslet, 'Manor of Cadland, Hampshire', *Country Life*, 1 October 1987.

90 We owe this observation to Gilly Drummond.

91 Clive Aslet, *Country Life*, 1 October 1987. The painting was sold by the family and destroyed in the Second World War.

92 EH Garden Register entry. However, the Landmark Trust handbook states that the 8th Earl of Cavan sold the Tower in 1844 to Dr Drummond, who bought it to prevent its development as part of the seaside boom.

93 Gilpin, *Forest Scenery*, 1808, 2, pp. 196-7.

94 Ibid., p. 203.

95 Stroud, *Capability Brown*, p. 242.

96 Ibid., pp. 221-2.

97 Brayley & Britton, p. 179.

98 Gilpin, *Forest Scenery*, 1808, 2, p. 219.

99 Brayley & Britton, p. 179.

100 Ibid., p. 282.

101 Ibid., p. 279.

102 HRO, 116M88/B18/1, 2 & 4; 116M88/C18/2 & 4.

103 EH Register entry.

104 Gilpin, *Forest Scenery*, 1794, 2, pp. 63-4.

105 EH Register entry.

106 John Plaw, *Ferme Ornée; or, Rural Improvements*, 1796, p. 7.

107 Ibid.

108 Ibid., p. 6.

109 Ibid.

110 Ibid.

chapter 6

1 Loudon first used the term in his review of W S Gilpin's *Practical Hints on Landscape-Gardening*, published in *The Gardener's Magazine* for December 1832, pp. 700-702. It can be reduced to 'the introduction of exotic trees and shrubs in artificial scenery' (p. 701).

2 JB Papworth, *Hints on Ornamental Gardening*, 1823, p. 100.

3 Ibid., p. 9.

4 For a discussion of this struggle see Timothy Mowl & Jane Bradney, *Historic Gardens of England: Herefordshire* (Bristol, 2012), pp. 103-152.

5 *The Gardener's Magazine*, 1835, p. 161.

6 John Plaw, *Ferme Ornée; or, Rural Improvements*, 1796, p. 5.

7 Plates 16 & 17.

8 JB Papworth, *Rural Residences, consisting of a Series of Designs for Cottages, small villas, and other ornamental Buildings* 1818, pp. 49-50.

9 Ibid., p. 50.

10 Jane Austen, *Persuasion*, 1818 (Oxford University Press, 1975 edition), p. 257.

11 Mary Ann Hanway, *Ellinor; Or, The World As It Is, A Novel*, 4 vols., 1798, 1, p. 26.

12 Quoted in Kim Wilson, *In the Garden with Jane Austen*, 2008, p. 4.

13 Quoted in Wilson, *In the Garden*, p. 34.

14 Henry Phillips, *Sylva Florifera: The Shrubbery Historically and Botanically Treated*, 1823, quoted in Wilson, *In the Garden*, p. 33.

15 The shrubbery design is preserved at the house. We are grateful to Sir James and Lady Scott for their hospitality at Rotherfield and for making the archives accessible for study.

16 For Repton's work at Stoneleigh see Timothy Mowl & Diane James, *Historic Gardens of Warwickshire* (Bristol, 2011), pp. 149-158.

17 Jane Austen, *Mansfield Park*, 1814 (Wordsworth Classic edition, 1992), p. 51.

18 Ibid., p. 53.

19 Ibid., p. 53.

20 HRO, 44M69/f10/82/1-16.

21 HRO, 44M69/P1/72.

22 HRO, 44M69/P1/76.

23 HRO, 44M69/P1/77.

24 Humphry Repton, *Observations on the Theory and Practice of Landscape Gardening*, 1803, in JC Loudon, *The Landscape Gardening and Landscape Architecture of the Late Humphry Repton* (Edinburgh, 1840), p. 284.

25 Stroud, *George Dance,* p. 200.

26 J Mordaunt Crook *The Greek Revival: Neo-Classical Attitudes in British Architecture 1760-1870*, 1972, p. 97; Dance's Stratton Park is discussed in Stroud, *George Dance*, pp. 200-3; plates 64-5. An inscribed lead attached to the portico records that it was erected in 1805. The later history of the house, its demolition and replacement by a modernist house designed by Stephen Gardiner, is discussed in JM Robinson, *The Latest Country Houses*, 1983, pp. 142-4.

27 HRO, TOP 101/1/1.

28 Stroud, *George Dance*, plates 67b & 67c. Both this and a further, single, lodge to the south with a Doric portico are now stranded between the two roads.

29 Baring Archives, DEP 23; we are most grateful to Lamin Koroma for her help with the archives. Repton's text indicates that the surviving elevation was one of a series, all in Tudor-Gothic style.

30 Stroud, *George Dance*, p. 212.

31 Dance's designs are preserved in Sir John Soane's Museum.

32 Stroud, *George Dance*, p. 213.

33 George Frederick Prosser, *Select Illustrations of Hampshire*, 1833, p. 29.

34 Ibid., p. 31.

35 Ibid., p. 31.

36 Norman Court appears in Hazlitt's essay 'On the Past and Future', published in his 1822 *Table Talk, Essays on Men and Manners*.

37 Prosser, *Select Illustrations*, p. 31.

38 Repton, *Observations* in Loudon, *Landscape Gardening*, p. 215.

39 For these buildings see Nigel Temple, *John Nash and the Village Picturesque* (Gloucester, 1979).

40 HRO, 117M91/SP190.

41 Christopher Hussey, "Somerley, Hampshire – II', *Country Life*, 16 January 1958.

42 Ibid.

43 JC Loudon (ed.), *The Gardener's Magazine*, 1835, p. 331.

44 For the rebuilding see John Redmill, 'The Grange, Hampshire – II', *Country Life*, 15 May 1975.

45 Quoted in Redmill, 'The Grange, Hampshire – II', *Country Life*, 15 May 1975.

46 *The Gardener's Magazine*, 1827, pp. 170-171.

47 Ibid., p. 171.

48 *The Gardener's Magazine*, 1826, pp. 108-112.

49 Ibid., p. 110.

50 Ibid., p. 111.

51 Prosser, *Select Illustrations*, p. lxxxviii.

52 *The Gardener's Magazine*, 1826, p. 107.

53 The gardens were photographed by William Savage in about 1870; his photographs are preserved in the Winchester Museums Collections.

54 David Watkin, *The Life and Work of C R Cockerell R A*, 1974, p. 174.

55 Quoted in HGT Research entry.

56 Prosser, *Select Illustrations*, p. 53.

57 Ibid.

58 Ibid.

59 *The Gardener's Magazine*, 1834, pp. 124-130.

60 Ibid., pp. 124-5.

61 Ibid., p. 127.

62 Ibid., p. 128.

63 Ibid., p. 128.

64 Derek Gladwyn, *Leigh Park: A 19th Century Pleasure Ground* (Midhurst, 1992); Chris Currie, 'A Late Eighteenth Century Map of Leigh Park near Havant and its significance to the development of the Nineteenth Century Garrett-Staunton Landscape', *Hampshire Field Club and Archaeological Society Newsletter*, New Series, no. 21 (Spring, 1994), pp. 4-6; William Butler, *Topographical Account of the hundred of Bosmere* (Havant, 1817).

65 Three of the Gilbert paintings are in the collection of the City Museum, Portsmouth. We are most grateful to the Collections Registrar, Katy Ball, for making these accessible for study.
66 James King, *A Poem on Leigh Park*, 1829.
67 Sir George Thomas Staunton, *Memoirs of the chief incidents of the public life of Sir George Thomas Staunton*, 1856, pp. 169-70.
68 Quoted in Gladwyn, *Leigh Park*, p. 35.
69 Gladwyn gives the date 1801 for the conveyance, while Currie states that the estate was surrendered by Sir John Frederick's widow, Ann, in January 1800. Kent is given as the architect of the new house by Staunton in his later reminiscences; this is corroborated by Prosser, *Select Illustrations*, p. 155.
70 Gladwyn, *Leigh Park*, p. 31.
71 Butler, *Topographical Account*, pp. 41-2.
72 Ibid., p. 44.
73 Ibid., p. 47.
74 Ibid., p. 48.
75 Peter Frederick Robinson, *Rural Architecture*, 1822, designs 8 & 9: 'As the author has been asked for some Designs for Swiss Cottages, he proposes occasionally to introduce them into his work, having studied the buildings of that Country, on his return from Italy, in the year 1816'.
76 For Lord Ongley's Swiss Garden see Mavis Batey, *Regency Gardens*, 1995, pp. 37-40; also Christine A Hill, *Old Warden: Tales of Tenants & Squires* (Stroud, 2014), pp. 69-74.
77 King, *Leigh Park*, p. 34.
78 HRO, 76M78/E/P6.
79 There are two sketchbooks made by C R Cotton in the Portsmouth Museum, which include evocative watercolours of the park.
80 Papworth, *Ornamental Gardening*, p. 64.
81 Wyatt Papworth, *John B Papworth: A Brief Record of his Life and Works*, 1879.
82 We are most grateful to Mrs Penelope Chamberlayne-Macdonald for an informed tour of both the house and grounds at Cranbury Park.
83 Papworth's drawing is of a dining room with architectural treatment on the back wall close to the Cranbury Library. Mrs Chamberlayne-Macdonald informed us that the Library desk and circular table are both thought to be by Papworth.
84 HRO, 44M73/E/P45: Plan of Cranbury by Alfred Lock of Southampton (1859).
85 Papworth, *Ornamental Gardening*, p. 105.

chapter 7
1 Bullen, *et al*, *Hampshire*, p.327
2 Ibid., p. 328.
3 'Heckfield Place, Hampshire', *Country Life*, 3 December 1898.
4 J A Hamilton, 'Lefevre, Charles Shaw, Viscount Eversley (1794-1888), Rev HCG Matthews', *Oxford Dictionary of National Biography* (Oxford: Oxford University Press, 2004), online edition, Jan 2008 [http://www.oxforddnb.com/view/article/25274, accessed 27 May 2015].
5 'Heckfield Place', *The Gardeners' Chronicle*, 9 December 1882.
6 Ibid.
7 DT Fish, 'The Late William Wildsmith', *The Gardeners' Chronicle*, 8 February 1890.
8 Ibid.
9 Ibid.
10 Brent Elliott, *Victorian Gardens*, 1986, p. 215.
11 *Country Life*, 3 December 1898.
12 Ibid.
13 Ibid.
14 *The Gardeners' Chronicle*, 9 December 1882.
15 Bullen, *et al*, *Hampshire*, p. 328.
16 Ibid, p. 327.
17 *Country Life*, 3 December 1898.
18 *The Journal of Horticulture, Cottage Gardener and Home Farmer*, vol. 5, new series (1882), p. 431.
19 *Country Life*, 3 December 1898.
20 Ibid.
21 Ibid.
22 Ibid.

23 Elliott, *Victorian Gardens*, p. 203.

24 Ibid.

25 Ibid., p. 204.

26 *Country Life,* 3 December 1898.

27 'Heckfield', *The Garden,* 29 May 1875.

28 Elliott, *Victorian Gardens*, p. 136.

29 *The Garden,* 29 May 1875.

30 'Notes of the Week', *The Garden*, 29 August 1874.

31 Ibid.

32 *The Garden,* 29 May 1875.

33 Ibid.

34 Ibid.

35 *Country Life,* 3 December 1898.

36 Ibid.

37 Ibid.

38 EH Register entry, from which most of the information on the park and gardens has been taken.

39 'Brockenhurst Park, Hampshire', *Country Life,* 23 November 1901.

40 EH Register entry.

41 *Country Life,* 23 November 1901.

42 EH Register entry.

43 *Country Life,* 23 November 1901.

44 Ibid.

45 Ibid.

46 Bullen, *et al, Hampshire*, p. 397.

47 Ibid., p. 398.

48 English Heritage Historic Buildings List Description.

49 Bullen, *et al, Hampshire*, p. 397.

50 EH Register entry.

51 Bullen, *et al, Hampshire,* p. 397.

52 EH Register entry.

53 Ibid.

54 'Minley Manor, Farnborough, Hants', *Country Life*, 23 December 1899.

55 Bullen, *et al, Hampshire*, p. 399.

56 *Journal of Horticulture and Cottage Gardener,* 29 November 1864.

57 Elliott, *Victorian Gardens*, p. 116.

58 *Gardeners' Chronicle,* 12 December 1891.

59 It is illustrated in 'Minley Manor, Farnborough, Hants', *Country Life*, 23 December 1899.

60 *Journal of Horticulture and Cottage Gardener,* 29 November 1864.

61 *Country Life,* 23 December 1899.

62 Ibid.

63 Ibid.

64 Bullen, *et al, Hampshire*, p. 399.

65 *Gardeners' Chronicle,* December 12 1891.

66 Elliott, *Victorian Gardens*, pp. 216-217.

67 *Gardeners' Chronicle,* 12 December 1891.

68 Ibid.

69 Ibid.

70 Ibid.

71 Ibid.

72 EH Register entry.

73 Ibid.

74 *Gardeners' Chronicle,* 12 December 1891.

75 Ibid.

76 Bullen, *et al, Hampshire*, p. 399.

77 Elliott, *Victorian Gardens*, p. 128.

78 Hampshire County Council Archaeology and Historic Buildings Record (AHBR): Site 51520.

79 Elliott, *Victorian Gardens*, pp. 204-205.

80 *The Garden,* 3 August 1889.

81 Ibid.
82 Ibid.
83 Ibid.
84 Ibid.
85 Ibid.
86 Ibid.
87 Elliott, *Victorian Gardens*, p. 217.
88 AHBR: Site 51520.
89 Bullen, *et al*, *Hampshire*, p. 477.
90 'Parishes: Sherfield-upon-Loddon', in *A History of the County of Hampshire: Volume 4*, ed. William Page (London, 1911), pp. 103-108 http://www.british-history.ac.uk/vch/hants/vol4/pp. 103-108 (accessed 4 June 2015).
91 Ibid.
92 Bullen, *et al*, *Hampshire*, p. 477.
93 'Sherfield Manor', *Gardeners' Chronicle*, 1 October 1904.
94 Ibid.
95 Ibid.
96 Ibid.
97 Ibid.
98 Ibid.
99 Bullen, *et al*, *Hampshire*, p. 477.
100 *Gardeners' Chronicle*, 1 October 1904.
101 Ibid.
102 Ibid.
103 Ibid.
104 Ibid.
105 Ibid.
106 'Reading Horticultural', *Gardeners' Chronicle*, 3 September 1904.
107 *Gardeners' Chronicle*, 1 October 1904.
108 'Winchester Chrysanthemum', *Gardeners' Chronicle*, 26 November 1904.
109 *Gardeners' Chronicle*, 1 October 1904.
110 Ibid.
111 EH Register entry.
112 Bullen, *et al*, *Hampshire*, p. 465.
113 Ibid.
114 'Tylney Hall', *The Gardeners' Chronicle*, 29 April 1905.
115 Ibid.
116 Ibid.
117 Bullen, *et al*, *Hampshire*, p. 466.
118 *Gardeners' Chronicle*, 29 April 1905
119 Ibid.
120 Ibid.
121 Elliott, *Victorian Gardens*, p. 115.
122 Bullen, *et al*, *Hampshire*, p. 465.
123 *Gardeners' Chronicle*, 29 April 1905.
124 *Gardeners' Chronicle*, 29 April 1905.
125 Hampshire County Council Archaeology and Historic Buildings Record: Site Number 51552.
126 Ibid.
127 Bullen, *et al*, *Hampshire*, p. 465.
128 *History and Gardens Information* (Tylney Hall Hotel, no date).
129 EH Register entry; Bullen, *et al*, *Hampshire*, p. 465.
130 EH Register entry.
131 *Gardeners' Chronicle*, 29 April 1905.
132 Ibid.
133 Ibid.
134 Bullen, *et al*, *Hampshire*, p. 466.
135 EH Register entry.
136 Ibid.

137 'Dogmersfield Park', *The Gardeners' Chronicle,* 13 October 1883.

138 'Dogmersfield Park, Hampshire', *Country Life,* 27 April 1901.

139 *Gardeners' Chronicle,* 13 October 1883.

140 Ibid.

141 Ibid.

142 *Country Life,* 27 April 1901.

143 Ibid.

144 *The Gardeners' Chronicle,* 13 October 1883.

145 Ibid.

146 *Country Life,* 27 April 1901.

147 *The Gardeners' Chronicle,* 13 October 1883.

148 *Country Life,* 27 April 1901.

149 Ibid.

150 Ibid.

151 HRO, 811/1.

152 Ibid.

153 Ibid.

154 Ibid.

155 Ibid.

156 Nikolaus Pevsner & David Lloyd, *The Buildings of England: Hampshire and the Isle of Wight*, 1967, p. 146.

157 EH Register entry.

158 Ibid.

159 Owen Johnson, *Champion Trees of Britain and Ireland: The Tree Register Handbook* (The Royal Botanic Gardens at Kew, 2011), p. 276.

160 Ibid.

161 EH Register entry.

162 Ibid.

163 'Recent Projects by Kim Wilkie', *The Architect's Journal,* 21 November 1996.

164 EH Register entry.

165 Ibid.

chapter 8

1 Gertrude Jekyll & Lawrence Weaver, *Gardens for Small Country Houses*, 1913, p. i.

2 Ibid., pp. iii-iv.

3 Ibid., p. ii.

4 Ibid., p. xvi.

5 A Stuart Gray, *Edwardian Architecture: A Biographical Dictionary* (Ware, Hertfordshire, 1988), p. 234.

6 Ibid. p. 235.

7 WR Lethaby, *Architecture, Mysticism and Myth*, 1891 (Architectural Press, 1974 edition), p. 7.

8 Ibid., p. 9.

9 See 'Avon Tyrrell, Christchurch, Hampshire', *Country Life*, 11 June 1910.

10 Lethaby, *Architecture, Mysticism and Myth*, p. 5. The house itself is perhaps the last example of a calendar house incorporating 365 windows, 52 rooms, 12 chimneys and 7 external entrances (Matthew Beckett's blog: thecountryseat.org.uk; accessed 21 September 2015).

11 *Country Life*, 11 June 1910. Lethaby returned to Avon Tyrrell in the early 1900s to alter the gardens (EH Register entry).

12 Lethaby laid out the gardens with input from Henry Ernest Miller (EH Register entry).

13 Jekyll & Weaver, *Gardens for Small Country Houses*, fig. 17.

14 Jane Brown, *Gardens of a Golden Afternoon: The Story of a Partnership: Edwin Lutyens & Gertrude Jekyll*, 1982, p.61.

15 Ibid.

16 Lawrence Weaver, *Houses and Gardens by E L Lutyens*, 1913 (Antique Collectors' Club 1981 edition), pp. 175-182.

17 Ibid., pp. 175-182.

18 Brown, *Gardens of a Golden Afternoon*, pp. 104-5.

19 Ibid., p.104.

20 Weaver, *Houses and Gardens by E L Lutyens*, p. 75.

21 Ibid.

22 Christopher Hussey, 'Marsh Court – I Hampshire', *Country Life*, 19 March 1932.

23 Ibid., p. 90.

24 Christopher Hussey, 'Marsh Court – II Hampshire', *Country Life*, 26 March 1932. Brown, *Gardens of a Golden Afternoon*, reports that 'no planting plans have been found' (p. 75), so we cannot be sure exactly what Jekyll might have specified.

25 Fenja Gunn, *Lost Gardens of Gertrude Jekyll,* 1991, pp. 36-40.

26 Brown, *Gardens of a Golden Afternoon*, pp. 141-145.

27 EH Register entry; however, the Armed Forces Chaplaincy Centre history to Amport House states that the topiary of this 'Knot Garden' represents the family coat of arms.

28 Brown, *Gardens of a Golden Afternoon*, p. 142.

29 We are grateful to Rosaleen Wilkinson for her help with Townhill and for an expert guided tour of the restored gardens.

30 Information on Townhill is derived from Rosaleen Wilkinson, *Townhill Park – The Life and Times of a Gertrude Jekyll Garden* (Totton, 2004); see also R Randall Phillips, 'Townhill Park – II. Near Southampton', *Country Life*, 21 April 1923, which has several photographs of the Sunk Garden and the Herb Garden.

31 David Ottewill, *The Edwardian Garden*, 1989, p. 122.

32 Ibid.

33 Ibid.

34 Ibid.

35 Lawrence Weaver, *Small Country Houses of Today*, 1910, p. 101.

36 Ibid.

37 H Avray Tipping, *The Garden of To-Day*, 1933, pp. 21-2.

38 Lawrence Weaver, *English Gardens*, 1925, p. 114.

39 Wendy Bishop, 'Harry Inigo Triggs', MA Garden History Dissertation, University of Bristol, September 2011.

40 Time did not permit a trip to Hailie, but we are grateful to Karen and Graham Potts for making it accessible to us had we been able to visit.

41 This area featured prominently in 'Ashford Chace, Petersfield, Hampshire', *Country Life*, 18 December 1920

42 Ibid.

43 Ibid.

44 Ibid.

45 Ibid.

46 Lawrence Weaver, 'Hinton Admiral, Hampshire', *Country Life*, 8 October 1910.

47 Peto's seats were inspired by carved stone exedra he saw in Pompeii; see Robin Whalley, *The Great Edwardian Gardens of Harold Peto from the Archives of Country Life*, 2007, pp. 16-17. It is not clear if Peto added the Pergola, but Robin Whalley confirms that he designed the Rock Garden that Weaver described in 1910 as 'quietly gay with all manner of saxifrages and hellebore' (*Country Life*, 8 October 1910).

48 Hampshire Gardens Trust Research file.

49 Ibid. Robin Whalley is sceptical about the attribution of the Italian Terrace and Sunken Garden to Peto; there is, apparently, no surviving documentation.

50 Janet Waymark, *Thomas Mawson: Life, gardens and landscapes*, 2009, pp. 125-127.

51 *Country Life*, 12 March 1910; see also Richard A Fellows, *Sir Reginald Blomfield: An Edwardian Architect*, 1985.

52 Fellows, *Blomfield*, p. 56.

53 Arthur Oswald, 'Melchet Court, Romsey, Hampshire', *Country Life*, 9 August 1930, fig.13.

54 Weaver, 'Hinton Admiral, Hampshire'.

55 Quoted in 'The New Planting in War Cloister' *The Wykehamist*, 2014, by the College Gardeners. Subsequent quotations are taken from this source.

chapter 9

1 EH Register entry.

2 Ibid.

3 Ibid.

4 Ibid.

5 Ibid.

6 EH Register entry.

7 GC Taylor, 'The Garden of a Great Gardener – Exbury', *Country Life,* 13 February 1942.

8 John Anderson, *Exbury Gardens and Steam Railway: A Guide to the Trees of Exbury* (Exeter, no date), pp. 86-90.

9 Taylor, 'The Garden of a Great Gardener – Exbury'.

10 EH Register entry.

11 Ibid.

12 Pevsner and Lloyd, *The Buildings of England: Hampshire and the Isle of Wight,* p. 342.

13 Ibid.

14 Ibid.

15 Allyson Hayward, *Norah Lindsay: The Life and Art of a Garden Designer,* 2007, p. 198.

16 Ibid., p. 7.

17 Ibid., p. 7; p. 78.

18 Ibid., p. 79.

19 Ibid.

20 Ibid., p. 199.

21 Ibid.

22 EH Register entry.

23 Michael Spens, *Gardens of the Mind: The Genius of Geoffrey Jellicoe* (Woodbridge, 2007), p. 62.

24 Ibid. p. 138.

25 Ibid. pp. 138-9.

26 Christopher Hussey, ' Hinton Ampner House, Hampshire', *Country Life,* 7 February 1947.

27 Ibid.

28 Nick Brooks & Oliver Garnett, *Hinton Ampner Garden* (National Trust, 2000), p. 5

29 Ibid.

30 Ibid.

31 Ibid.

32 Hampshire Archaeology and Historic Buildings Record, Site No. 52219.

33 Brooks & Garnett, *Hinton Ampner Garden,* p. 17.

34 Ibid. p. 10.

35 Ibid., p. 14.

36 Ibid., p. 18.

37 Ibid., p. 10.

38 Roy Lancaster, 'Wade through a Water Masterpiece', *Country Life,* 25 July 2002.

39 Ibid, p. 60.

40 Ibid, p. 58.

41 EH Register entry.

42 Roy Lancaster, 'The Hillier Arboretum', *Country Life,* 7 September 1978.

43 Ibid.

44 EH Register entry.

45 Bullen *et al, Hampshire,* pp. 139-140.

46 Ibid., p. 540.

47 Ibid.

48 *West Green House Garden* (National Trust, no date).

49 Ibid.

50 David Watkin, *Radical Classicism: The Architecture of Quinlan Terry,* 2006, pp. 140-141.

51 Bullen *et al, Hampshire,* p. 541; see also Frank Russell (ed.), *Quinlan Terry,* 1981, pp. 10-11.

52 *West Green House Garden.*

53 Ibid.

54 EH Register entry.

55 http://www.victoriacountyhistory.ac.uk/explore/items/mountbatten-house-hanging-gardens-basingstoke (accessed 1 September 2015).

56 T Aldous and J Winter, 'Roof Gardens: Gateway House', *Architects' Journal,* vol. 171 (24 August 1977), pp.631-637.

57 http://www.victoriacountyhistory.ac.uk/explore/items/mountbatten-house-hanging-gardens-basingstoke (accessed 1 September 2015).

58 EH Register entry.

59 http://research.hgt.org.uk/item/the-beeches-the-cement-garden (accessed 3 September 2015).

60 A Shaw, 'Fantasia on a theme of stone and firs', *Andover Advertiser,* 28 June 1985.

61 The garden was one of the six finalists in the RHS/*Daily Mail* Garden of the Year competition in 1995, out of no fewer than 3,200 entries, a mark of its originality.

62 Rosamund Wallinger, *Gertrude Jekyll's Lost Garden: The Restoration of an Edwardian Masterpiece* (Woodbridge, 2000), p. 11.

63 Bullen *et al, Hampshire,* p. 529.

64 Ibid.

65 Wallinger, *Gertrude Jekyll's Lost Garden*, p. 17.

66 Ibid., pp. 24-25.

67 Ibid., p. 27.

68 Ibid., p. 135.

69 Ibid., p. 50; p. 203.

70 Ibid., pp. 66-68.

71 Ibid., p. 85; p. 99.

72 Ibid., p. 29.

73 Ibid. Another recent recreation of a Jekyll garden has been undertaken at Durmast House, Burley in the New Forest, by Mr and Mrs Daubeney. Jekyll's 1907 design was for her cousin, Miss Nelly Baring of the banking family. The Daubeneys went to see the plans, which are at the University of California at Berkeley, in 1999, since when they have directed the restoration.

74 Nikolaus Pevsner and David Lloyd, *The Buildings of England: Hampshire and the Isle of Wight,* 1967, p. 529.

75 Ibid., p. 529.

76 Sylvia Landsberg, *The Tudor Garden* (Southampton City Council, no date), p. 8.

77 Robin Whalley & Anne Jennings, *Knot Gardens and Parterres*, 1998, p. 45.

78 Thomas Hill, *A most briefe and pleasaunte treatise, teachyng how to dresse, sowe, and set a garden*, 1558.

79 Thomas Hill, *The Arte of Gardening*, 1608, p. 15.

80 Whalley & Jennings, *Knot Gardens and Parterres,* p. 38; p. 40.

81 Landsberg, *The Tudor Garden*, p. 6. J H Baker, 'Lyster, Sir Richard (*c.* 1480-1553)', *Oxford Dictionary of National Biography*; online edition, May 2013 http://www.oxforddnb.com/view/article/17300, accessed 3 Aug 2015.

82 Landsberg, *The Tudor Garden*, p. 8.

83 Pevsner & Lloyd, *Hampshire and the Isle of Wight,* p. 529.

84 Landsberg, *The Mediaeval Garden*, p. 121.

85 Ibid., p. 122.

86 Ibid., p. 60.

87 Ibid., p. 124.

88 Ibid., pp. 124-125.

89 Ibid., p. 124.

90 Jennings, *Mediaeval Gardens*, p. 21.

91 Landsberg, *The Mediaeval Garden*, p. 125.

92 Ibid.

93 Jennings, *Mediaeval Gardens*, p. 21.

94 Landsberg, *The Mediaeval Garden*, p. 126.

95 Pevsner & Lloyd, *Hampshire and the Isle of Wight*, p. 487.

96 http://www.parks and gardens.org/places-and-people/site/4897/history (accessed 17 November 2014).

97 Ibid.

98 Ibid.

99 Ibid.

100 Ibid.

101 Ibid.

102 Ibid.

103 http://www.winchester-cathedral.org.uk/our-heritage/cathedral-close/dean-garnier-garden/ (accessed 20 August 2015).

104 Ibid.

105 Ibid.

106 Hampshire Gardens Trust research notes.

107 http://www.winchester-cathedral.org.uk/our-heritage/cathedral-close/dean-garnier-garden/ (accessed 20 August 2015).

108 Hampshire Gardens Trust research notes.

109 Bullen *et al, Hampshire,* p. 560.

110 Ibid.

111 Ibid.

112 http://www.archaeology.co.uk/articles/news/a-great-discovery-remains-of-king-alfred-or-his-son-found-in-winchester.htm (accessed 10 August 2015).

113 Bullen *et al, Hampshire*, p. 701.

114 Ibid., p. 702.

115 http://www.hyde900.org.uk/2014/01/17/burials-and-bones/ (accessed 10 August 2015).

116 http://www.archaeology.co.uk/articles/news/a-great-discovery-remains-of-king-alfred-or-his-son-found-in-winchester.htm (accessed 10 August 2015).

117 Ibid.

118 Bullen *et al*, *Hampshire,* p. 702.

119 Kim Wilkie, *Led by the Land: Landscapes by Kim Wilkie*, 2012, p. 95.

120 Ibid.

121 Ibid., p. 138.

122 Page's plans are preserved at the house.

123 The model is preserved at Rotherfield. We are grateful to Sir James and Lady Scott for their warm hospitality and for making the model accessible for study.

124 Wilkie, *Led by the Land,* p. 142.

125 Ibid., pp. 109-110.

126 Ibid., p. 137.

127 Wilkie has created a less dramatic design at Hurstborne Park, in front of the house, which he describes as a 'subtle knot garden of turf cut down into the grass', which only appears in morning and evening light; see *Led by the Land*, pp. 128-9.

128 Ibid., pp. 61-65.

129 Ibid., pp. 66-71.

130 Ibid., p. 66.

131 Ibid.

132 This, and subsequent quotations, are taken from an overview of Bury Court, written by John Coke, for a German garden magazine, *Gartenpraxis*. We are grateful to John for supplying us with his typescript.

133 Ibid.

134 Ibid.

135 For Adam's career see Richard John, *New Classicists Robert Adam: The Search for a Modern Classicism* (Victoria, Australia, 2010).

136 Particularly George Saumarez Smith's award-winning Summerhouse at Langton House, Alresford.

137 The Millennium Pavilion is discussed in John, *New Classicists*, pp. 30-32.

Gazetteer

The following is a list of the gardens of significant historic importance which are covered in this book and are open to the public.

Abbreviations

C   Council/Charity owned
CC   Conference Centre
P   Privately owned but open occasionally or regularly
NGS Privately owned but open occasionally as part of the National Gardens Scheme
NT   National Trust
EH   English Heritage
H   Hotel
PP   Public Park
U   University

Amport House	P
Basing House	C
Beaulieu Abbey	P
Bishop's Waltham Palace	EH
Breamore House	P
Broadlands	P
Bury Court	NGS
Cadland House	P
Chawton House	P
Chawton Cottage	P
Cranbury Park	NGS
Dean Garnier Garden	C
Dogmersfield Park	H
Elvetham Hall	H
Exbury House	P
The Grange, Northington	EH
Heckfield Place	H
Highclere Castle	P
Hinton Admiral	NGS
Hinton Ampner	NT
Houghton Lodge	P
Hyde Abbey	PP
King John's House, Romsey	C
Lainston House	H
Lake House, Northington	NGS
Leigh Park	PP
Longstock Park	P
The Manor House, Upton Grey	P
Mottisfont Abbey	NT
Netley Abbey	EH
New Place	CC
North Stoneham Park	PP
Odiham Castle	C
Paultons Park	P
Pylewell Park	NGS
Rhinefield House	H
Rotherfield Park	NGS
Queen Eleanor's Garden	C
St Cross Hospital	C
St Swithun's Priory	C
Sir Harold Hillier Gardens	C
South Stoneham House	U
Stratfield Saye	P
Titchfield Abbey	EH
Townhill Park	NGS
Tudor House	C
Tylney Hall	H
The Vyne	NT
The Wakes, Selborne	P
Walhampton House	NGS
Warbrook House	CC
Warnford Park	P
West Green House	NT
Winchester Castle	C
Winchester College	P
Wolvesey Castle	EH

The Gardens

Not all gardens shown are open to the public

Stratfield Saye
Macartneys
Highclere Castle
Sherfield Manor
The Vyne
Tangier Park
Berrydown Ct BASINGSTOKE
The Beeches
Hackwood Pk
Herriard Pk
Preston House
Moundsmere Manor

Bramshill House and Warbrook House
Heckfield Place
Tylney Hall
Minley Manor
FARNBOROUGH
Manor Ho. Weir's Barn and West Green House
Upton Grey Odiham Castle
Elvetham Hall ALDERSHOT
Dogmersfield Park

Amport House ANDOVER

Longstock Park
Stratton Park
The Grange
Lake House
STOCKBRIDGE
Abbotstone
Marsh Court
Houghton Lodge
Lainston House

Bury Court
ALTON Headley Park
Chawton Ho & Chawton Cott.
Old Alresford House
NEW ALRESFORD
Hailie (Bramshott Rectory)
Rotherfield Park Little Boarhunt
The Wakes Ashford Chace

Norman Court
WINCHESTER
Compton End
Hursley Park
Sir H Hillier Gdns
Melchet Court Cranbury Park
Mottisfont Abbey ROMSEY
Shawford Park
North Stoneham
Broadlands
Paultons Park
SOUTHAMPTON

Hinton Ampner
Westbury House

PETERSFIELD

Warnford Park
EASTLEIGH The Holt
Bishopstoke
Rectory
Bishops Waltham Palace

Hale Park
Breamore House
Somerley Park
RINGWOOD
Cuffnells Park
LYNDHURST
High Coxlease
Rhinefield House
Brockenhurst Park
BROCKENHURST
Avon Tyrrell
Walhampton House
Hinton Admiral
LYMINGTON
HRISTCHURCH

Netley Abbey
HAMBLE
Titchfield Abbey
Beaulieu Abbey
Cadland House
Exbury House
Eaglehurst/
Luttrell's Tower
Pylewell Park

New Place
Rookesbury Park
Southwick Park
FAREHAM
Leigh Park
GOSPORT
Warblington Castle
PORTSMOUTH

BASINGSTOKE
Basing House
Mountbatten Ho

ROMSEY
King John's House

SOUTHAMPTON
South Stoneham House
Townhill Park
Tudor House

WINCHESTER
Dean Garnier's Garden
Hyde Abbey
St Cross Hospital
St Swithun's Priory
Winchester Castle
Wolvesey Castle
Winchester College

Index Page numbers in **bold** refer to illustrations and captions